To Bo[b]
Merry Christmas
Dec. 1993
Love
Brenda

FORGIVE ME MY
PRESS PASSES

KRIEGER©

FORGIVE ME MY PRESS PASSES

by

Jim Taylor

Horsdal & Schubart

Horsdal & Schubart Publishers Ltd.
Victoria, B. C., Canada

Cover: Background layout by Deborah Taylor, Vancouver, B. C. Background photograph by Gael Howard, Vancouver, B. C.

Frontispiece cartoon by Bob Krieger, Vancouver, B. C. Courtesy of Bob Krieger.

The articles in this collection appeared first in either *The Province* or *The Vancouver Sun*, Vancouver, B. C.

This book is set in Galliard Book Type.

Printed and bound in Canada by Kromar Printing, Winnipeg, Manitoba

Canadian Cataloguing in Publication Data

Taylor, Jim, 1937 -
    Forgive me my press passes

    ISBN 0-920663-22-2

    1. Sports — British Columbia — Vancouver.   2. Sports.
I. Title.
GV585.5.V2T39 1993   796'.09711'3   C93-091624-7

CONTENTS

* * *

For Stan Murphy (1917-1971)
who opened the door and pushed me through,
and
Jim Tang
who let me stay

* * *

INTRODUCTION

"You made up that stuff about the moose," a reader said accusingly. I get that a lot.

No, I didn't, I assured her. The Seattle Mariners did hold a mascot contest, and the winning name was Mariner Moose, and now they were holding auditions to find someone to jump into the moose suit. Who'd lie about something that serious?

"You're always making stuff up," she insisted. "Like the day you claimed the Lone Ranger got married and lived in a condo and his business cards said 'Lone (Larry) Ranger', and his wife tried to apply for a credit card and when they asked what her husband did for a living and she said he rode across the American west on a great horse named Silver, shooting silver bullets at bad guys, she got turned down."

Well, okay, maybe *that* one.

"And the interview with the race horse that was about to be put out to stud, and he said it was about time because he was sick of listening to kids learning about sex out behind the barn while he had to sit in the barn getting all sweaty. You didn't really talk to that horse."

No, but...

"So are you crazy, or what?"

Perhaps an explanation is in order.

I love writing about sports — but I hate the term sports columnist. By definition, it draws fences. I'm a people writer. The people I write about happen to be people involved in sports. If sport died out tomorrow, I'd shed a few tears, treasure the memories, and go write about something else.

Sport can be dramatic, exciting, stimulating, moving and wrenchingly sad. There are columns here covering all of that, and I am among God's more fortunate creatures to have been there to write them. It can also be fall-down funny. Given a choice, I'll take funny every time.

Reporters have to ask "Who, What, Where, When, Why and How". The columnist, lucky sod, can ask "What if...?" What if the Lone Ranger did get married? How would he live? If a prize race horse could talk, what would he say before they started trucking in the fillies for candle light and whinny? What if they put cannons on the America's Cup yachts?

But it's getting tougher every day. Because no matter how far off the wall I bounce, the real world bounces harder. For instance, there is the Case of the Undercover Horse.

FBI agents recently told a federal grand jury in Rochester, N.Y., that they used an undercover horse to expose a race-fixing scam at Finser Lakes Race Track in Canandaigua, N.Y. The horse was stabled, trained and raced at the track while its handlers secretly gathered information on the fixers.

Then the FBI agent said — and I am not making this up — "Because of the pending case, we cannot name the horse or discuss its record."

Well, that can mean only one thing. They've set the horse up in one of those witness-protection programs. Relocation, new identity, the works...

"Hold still, girl. This plastic surgery is a bitch, you stompin' around like that. There! Nobody'd ever guess you used to be a mare. Just don't be hangin' around the singles barn or some filly might call your bluff.

"Now, your new name is Ed. We got you set up in a riding academy out in California. The Mob'll never look for you there. Your cover is, you're part of a learn-to-ride class. Kids only. And don't worry about the fat one who comes Saturday mornings. That's Agent Freddy. He'll be bringing you your weekly cheque.

"This is the last time you'll see me until the trial. And don't worry. The van that brings you to the courthouse will be bulletproof and we'll have the place surrounded by plainclothes agents dressed as jockeys and touts. You're our only witness, and they'll stop at nothing to keep you from testifying, so don't stick your snout in any strange nosebags..."

Go ahead, lady. Phone again and tell me it didn't happen that way. But remember, that's what you said about the moose.

Jim Taylor, July 1993

Chapter One

NOBODY KISSES THE MASKED MAN

Early in the game I was blessed with editors who noticed that from time to time I came down with the Weirds.

The stories I wrote sometimes had little to do with the game I was covering. Comic-book characters kept showing up in them. Or old movie or song titles. And there were a lot of "What ifs..." like "If Noah had remembered the unicorns, would race horses have horns?" and "What if a coach said 'There's no tomorrow' — and there wasn't?"

Instead of beating the weird streak out of me, they pulled me in and out of the sports department and gave me weird things to write.

I climbed into a suit of armour to report that knighthood probably died out because the suits had no pants and they were too embarrassed to get off the horse. I stood in line at the doll counter in the toy department at Christmas and asked the girl behind the counter for a Poverty Pete doll — "You know, Barbie's father, the guy who pays for all those clothes."

I interviewed wrestler Whipper Billy Watson while he held me at arm's length over his head, and a parakeet named Petey Parsons who'd finally been taught how to say his name *and* address, untaught and re-programmed with the new address when they moved, and now was going nuts because the city was changing the name of the street.

When the Social Insurance numbers came in, I taped mine in big letters across my forehead, had my picture taken and faked a psychi-

1

atric appointment ("Hello, doc. My name is 702-044-405. You can call me 7.") claiming the Thought Police were after my wife and me because we wouldn't name our baby daughter Twelve.

They didn't just *let* me do all these things. They encouraged me to do them and gave them big play when I did, even when they moved me back into the sports department. "Writing is writing," they said. "If you think something is funny, go ahead and write it that way. There are probably people out there who'll think so, too."

Usually, there were. Not always, and sometimes not many, but usually some. A good thing, too, because the Weirds never did go away...

ADIOS, OLD UNDERWOOD

September 14, 1976

It was a simple ceremony. In the quiet of the basement, we laid a friend to rest.

We'd been together 22 years, my Underwood and I, good years and bad. Now it was rolled into the special drawer in the old walnut-veneer desk for the last time, the two-colour ribbon locked in final, funereal black.

I am writing now on something called a Computek Video Display Terminal. Paper is a thing of the past. The words appear on a screen in front of me, like a verbal game of Pong. It is a wondrous machine capable of wondrous things, and I wish it would go away.

The VDT can change typeface at the touch of a button, opening up vast new worlds in expressing profanity. A simple old-fashioned bleep can now be a BLEEP or even a *bleep*. Where were you, VDT, when I wrote of Renee Richards?

Okay, so it's three-faced. Big deal. Can it make soldiers? My Underwood could. For both my children the Underwood was a magical baby-sitter, big eyes watching inky fingers create armies that marched across the page.

Remember? You started with an & for the body, making sure the ribbon was on red. Then you switched to black, back-spaced and hit the /. Suddenly, your redcoat had a rifle. Back-space again, roll the paper down slightly, hit the ' and he had a hat. Back-space, roll the paper up, hit the " and he had legs — not curling, sissy legs like the ones you see here; straight, firm, military legs. And for your captain, you could make his hat a *. Can you do that, VDT? The hell you can.

Could you look at the stuff written by a scared-green kid on his first assignment and save him from making an utter fool of himself? My Underwood did.

I was 16 years old, and a journalism teacher named Stan Murphy had kicked my tail down to the *Daily Colonist* to apply for a job I didn't want: part-time high school sports reporter. I took it, because it was a way to get into newspapers and the $30 a month for covering only three softball games a week plus Sunday doubleheaders was too good to pass up.

The first time I sat down to write, I carefully measured the width of a newspaper column and tried to set the margins exactly that wide. I was not in school on scholarship.

My Underwood refused. You can say the margins jammed if you like, but I know better. The machine would not let me do it. So I went to the office to write and a lot of good people set me straight. Can the VDT do that? Maybe — but *would* it?

We fought sometimes, my Underwood and I. Spelling was never its strong point. But we always made up, and if it came out misspelled — what the hell, you could always blame the printers.

Red Smith, the greatest sports columnist who ever lived, said once that writing a column was easy. "All you have to do," he said, "is sit down in front of the typewriter and stay there until little drops of blood appear on your forehead." Well, there's a lot more forehead now, but somehow I can't see Red sitting down in front of a Computek Video Display Terminal. We live in discouraging times.

It isn't just the machine. Even the terminology has changed. With the Underwood, you dealt with "carbon paper," "takes" and "the Goddamn ribbon is jammed". No more. When the VDT breaks down nobody says, "The VDT's broken down." Instead, we are told that there's been a "host collapse."

I know about host collapse. I am one of the great collapsing hosts of our day. Four drinks and it's horizontal city. So I figure the machine is drunk, which is kind of, well, *humanizing*.

Not so. The host is actually the mother computer, the one that sits out back like the queen bee, digesting pollenized copy and spitting it out by the sheet. If the machine wants coffee, study session or pregnancy leave it "crashes", another Computek word meaning "Congratulations! You have just wasted two hours." We are sitting here, the very flowers of Vancouver journalism, locked in a million-dollar game of Mother, Mother, May I?

My Underwood knew its place. It sat there on the desk waiting for me to use it, and crashed only once. I was trying to carry it upstairs to display to visiting friends and it fell to the floor. (See: "Host Collapse.") I put it back on the desk and it worked just fine. The floor, however, needed refinishing.

The Underwood's day is gone. Knowing that doesn't mean I have to like it. You do not idly trade away your first love. Not when you know she's still got a lot of good miles on her.

I'll work with you, VDT, but I'll never trust you. And frankly, the same goes for your mother.

ELVIS WHO?

August 18, 1977

I, too, have an Elvis Presley story. All together now: "EEEEEEEECCCCCCHHHHHH!"

It's a sports story, sort of, in that it involves the birth of my incredible ability to pick winners, that instinctive knack that has made me justifiably famous. Because it all started with Elvis, on a day in 1955.

I was 18 years old, writing sports for the *Daily Colonist* in Victoria. Little League baseball, senior men's softball — all the big stuff. But I wasn't a sports fan, not really. Deep down, I was a closet jazz buff.

It wasn't easy, being a jazz fan in the middle of the rock 'n' roll craze, but my friends understood. They called me a dirty weirdo Commie freak and let it go at that. Besides, they were never in danger of actually hearing the stuff, because I could never afford the records.

Then Leonard Feather, one of the world's greatest jazz authorities, produced a five-volume *Encyclopaedia of Jazz on Record*, featuring the original recordings. I had to hear it. So, being young and stupid, I filched some *Colonist* stationery, wrote to Decca Records, and asked if I could *borrow* a copy in order to write a review.

They sent me the records plus a letter saying I could keep them. All they required was a copy of the review. And a great light dawned. Somewhere out there, people were *giving away records*.

I became a record columnist. Part time, of course. I couldn't give up the security of that $95 a week writing sports. The column appeared each Sunday. At first it was called "Needle Dust". (See, record player needles get little bits of dust on them and the column was little bits about records, and...) It took the news desk only 14 months to come up with a better name. They called it "Off the Record". We were a progressive paper.

The record companies started sending me records. Dozens of records. *Hundreds* of records. Free. Most of them were crap. Occasionally there'd be a nugget, but I had no selectivity. They just came. One package contained two LPs: "Ella Sings Gershwin" and "Screaming Jay Hawkins Sings Religious Songs". The singles were no better — rock, mostly, because that was what was selling. My all-time favourite was a 45 by Gene Autry. On one side was "God Is My Saddle Partner". The flip was "When I Looked Up and He Looked Down". Bill Haley survived the challenge.

Then came Elvis.

From the start I loathed him, and said so. Fan club presidents, ponytails quivering with indignation, stopped chewing gum long enough to print me misspelled letters:

"You're like a lot of people whom I have heard of. For instance, the many people of whom he was going to make a movie with, they were all set to hate him but they changes [*sic*] their minds fast when they got to know him."

But they couldn't fool me. The guy was a passing fad. How long could a Presley last when Warren Covington was regrouping the old Tommy Dorsey band and recording the "Tea For Two Cha Cha"? So I sat down and wrote the "Needle Dust" that would blow Victoria wide open.

My mother, who wanted me to seek honest work, saved a copy. In fact, she must have saved 1,000 copies. Every time she produces one I burn it, and in 20 years she's never run out. She is a nice lady, but she loses hard.

Now that The King is dead, I thought you might like to see my first big prediction, the one that started it all:

PRESLEY? WHO'S HE? By Jim Taylor

"Rock 'n' roll has hit Victoria hard in the past two months, but it has also hit it late. Elsewhere in the country the music is dying out.

"According to national sales charts, only three rock 'n' roll tunes are in the Top 10. "My Blue Heaven" and "I'm In Love Again" by Fats Domino are numbers three and four, respectively, and Elvis Presley scores with "I Want You, I Need You, I Love You" in the number nine slot. Otherwise, the trend is toward ballads like Gogi Grant's "Wayward Wind", number one, and "Moonglow", number 2.

"The thought here is that rock 'n' roll will never die out completely but, like progressive jazz and Dixieland, will gradually fall in the rating of the general public and be limited to its own select group of listeners.

"And as for singers like Elvis Presley, within six months to a year the name Presley will bring forth, instead of screams of delight, one comment:

" 'Who?'."

BINGO, BANGO, BONGO

May 25, 1978

Lil Tishler wins bingo, bango, bongo competition — Women's Golf, *The Vancouver Sun.*

The last time I read the words bingo, bango, bongo they were followed by "I don't wanna leave the Congo, oh-no-no-no-no-no." The next line was "Bingle bangle bungle, I'm so happy in the jungle I refuse to go." They don't write songs like they used to.

Maybe you don't read the Women's Golf section. Millions don't. In fact, there are days when I wonder why we run it at all. Days ending in Y. But we do, and in one sense it is educational. Where else in the newspaper would you stumble on bingo, bango, bongo? It fairly leaps out at you:

"Bingo, bango, bongo winner was Lil Tishler. Nancy Zlotnik, Marg Logan and Zoe Gropper were runners-up."

Well, what's a man to think? Somewhere out there are women who bingo, bango, bongo! And they *advertise*.

Women's Golf didn't give details. How does one bingo, bango, bongo? Is it anything like va-va-voom? Is it safe for guys over 40? I had to find out. And I did.

Bingo, bango, bongo is a three-part contest played during a normal round of golf in which points are awarded for things other than your score. When one bingos, she has become the first person in her foursome to reach the green. This does not necessarily qualify her to bango. (There is a lot of controversy over this.) The bangoperson is the one whose shot to the green is closest to the hole.

So the foursome is on the green. One person has a point for bingo and another a point for bango — unless of course the person who bingoed also bangoed. Right about there things start to get tense. Because *anyone on the green can bongo!* It matters not that you have neither bingoed nor bangoed. If you are the first to sink your putt you have bongoed and are suitably rewarded.

Thus there are a possible 18 bingo points, 18 bango points and 18 bongo points. At the end of the day the girls total up their points, pick the winner and retire to the press tent for interviews. ("Well, I had my bingo going pretty good and my bongo was deadly. But my bango! — if I don't get my approach shots going I may never bango again.")

Do not confuse Women's Golf with athletic endeavour — at least, not the women's golf found in Women's Golf. It is recreation, pure and simple, about as newsworthy as you and me going outside and playing frisbee. But it certainly is educational.

Have you ever in your life played Throw Four? Or Best Nine, Half Handicap? How about Honeypot? Steeplechase Best-Ball? Cryers' Tournament? Have you known the thrill of being "first round grand slam low net winner in the first division"? Led the "A" division in fairway shots? They are all there every Wednesday in Women's Golf.

Every Tuesday at 2:30 p.m. a womanperson comes from the library, sits by the sports department phone and takes the results. She leaves in 2 1/2 hours, eyes glazed, lips lightly frothed, muttering things like "Tombstone Competition, Monthly Medal, Irons Event..."

We don't expect to have her long.

I have given considerable thought to the competitions listed in Women's Golf. Some of them I don't quite understand. The Tombstone Event, one assumes, is for women who play sore losers. The therapeutic benefits of the Hidden Hole Event are obvious, since women who spend their round hacking through the rough could always claim they were looking for it. But how does one play a Hidden Hole? If you can play it, it obviously isn't hidden at all.

Still, some events have possibilities.

There is nothing wrong with an Irons Event for women. They could tie it in with a Stove Event, a Fridge Event and a Mop Event and stay home. Unfortunately, this would make them ineligible for the Longest Drive title, currently held by a lady who lives 32 miles from the course.

Nor could anyone find fault with the Throw Four competition in which you play a round, throw out your four worst holes, and add up your score. Think how much tension you could add to the Masters. Jack Nicklaus is just pulling on the green blazer when Johnny Miller, who is 18 strokes back, putts out, scratches four bogeys and rips the coat from Jack's back. It's got everything: drama, suspense, pathos...

I took a Women's Golf result on the sports phone once. Somebody won with a round of 123.

"That seems rather high," I suggested.

"It's gross," she explained.

"It certainly is," I agreed.

Fortunately, I'd given an alias.

THE STADIUM BUILDERS

September 1, 1981

It took five years of governmental and public arguing, lobbying, whining and bitching to get a covered stadium for Vancouver, and the price mounted with every passing day. Has it always been this way with major projects, I wondered, and what happens if they never quit talking...?

STONEHENGE: circular setting of large standing stones, built during the late Neolithic Period and Early Bronze Age (*c.* 1800-1400 BC) near Salisbury, Eng. Believed by some to be Druid Temple.

The scholars are wrong. Stonehenge wasn't a temple; it was going to be a stadium. Then the Druid Council held another public meeting.

The circle of stone supports was up, the cross-stones already laid on top. The project was being fast-tracked to get construction finished in time for the big game between the Picts and the Celts. Politicians battled for the right to throw out the first virgin.

But like all major construction projects, the stadium had its opponents. They waxed loudly, if not eloquently, and council was full of rookie Druids. Thus, while more stones were rolled into place and construction proceeded apace, the opponents rose once more.

There were the Shelter Druids:

"This BC Place," they thundered. "A playpen for gladiators!

What about housing? Has council forgotten the people? We need low-rental caves!"

And the Transit Druids:

"What about parking? You can't get 100 chariots down here, let alone 1,000. No Druid in his right mind will park rods away and walk!"

And the Environmental Druids:

"Even if you do get the chariots down there, the pollution will be unbearable. One step out of the chariot and you're up to your toga in horsebleep. And licensing the sale of food in the stands — madness! Gnawed bones all over the place. Flies, stray dogs..."

And the Health Druids:

"You know what will happen then, don't you? The shamen and the witch doctors will start screaming they're overworked. They'll want more shells, a better quality of blue body paint. They'll refuse to work! Who'll put the leeches on then?"

And the Economy Druids:

"Even with the slaves it can't be kept within budget. Who's going to pay for the overseers to handle the slaves to clean up the mess? Who's going to pay for the paths up the hill to the stadium? Who's going to pay for the upkeep? All this talk about a major league circus! All the good gladiators stay in Rome and everybody knows it. Expansion is a pipe-dream!"

And the Lifestyle Druids:

"The people don't want stadiums. We're on the threshold of a communications breakthrough: the stone tablet weight problem has been whipped. Tablets are going to be made of wax. You know what that means? Home delivery! Who'll want to go to a game when you can have the results dropped right at your cave-mouth?"

And the Futurist Druids:

"People today want a better way of life. Council must abandon the old ways and look ahead. This is 1800 BC. It'll be AD before you know it."

And the Conservative Druids:

"I move we table construction until all facets of the project can be thoroughly re-studied. There's plenty of time. Let's get all these problems solved first. Then we can rethink the whole BC Place concept. Better still, another Druid Council can rethink it, and you'll all be off the hook."

Council listened to them all, and announced its decision:

"Your Council is aware of its responsibilities. You want firm leadership by men of decision. If you can't stand the heat, stay away from the campfire. Therefore, it is our decision..."

He paused for effect. Then:

"...to call another public meeting!"

And they did.

They called one in 1700 BC, put a circle of stones in the middle and built a road joining the outside circle to the River Avon. Archaeologists call it Stonehenge II.

They called another one in 1400 and dismantled the stones put up for Stonehenge II.

They met, and they met, and they met. A lot of loud-mouthed Druids got to do a lot of talking. A lot of councils got off the hook. And today, near Salisbury, England, you can still see the fruits of their labours.

One useless pile of rocks.

There is a post-script. After the B.C. Place domed stadium was built in Vancouver in 1983, provincial premier Bill Bennett spoke at a banquet and gave me credit for my efforts to get it built. Noting that my hair was no longer apparent, he said:

"I got the idea for the domed stadium when I went camping with Jim Taylor and saw him crawling out of the tent. Fortunately, he crawled out head-first. If he'd backed out, we'd have had two domed stadiums."

LIPSTICK FOR KEMO SABE

Sepember 25, 1981

Unless you consider sex a sport, this is not a sports column. Sorry, but this is an emergency. The Lone Ranger may be about to kiss a girl.

I've been worried about him since the day he turned up on the *Province*'s comics page. He just isn't the same old Ranger. Even Tonto's noticed it. He says so right there in his dialogue balloon, which is all wiggly so you'll know he's thinking:

"Strange! I've never seen such a look in his eyes! Could it be the woman...?"

Now, if Tonto can see there's a problem, it's got to be fairly obvious. He's not exactly out there on an equestrian scholarship.

For 35 years he's been letting the Ranger stay out on the prairie making camp while he goes into town to get beaten up and thrown out of saloons. You'd think, just once, he'd say "This time, I make camp."

Mind you, the Ranger's no mental giant. Tell me about a guy who finds a silver mine and uses the stuff to make bullets. But he's been a hero to generations of North American kids, and I'd hate to see him fall.

And I'm afraid he is falling. For a girl.

It started innocently enough. Just an average day at the office, shooting the guns from the hands of a bunch of stagecoach robbers. But out of the stagecoach steps this girl. And the Lone Ranger takes one look and thinks:

"Great thunder! It can't be her!"

He hasn't been the same since. His dialogue is smarmy. He just stands there, ga ga, while she natters on and on:

"I must say you are a singular sort of man! Why, you'd probably be arrested on sight where I come from! Nevertheless, I am in your debt, though I doubt our paths will ever cross again...!"

The old Ranger would have Hi-yo'd half way across the state by the time she hit the first exclamation mark. I think he's got the hots for this chick.

Well, I'm no prude. If she's just some dance-hall girl he met at a barn dance and took up into the loft, that's one thing. It gets lonely out there on the prairie with two horses and a guy whose idea of conversation is "Hmmmm, kemo sabe, Cavendish gang, them heap bad!"

But what if it's something more? What if she's the marrying kind?

Lord knows she talks enough. She ever gets her hooks into the Ranger, he'll be up to his neck in credit cards and Rotary luncheons, wearing a badge on his shirt that says "Hi! I'm Lone (Larry) Ranger."

Sure as hell, she'll be after him about the mask. ("Sometimes I think you love that mask more than you love me!") She probably won't want Tonto along on the honeymoon.

Nah! They wouldn't let that happen. Not to the Lone Ranger. Still, they did ditch Clayton Moore when they made the movie and hired that guy Klinton Spilsbury who looked like he should be out winning a bake-off. What if...?

I decided to check with the comics-person.

The comics-person is the power behind any newspaper. She gets the comics a week or more in advance. She knows what's coming down in *Mary Worth*. She's got the inside dope on *Judge Parker*. She has the exact date when that kid in *Gasoline Alley* stops thinking he's a dog. That's power.

And she never tells.

But this was an emergency. This was the Lone Ranger.

"Think of all those kids out there," I pleaded. "Think of the valuable lessons the Ranger has taught them, like girls are for staying back at the ranch cooking, and horses get great mileage and don't burn oil. What are they going to think, what will it *do* to them if the Lone Ranger has an *affair*?"

I hounded her until she cracked.

Some time in the next few days, the girl from the stagecoach is going to be crying and hugging this guy who says he loves her. Only his back is turned. All you see is his haircut and his hat.

"Is it *him*?" I cried. "Is it the *Ranger*?"

She just smiled.

"That panel hasn't arrived yet," she said.

I think it has. I think she knows. I wish we were out on the prairie. I'd send her into town while I made camp.

ENTER JOGGER, EXIT SEX

April 20, 1982

The Runner, acknowledged bible of the sweat set, has published the results of a survey claiming that 26.5% of the 3,140 runners polled said they'd rather give up sex than running. Good-bye, Participaction.

The survey also claims that:

(a) 47.5% of those surveyed spent more time thinking about running than about sex;

(b) 82.2% think about sex while running;

(c) 18.9% think about running during sex;

(d) 62.7% say a perfect Sunday afternoon consists of a run, a shower with one's mate, a bottle of wine and soft music;

(e) 11.1% figure a great Sunday schedule starts with a run and a shower followed by a few beer and an afternoon in front of the TV watching a track meet.

It is a depressing picture, even for those of us who've long viewed runners with suspicion. (Did you ever wonder why Earl Cameron wears a trench coat in those walk-a-block-a-day commercials? Or what he's got on under it?) Anyone with such single- or simple-minded dedication must be running from something. Now *The Runner* implies that the pursuer could be a sex-starved mate.

"Well, darling, we've had the run, and the nice warm shower. The wine is at room temperature, which is more than I can say for me. The music is soft and low. I've sent the kids on a marathon. In Greece. How about..."

"Not now, dear. I've got a shin splint."

Examine the survey's figures closely and you come to some inescapable conclusions about the sex life of a runner. For instance:

If 82.2% think about sex while running and 26.5% would rather give up sex than running, it means that even without duplications 8.7% of the people running are jogging along thinking that what they're doing on the road is a lot better than what they could be doing at home.

Not that it doesn't make sense to think about sex as you pound mindlessly across the landscape. When you run, you need rhythm. It's also helpful to have a song or jingle running through the mind. We've all seen the rowing commercial on TV. Why not the same tune for runners, with slightly altered lyrics:

"Another one sights the bust;
"Another one sights the bust.
"And it won't be long 'til her chaperone's gone,
"Another one sights the bust..."

On the other hand, the trained scientific mind boggles at the ambiguity of the news of the 18.9% who say they think about running during sex. Do they mean that during sex they think about running — or that they think about what it might be like to be running during sex? If the latter, the word marathon could take on a whole new dimension.

That 47.5% of those surveyed would confess to giving more thought to running than to sex is not surprising. There are similarities — both activities tend to be sweaty — but running should require more thought. It takes longer and requires more equipment.

A runner is constantly on the prowl for the latest in shoes, sweatsuits, stopwatches and invigorating drinks. A sexer, if one may use the term, leans more toward depleting his wardrobe than adding to it. Shoes of any kind are considered more hindrance than help, and at the very least bad form. The sexer bringing a stopwatch to bed may never get a chance to click it. A partner expecting brandy and a cigarette may not view with love a proffered salt tablet and Gatorade.

Naturally, there is the possibility that the survey is a crock. A 3,140-runner sampling may not be statistically relevant. Some of those surveyed could have reacted to the infringement on their private lives by pulling the leg of the surveyor. Certainly, runners as a group will deny most of the findings.

There is, however, that famous story of the runner who asked his doctor how to improve his sex life and was told to run five miles a day.

Three days later he phoned.

"It ain't workin', doc," he complained. "I'm 15 miles from home and I ain't had a proposition yet."

DEAD IN THE WATER

May 20, 1982

Canada's America's Cup yachting challenge seeks funds as most of its $2 million "seed money" exhausted. — *The Province*, May 18, 1982.

"Good afternoon, madam. Is your husband in?"

"Whadya mean, in? It's 10.30 in the morning. He's working. Does street repairs for the city. Jackhammer, y'know? Seven hours a day and what it does to his kidneys you wouldn't believe."

"I see. Well, I'm here to solicit your help in launching Canada's America's Cup challenge, and..."

"If it's America's Cup, let America pay for it."

"Uh, no, you don't quite understand. The America's Cup is a race. A yacht race. You take these enormously expensive 12-metre yachts to Rhode Island, and four or five countries race for the right to see who races against the Americans for the Cup. We've got 38 men in Florida, and..."

"Can't get jobs here, eh? I know the feeling. If my Fred doesn't have a cousin in Public Works he maybe doesn't get the shot at the jackhammer and — RALPHIE! Stay out of the cupboard! — That's

14

Ralphie, the baby. The other three kids are in school. Now, whadya need — 50¢ or a buck for a raffle ticket or something? I guess maybe I can spare it. Live a little, I always say."

"Well, no. Actually, we need, oh, maybe three million dollars minimum."

"Sorry, I'm a little short this week. I went crazy at the supermarket and bought meat. Say! What kind of a boat is this, anyway? Got a john and everything?"

"Uh, it's two yachts, actually. We're practising with the *Clipper* and the *Intrepid*. Only until the one we're having built is delivered, of course."

"Of course. Sorta like Fred and me, living out here in the boonies and driving the one car until someone gives us the money to drive to the British Properties in our twin Porsches."

"You don't understand, madam. This is the most prestigious yacht race in the world! With a good showing, we can put this country near the forefront of world yachting!"

"They must be pretty excited about that in Saskatchewan."

"Madam, we have already raised two million dollars to launch this project, and it's all but gone. What if...?"

"You spent two million dollars to launch a *boat*? You never heard of a car top or a trailer? You back the car down to the launch, take a few friends with you, and all it costs is a couple sixpacks. Fred and me did it once. Got invited on this guy's 12-footer. Fished all day. 'Course, we had to pay a sitter to stay with the kids, and what with our share for the beer and sandwiches it came to a few bucks, but once in a while you gotta go first cabin, right?"

"*Yacht*, madam! *Yacht*! And what I'm trying to point out is that if we don't get the rest of the money those 38 men who've sacrificed and devoted two years of their lives to this project may not be able to..."

"To spend the time sailing in Florida and Rhode Island. I know. Well, times are hard. Listen, who started this thing, anyway?"

"A dedicated group of Calgary businessmen who..."

"So how come you're looking for money in Coquitlam, B.C.? All the oil wells hit water or something?"

"We have to be based in B.C., madam. Those are the rules! We have to base in an area where there's an arm of the sea. That's why we formed the Secret Cove Yacht Club. We're going to put Secret Cove on the map. Some of the Calgary men have condominiums up there, I believe, and there are plans to build a marina..."

15

"Oh, good. And I guess if Fred and me give you some money to help you race in Rhode Island, when you get the marina built we can come up and ride in your boats."

"Well, no..."

"Free fishing trip once a month to stock up the old freezer and beat the grocery bill?"

"Madam, we can't just... Look, perhaps I should come back when your husband's home..."

"Good idea, mister. You come around about seven tonight after his kidneys stop hurting and the kids stop howling and you explain to him like you did to me. I may even keep the kids up."

"Why?"

"They've never seen a guy with a jackhammer up his nose."

HERM THE SPERM

May 29, 1982

Founder of sperm bank for high I.Q. donors and Nobel Prize winners now wants athletes to donate their sperm.— News item.

"Hi there, pretty momma. Herman's the name and spermin's my game. Where do ah sign the RE-lease for the RE-lease?"

"Uh, I beg your pardon, sir?"

"I'm a *donor,* momma! 'Cut out the jive, keep the strain alive', that's my motto. Saw your ad askin' for athletes to come in and contribute and said to myself 'Herm Hotshot, when it comes to genes you are one mean machine! Get over there and spread yourself *around!*' Now, where's my cookie?"

"Cookie, sir?"

"Yeah, cookie. You know — like at the blood bank? You give 'em a pint of supreme and they give you a cookie. Kinda makes the time pass, y'know? You got any Famous Amos?"

"Uh, perhaps you'd best talk to our Mr. Andrews. He's in charge of, uh, deposits."

"Right on, momma. I sure ain't here to make no WITH-drawal!"

"Good afternoon, sir. How may I be of service?"

"Man, I got me a *mortgage* faster'n this over at the other bank. What's the DE-lay? You want to perpetuate what I got, or not? You ain't the only one after me, y'know. I got me a big offer up in the

16

CFL — the Controlled Fetus League. I can go up to Vancouver and sign with the Bank of B.Semen just like that! They give ballpoint pens plus a little pocket-size, battery-operated sperm counter if you bring a friend. I been in your joint ten minutes, I ain't even got me a crummy calendar!"

"Now, now, Mr...uh...Hotshot. Of course we're interested in obtaining your...contribution. But as you must understand, we can't take just any Dick or Peter who happens along. We here at Mutual of Orgasm have *standards*. Do you know, before we started screening applicants we were getting donors who couldn't run a 4.4-second 40?"

"Gowaan!"

"It's true! Flabby biceps, scrawny deltoids...there's no end to it. Here we are, trying to build a bigger, stronger, faster human being through scientific selection and they're trying to fob off shoddy building blocks. That's why we have this battery of tests..."

"Hold it, man! You ain't hookin' me up to no battery. Couple of seconds of that, you could cancel out the old bankbook..."

"No, no, Mr. Hotshot. These are merely a series of test questions to measure your athletic ability and intelligence. First, word association. I'll say a word, and you answer with the first word that comes into your head. Right?"

"Wrong!"

"No, no!"

"Nanette!"

"I mean, don't start yet! All right, first word: 'Pi'!"

"Lemon!"

"Wrong, Mr. Hotshot. It's a mathematical question. When I say 'Pi', the correct answer is 'Pi r squared'."

"That's stupid. Pie are round! CAKE are square!"

"Uh, yes... Now, then, I understand you are a basketball player. That's in your favour. Here at the sperm bank we realize that basketball requires a combination of speed, skill, size and intelligence — all desirable traits in the selection of top-grade donors. Do you feel you are capable of, uh, passing on those traits?"

"Andrews, my man, you are lookin' at one of the all-time great passers. Sign me up and you are gettin' the absolute Kareem of the crop!"

"Fine. Now, how is your floor play?"

"Great, man! Flowers, candy, lemon gin..."

"Mr. Hotshot, I'm afraid this has gone far enough. Yours is not the type of sperm we are seeking. You lack the proper degree of intelligence. You are, to put it mildly, an utter jock! We have ladies of quality in cities all over the nation waiting for a test tube from Mr. Right. How do you think they'd feel, accepting something from a man who has nothing to offer but size, strength and good looks?"

"Gee, I dunno. Tell you what, though: You gimme a few phone numbers, I'll find out and report back."

THE DISH MEETS THE DISH

December 5, 1982

The dish in the living room is not impressed with the dish on the roof. "Your legs will atrophy," sniffs the former Deborah Easton. "You'll be nothing but bald head and belly."

The dish in the living room does not like spectator sports. She doesn't read sports pages. She knows I'm a sports writer because 22 years ago when I married her, I told her. The idea of putting a 300-pound birdbath on the roof to reach into space and grab other games was not greeted with huzzahs. But it's there and it hasn't changed a thing. I'm pigging out on sports. She's still in the living room. I think.

If anything, I'm better organized. When you jump from 13 channels to roughly 140 and one of them is a 24-hour sports channel, you've got to be, or you'll miss something. Take the other night. I got so interested in watching Kentucky play UCLA in college basketball that I missed an entire period of Oilers-Flyers hockey. And last night I fell asleep with a minute or so left in the UCLA-Notre Dame game and blew the final of the Wendy's Classic tournament.

But not to worry: ESPN will give it to me again. And again, and once more after that. Showing sports 24 hours a day forces some repetition. Still, if you don't know the score, watching Herschel Walker and Georgia beat Georgia Tech at one a.m. is just as much fun as watching it live.

Whatshername just called me. "When do you want dinner?" she asked.

"Half time," I said. "Here."

"You want to eat it," she asked sweetly, "or wear it?"

A hard loser, old Della...er, Deborah. Take the night we had a dish brought over for a demonstration.

18

The guy backed it into the driveway on a flatbed truck, made some adjustments, turned on a set in the van — and suddenly, while my neighbours were getting ready to battle traffic to watch the mighty Canucks play Hartford, I was standing in my driveway watching the Sabres and Canadiens play to a 7-7 tie.

"Where's the movie channel?" Dolores asked.

The guy started flipping channels as I went in to get a coat. When I came out, Daphne had a message.

"The Playboy channel works," she said.

"You mean the one with the X-rated movies and live nude centrefolds?"

"That's the one."

"I better check it out, just in case," I suggested.

"Trust me on this," she said. "It works."

"But, this thing is EXPENSIVE! It's gonna cost me a lot of money."

"Not as much as it's gonna cost you if I catch you watching that channel," she replied. You can take the girl out of Victoria, but...

We did not rush into the dish purchase. First the man had to do a site check. There were problems: There was no room in the back yard for the dish. The neighbours, a nice, quiet lot, might not want a ten-foot circular birdbath decorating the front.

"On the roof," the man said. "We'll put it on the roof."

Our house has slanty roofs in all but one area about 15 feet square. "Amazing," the man said. "That's exactly where the dish would have to go."

"You see?" I said, pivoting triumphantly. "That proves it!"

"Proves what?" Denise asked.

"God wants me to have a dish!"

So we bought it. I had to agree to buy a VCR so we could tape movies, and run outlets to a set in another room so she could watch them "while you watch those idiots sweat," but it's in. I can watch NBA and college basketball, all the New York Islanders' games and most of the Oilers', NFL football 'til it comes out of my ears — if you wear a jock to play it, I can watch it.

And it's wonderful. There are, however, minor drawbacks. The December issue of the monthly satellite TV listings (magazine-sized, 133 crammed pages per month) hasn't arrived yet, forcing me to spend as much time searching as watching. I even phoned the publisher in Haley, Idaho, to question the delay.

"Canada?" she asked. "What providence [*sic*] are you in?"

"Divine," I snarled.

"That's our worst one for delivery," she cooed.

But I'll get by. After all, I've got a family, and there's nothing nicer than meaningful family dialogue. Just the other night my 18-year-old son said, "Dad, I can't find the Playboy channel."

"Gosh, son," I replied, "let old Dad help you."

I pushed a few buttons — and suddenly we were looking at a man with a microphone doing a Howard Cosell while several nude couples cavorted on cots. "Welcome," he said, "to the Heterosexual Olympics!"

"UUHHH!" said the young lady who lives with us.

"Migawd!" said Whatshername.

"Dad," my son said, "I think you found it."

MARATHON REVISITED

December 9, 1982

Alberto Salazar and Bill Rodgers to run original marathon route wearing the kind of armor Greek soldiers may have worn in 490 BC. — *The Province*, December 8, 1982.

News that the great marathon argument is about to be settled triggered a certain amount of dissension between Fred and Martha Schwartz, who pride themselves on keeping abreast of world events.

"Makes a man feel proud," Fred said, "knowing that while most of us are wasting our time making a living there are still folks willing to sacrifice to expand the limits of human knowledge, to seek the answers to questions that have plagued mankind for centuries."

"Like what, dear?" Martha asked.

"Like, was the original marathon fixed? Did that guy Pheidippides run the whole route the first time, or did he take a shortcut? We gotta know these things, Martha, or a whole bunch of scholars are gonna go to their graves wondering, and we'll be responsible."

"Pheidippides? I didn't notice his name in the Vancouver Marathon. Is he one of the new boys?"

"Jeez, Martha, haven't you ever read any of your classicals? Pheidippides was the first guy ever to run the marathon. He was a soldier fighting for this hotshot Greek general, and when they beat the crap out of the Persians at Marathon, the general sent Pheidippides running off to Athens to tell the politicians so he could maybe parlay it into a job in the Senate. Pheidippides ran like hell, all 26 miles, 385 yards, delivered the message, and dropped dead.

"But some people say he didn't run the whole route, that maybe he cut through the hills, in which case his time would be phony and the International Track and Field Association would have to take away his medals."

"But, Fred, if he was running to deliver a message, what difference does it make how he got there? That's what I could never understand about all those people being angry at that Rosie Ruiz person. She wanted to get somewhere, she took a shortcut or maybe a subway. Seems entirely sensible to me."

"You don't understand! These two hotshot runners, Salazar and Rodgers, have decided to run the original route wearing armour like the kind Pheidippides wore, and..."

"Pheidippides. My, that *is* a long name, isn't it? Good thing they put numbers on their backs instead of names. Otherwise, he'd have to be continued on the next runner."

"Martha, will you *listen*? It wasn't a race! This one won't be, either. They're running to settle the argument, to prove once and for all whether a guy in armour could run that far or whether he got exhausted and died because he left the road and ran through the hills, or..."

"Uh, Fred, settle whose argument? I never hear about it at bridge club. Do the boys on the Public Works crews argue about it much?"

"Well, no, but..."

"Until you read the paper had you ever heard of *anybody* arguing about it?"

"Not exactly, but... Look! What they're trying to do is recreate the original run under the original conditions. Armour and everything, except of course they'll be wearing proper runners, likely so the shoe people will pick up the tab."

"Why? Did Nike provide shoes for Pheidippides? Did Adidas have a model with those thongs that wrapped up around the leg like you see the soldiers wearing in all those religious movies? Richard Burton looks lovely in them. Mind you, he has marvellous legs and I've never met Mr. Pheidippides, so..."

"It was in 490 BC! Running shoes weren't invented yet!"

"Well, then I certainly think Mr. Salazar and Mr. Rodgers should wear thongs. Either that, or dress sensibly in one of those toga things that look like a woman's nightdress. They're cool, comfortable...but no, I guess they wouldn't dare do that. Bad for their image and all."

"Okay, I'll bite. Why not?"

"Well, you know what they say, Fred: 'Beware of Greeks wearing shifts'."

GO BACK TO HIM, MARTHA!

December 12, 1982

One night in 1982 Vancouver sports entrepreneur Nelson Skalbania — former owner of two pro hockey franchises, one pro soccer franchise and, briefly, the playing rights to a 17-year-old hockey player named Wayne Gretzky — rose at an intimate dinner for 150 to announce his bankruptcy and plead with his wife, Elena, to come back to him. The Vancouver media went nuts.

Radio and TV people hounded him for interviews. One columnist wrote a tear-stained open letter pleading for a reconciliation. Me? I found myself wondering how much fuss there'd have been if they hadn't been jet-setters...

Friends and fellow-workers sat in stunned silence Friday night as Fred Schwartz, video sports-game whiz and high-stakes Monopoly magnate, tearfully confessed that his empire had crumbled and his wife had left him.

The admission — made at the weekly beer-and-bunfeed in the Legion Hall — completely upstaged feature speaker Melvin Fry, whose long-awaited speech entitled "How We Gonna Raise Dough for the New Bumper Pool Table?" received only token applause.

"I'm tapped," Fred announced. "But that ain't important. What's important is, Martha's left me. As soon as I realized she was gone, I knew what a big hole had been ripped in my life. So Martha, wherever you are, I'd really appreciate it if you'd come back. And bring the car keys."

The meteoric rise and fall of Fred Schwartz, first revealed in a hard-hitting *Province* series after an anonymous caller submitted his name as a candidate for help from the Empty Stocking Fund, is classic Canadiana.

Fred Schwartz didn't always have the big job pushing the jackhammer for Public Works. He and Martha didn't always live in the famous two-bedroom Coquitlam bungalow, or drive the Nash Metropolitan, or spend two or three hours a month fishing off the ten-foot rental with outboard. The luxuries didn't start rolling in until the night Fred hit big at Bingo and won a hand-held electronic football game.

It opened up a whole new world.

Suddenly, people were fighting to sit next to him at lunch, offering to share their peanut-butter-and-banana sandwiches — important people like Sam from Hydro, who's in charge of water pressure. If Sam throws a switch, not a john in Vancouver flushes. That's power. And he wanted to play football with Fred Schwartz.

"Games!" Fred thought. "Sports games! A man who's a bigshot sports-games type can call his own shots!"

He sold his car for $200 and bought electronic baseball, hockey and soccer. Overnight, he became one of the Beautiful People. There wasn't a Legion where he could buy his own beer. He was king of the video games. He could have relaxed and lived comfortably forever. A nine-to-five job and nights at the Legion — what more could a guy ask?

But the bug had bitten deeply. He wanted more. One fateful Monday night he gathered all the hand-held games, went to a video shop and flipped them in a package for an Intelevision, an Atari and a Coleco. For collateral he put up the house.

He began to gamble. After all, they were playing on his home machines. A quarter, then 50¢, then a buck — why not? His credit was good. Every Legion branch knew that. They all had his markers.

When he wasn't gambling electronically he was moving equally vast sums of money in lightning real estate deals.

"That's what did me in," he told the crowd Friday. "The economy and Monopoly. They cost me everything, and now they've cost me Martha."

Close friends call his downfall a tale of three houses: One on Baltic, one on Marvin Gardens and one on Boardwalk. "He kept flipping small properties for big ones," they sighed. "Every time he got $200 for passing Go he'd throw it into another mortgage, borrow from the bank, grab another property. And houses weren't good enough. Not for Fred. Oh, no. He had to have hotels. And one day, everything just started to crumble."

It started, they claim, with a custody fight.

Martha, weary of staying home while Fred hit the Legions, began making the trips with him and joining in the game. Soon she owned Boardwalk. The crunch came when she insisted it was her turn to use the Milk Bottle token. Fred refused.

"You had it last time," he snarled.

Martha leaped up, snatched her hotel off Boardwalk, warned him to keep his Milk Bottle off her property, and fled.

Right then, the life seemed to go out of Fred Schwartz. All the fun things — the foreclosures, the squeezing out the player next to him, the sheer joy of watching an opponent languishing in Jail while you refuse to lend him the $50 to get out — suddenly seemed so meaningless without Martha there to share them.

He began making mistakes. Three hotels on Mediterranean, one house on Baltic. Chance and Community Chest hit him for Income Tax. People weren't buying him beer anymore. The Atari, the Intelevision, the Coleco all went to pay his pub tabs. In a matter of weekends his empire crumbled. Friday night at the Legion it all spilled out.

His friends hailed his courage. ("Out to here," the bartender said, holding his hands a foot out below his belt. "He's got 'em out to here.") The Saturday afternoon newspaper carried a fervent editorial plea: "Go Back to Him, Martha! It's Your Roll!"

Saturday night, he and Martha were seen together in the living room of the Coquitlam home. Fifty television cameras and six reporters surrounded the house, demanding a picture and a statement.

Martha came out on the porch. "I'll give you a statement," she said. "This is private property. Get the (bleep) off my lawn or I'll call the cops."

Departing reporters heard Fred's voice from within:

"Honey, you rolled a six. Shall I move the Milk Bottle for you?"

Life, it's assumed, went on.

ADVERB, R.I.P.

January 15, 1985

Mourners at the bedside of the dying English language shivered Sunday with the knowledge that their vigil soon will be ended.

It's been a long and bitter battle. The language of Shakespeare, of Keats and Shelley and Hemingway, of Red Smith and Paul Gallico and Mike Royko has not gone down without a fight. Like the men of the Alamo it will go out with guns blazing, buried under sheer weight of numbers, leaving behind a people reduced to communication by cliche and primordial grunt.

It will be murder, of course. Television pulled the trigger while newspapers and radio held the arms. They shot off the adverb first, leaving the "ly" bleeding on the diamonds and rinks and gridirons and golf courses of North America, putting the boots to it each time it attempted to rise. Before long, people will have forgotten it ever lived.

For a moment on Sunday afternoon, watching Lanny Wadkins battle Craig Stadler through 23 holes to win the Bob Hope Desert Classic, I felt a faint surge of hope. I'll swear John Brodie said Stadler had played a shot "beautifully", not "beautiful", as is his habit.

It must have been wishful thinking, for minutes later we heard this message from Lee Trevino, up in the tower, to Bob Goalby, out on the course: "Bob, you said he's putting good. I'd say he's putting fantastic!"

Before the day was over we also learned that both men "have played fabulous", that "he didn't hit it very good," and that "everybody thinks he's not going to do too good." This is merely a random sampling — time, space and stomach precluding full disclosure.

Personally, I blame Dizzy Dean. He started it. Some network executive decided that Dean's mangling of the language was colourful and before we knew it the past tense of slide was slud.

I didn't mind. It *was* colourful. When ol' Diz said "He brung that one in flat overhand," it even sounded cute. When they made the movie of his life story and built in the fight with the school board and the old maid school teacher who said "We'll keep teaching them English, Mr. Dean. You keep learnin' them baseball," I probably cheered with everyone else. How were we to know it was the thin edge of the wedge?

How could we suspect that, 30 years later, the B.C. Dairy Foundation would run a TV commercial promising that if we'll get fit "You'll look good! Feel good! Do good!"

In the wildest of dreams could anyone have foreseen a Howard Cosell, who was paid more than one million dollars a year to cut the language to ribbons by stringing words together without regard for order or sense?

The plague has swept the land. Name a sport. I guarantee its athletes move quick and play determined. They run a play like it was wrote on paper. They play OH-fence and go on DE-fence. The good

25

ones have some quick and the lazy ones have to get themselves some intense. The best get invites to bowl or all-star games.

Newspapers have a tiny excuse. When we quote someone we're supposed to use their words, not ours. Some don't, which is why a freshman running-back from Florida uses the same phrases as a cricketer from Australia. But announcers are supposed to be giving us their words, not the athlete's. Is it asking too much that they use sentences, or words that have the meaning they give them? Must we let our kids grow up thinking that "y'know" is the access code without which the tongue cannot come on line?

It's such a fine language, full of fire and flowers and music. There isn't a situation, sporting or otherwise, it lacks the words to describe.

Sunday it was beaten senseless with a golf club. Next Sunday — Super Sunday — it will be stomped into the dirt by cleats. You wonder how long it can keep getting up, and how many will care when it can't.

GO, SLOBBIES, GO!

June 18, 1985

Our paper is full of trendy organizations these days — Yuppies, Puppies, Yubbies — a classic example of journalism at its shoddiest.

I have nothing against Young Urban Professionals, Young Urban Breadwinners or any of those other groups who seem to feel it's not what you do, it's how you dress, eat, think and drive while you're doing it. But *The Province* has overlooked the biggest, most dedicated group of all, and frankly I think it's a damned shame.

I refer, of course, to the Slobbies.

Slobbies are the athletic counter-culture, Nature's attempt to achieve some sort of balance before the jock-minded take over the earth and turn it into one big Vic Tanny's. We started out, most of us, as charter members of SLOBS, the Society to Let Our Bodies Stagnate. Maturity and evolution have brought us to where we stand — actually, sit — today: Slobbies — the Society to Let Our Bodies Indulge to Excess.

Slobbies are neither trendy nor social minded. Not for us the gay, mad whirl. (Remember when you could say "gay, mad whirl" without getting queer looks? Remember when you could say "queer"?) It's all too tiring. But, like the Yuppies, Yubbies and the rest, we have our standards and our code:

26

* Slobbies think softball is a physical condition.

* Slobbies never drink mineral water, and think diet soft drinks and lite beer are Commie plots.

* Slobbies believe golf would be a great game if they eliminated clubs, balls, tees and the first 18 holes, and proceeded immediately to the 19th for the drinking and lying.

* Slobbies are in love with the fat little blonde tap dancer in the Molson Golden commercials.

* Slobbies' lone concession to exercise is to watch the *60-Second Workout* on TV. Watching the girls in tight leotards increases their pulse rate.

* Slobbies don't care what kind of car they drive, as long as they don't have to walk.

* Slobbies know that when one of their members shows up the day after his birthday in matching joggers and track suit, his wife is after the insurance money.

* Slobbies know that joggers are people too stupid to figure out why they're sweating.

* Devout Slobbies believe that if God had meant man to cover ground at anything faster than a walk, he'd have an exhaust pipe sticking out his fanny. Slobbies' heaven is a condo with a TV set, a sofa, a chocolate layer cake and a six-pack.

* Fashion-conscious Slobbies believe a real track suit should have a pocket for the Racing Form.

* Slobbies feel that anyone stupid enough to go looking for a wall of pain deserves to find it.

* Slobbies know Rosie Ruiz had the right idea.

* Slobbies believe the Charter of Human Rights is an all-male fishing trip with a stocked cooler and at least one tourist who believes you can draw to an inside straight.

* Slobbies are constantly recruiting new members for the women's auxiliary (the lovely Slobbettes) as part of their poignant, never-ending search for Ms. Right — a curvaceous and pliable lady, strong of wrist for the removal of twist-off caps and willing to do wonderful things with lasagna.

We are not Yuppies or Yubbies any more than in the old days we were Yippies or Hippies. We are Slobbies, and proud of it. We'll even drink a toast to ourselves. If you're buying.

SO LONG, SLOBBIES

March 17, 1987

It was the 50 pink plastic flamingos on my front lawn that made me suspicious. You can't fool me. I'm a trained reporter.

The 51st flamingo sitting on the front porch offered another clue. It had a scroll around its neck informing me I'd just been flocked. In a flash I knew what had happened: My wife had snitched. Twenty-six years of marriage and you wake up one morning to find the chick lying next to you has turned into a stool pigeon.

Saturday wasn't really my 50th birthday. Monday was. My friends had simply gathered early to allow me two extra days of pain. They did it with their usual style — flamingos on the front lawn, huge inflated crocodile in the swimming pool eying the duck decoy I keep there in the hope that dinner will land for a closer look, nasty cards, hair jokes. Boy, who said sentiment is dead?

Down deep inside, the smooth, suave, disturbingly handsome Jim Taylor, he of the wavy hair, the pencil-thin black moustache and the pneumatic blonde on each arm, accepted the gifts with thanks. For the exterior JT, it was a time to make a painful announcement:

I have to resign as president of the Slobbies.

It's not an age thing. As founder of the Society to Let Our Bodies Indulge to Excess, I had long since ruled it a life appointment. Two weeks ago, diabetes cast a veto. It refused to share living space with a guy who considered cake an entree. Upon reviewing my options, the vote was 2-0.

For a guy whose favourite cowboy hero was Wyatt Urp, it was no easy decision. But it wasn't until the nice physiotherapist at the clinic said the E word that it really hit me. We were all sitting there clutching our little diet charts and getting over our surprise at learning that the ketones weren't a '50s rock group — Gary Glucose and the Ketones: Didn't they do "Sugar Shack"? — when she came right out and said it.

"How would you class yourself in terms of exercise?"

I wanted to wash her mouth out with soap. Don't they teach young girls better than that? Where are you, Emily Post, when we really need you? But she wanted a straight answer, so she got one.

"Couch potato," I said proudly. She was not impressed, not even when I casually mentioned that I held the Easter Hot Cross with butter clusters. She just pointed her index finger at me and said the E

28

word over and over again. She didn't care that it would cost me ten columns a year becoming a closet ex . . . exer... Jeez! I can't even *say* it, and now I have to do *it*?

"Not jogging!" I cried desperately. "Joggers are crazy! They go *looking* for the Wall of Pain. They sweat on my lawn! Marathoners cross the finish line and throw up — and they think it's fun!"

"No jogging," she agreed. "But plenty of long, brisk walks."

Migawd! First the E word, then the W word. The woman has no shame. Why couldn't she use decent words like ride, or taxi, or bus? They worked fine for Rosie Ruiz. Why not for me?

But I'm doing it. I'm riding Nick the Matchmaker's Ankle Express. One foot forward, then the other, then the first one again. Step on a crack and I break my mother's back. I am even (sob) riding an exercise bike. Only while watching hockey games, of course. A man has his limits. It's got lousy mileage, but so do I.

There are side benefits. In moderation, I can eat almost anything but desserts. And if I stumble or want to quit, there is a loving nag here to spur me on. A man can't ask for more than that.

But I can't be a Slobbie anymore. A man who turned his back on a rich, gooey 50th birthday cake is no longer fit to lead.

PRESENTS FROM THE PAST

December 11, 1975

The man on television is talking about air hockey, in which the puck floats on an invisible cushion of air at phenomenal speed for only $40 (batteries not included). It is the low-priced model. Those not up to inserting batteries can buy deluxe models with special table and plug-in, which start at $165.

He is followed by an identical man pushing one of the new games you plug into your TV set, battling with electronic blips on your own TV screen, playing hockey or football or tennis by remote control for around $125.

They are magic, these games, if you happen to be an adult. The children merely accept them. They've seen them and everything else on TV. They work, never mind how. In all the talk of family hours and violence, television's greatest crime against children goes unpunished: it has killed their sense of wonder.

But for a guy closing in on his 40th year, the wonder remains. The screen blurs as the mind reaches back to other Christmases, other lists of things you couldn't afford and knew you'd never get. Except that it was Christmas, and dreaming came easily.

And he wonders: If he could bring them back now, all the things he played with that were so essential to being a kid, and place them under the tree for his own kids, could they begin to understand...?

The baseball might puzzle them — the one with the electrician's tape wrapped around it, layer upon layer. You couldn't play baseball without electrician's tape. Games on gravel roads and vacant lots played hell with the stitching, and the baseballs kids could buy were never meant to last. The cover came off and the tape came on, a ritual of spring.

And the glove, the one with the real pocket and the leather pad between thumb and forefinger. "Molded Pocket", it said, right there where the ball would stick. It wouldn't look like much now, up against the autographed Little League models, but a lot of love was rubbed in with the neat's-foot oil.

It would be difficult, too, to explain what his big brother was doing under the tree. A big brother was an essential. You opened your presents and kept an eye out while he opened his because if he got a new something it meant you'd get his old one — a pair of skates, maybe third-hand already; a set of pads. If your brother played goal you played goal, too, and dreamed of inheriting those pads.

There was street hockey then as now, but no nets, no superblades, no special puck. You wanted a puck, you waited for a cold day and a passing horse. How do you put that under a tree? The kids would figure you'd flipped.

The football would draw snickers. Hard rubber, so heavy throwing it was like shot-putting, and when you caught it your hands stung. The day your buddy got one that was inflatable he was automatic captain and king of the block. But a hard rubber football? Gross, Dad. Not cool.

But more than anything else he'd like them to see the hockey game, which wasn't his.

He was nine, and his best friend owned it. A glorious thing it was, solid wood, the sides painted red, the rest left wood colour. Two knobs at each end and a pinball-type spring that shot a steel marble onto the wooden ice surface.

One knob controlled your two defencemen and three forwards, who were bolted to the ice. Only their sticks — coat-hanger wire formed in a V — moved when the knob was pulled, and every stick moved at once. The other knob controlled the goalie, who slid from side to side in his crease, a straight, rounded peg of wood with no stick.

It was smaller than today's fancier plastic models but it always seemed huge — too huge for a nine-year-old to borrow casually and take home for an hour. Besides, the house was seven blocks away from his, it was winter, and by the time school ended it was dark. He was terribly afraid of the dark. But he wanted desperately to have it in his own house, if only for a day, and his friend said he could if he'd come and get it.

So one night after supper he took his sled and raced the seven blocks through the darkness. It was snowing lightly, so the wondrous game had to be wrapped in newspapers. And because it was a precious thing it could not be run home lest the sled tip and plunge it into a drift.

He walked it home. Slowly, carefully, stopping from time to time to rearrange the newspapers and keep the snowflakes out.

Monsters lurked in the shadows. He knew they were there, waiting. The crackling frost made footstep sounds. Security lay in flight. But he walked, and he got the game home and was allowed to keep it for one entire week.

He sighs now, thinking how much he'd like to put that game under this year's tree. But they don't make them anymore. He's looked, even tried to find one second-hand. They are gone.

Maybe it's just as well. It would have no magic buttons, no individual controls, no flashing lights. They'd find it a pretty dumb game.

THERE AUTO BE A LAW

August 25, 1990

My first car was an Austin A40 so small I could date only midgets. When we parked on Clover Point the other kids stopped necking to yell "Good luck!"

My second car was a '53 Chev, gearshift on the steering column so a guy could scrunch casually over to share the passenger seat without risking rupture. Two kids found it in a bowling alley parking lot, hotwired it, drove it until the tank was empty and pushed it over a cliff.

My third car was a brand-new, 1959 MGA convertible, white with red upholstery, side pockets in the doors. On the night of what

I had tentatively scheduled as D-Day, the girl in question over-wined, over-pizza-ed, and almost got her head out the door before she threw up.

Unbeknownst to me, she'd filled the side pocket of my new car. The next day I covered a golf tournament, leaving my car in the parking lot with the top down. The temperature hit 95 Fahrenheit. When I came back at seven p.m. the lot was crowded but there was a huge empty space around my car. From 30 feet away, you knew why.

I hosed it down from a distance and kept it — short, stubby, infuriating stick shift and all. Eventually, you could learn the four speeds forward by reading my navel.

By my fourth car I was married, making model and style academic. (It was an Envoy that should have had "Sardines" stamped on both doors. I kept waiting for someone to reach in and close my eyes.) But the first three scarred my psyche: I cannot get the least bit revved up about car racing of any sort. A guy spends four years in high school trying to park and now he should watch a bunch of guys who don't even want to stop?

Obviously it is my loss. There isn't a faster-growing sport around. Me, I'd as soon watch a freeway.

Part of it is ignorance and a searing memory of the day I attended a Sports Car Club press conference featuring a car called the JM-2. I spent five minutes studying the rear of the car, trying to look knowledgeable. "That's not the back," someone said kindly. "That's the front."

Or maybe it's all those sponsors' decals: Beer, cigarettes, motor oil, airlines — you name it, you'll find it plastered somewhere. It's bad enough on the cars — assuming there is a car under there somewhere. The drivers look like stamp albums. Meet one and you don't know whether to light him, drain him, fly him, pour him or shake his hand.

Then again, it could be the jargon gap. "Rear wing", "tub", "down force", "G-force" — are we talking cars here, or space shuttles? The world has passed me by. What would I say to these guys? Give them the spec sheet on the old A40?

CHASSIS: leaky. WHEELS: four. BRAKES: occasionally. STEERING: eventually. FUEL CAPACITY: always more than fuel money.

Lovely old car, the A40. It had but one real drawback. Driving or parked, we rarely got as far as we'd hoped. But then, at 17, who did?

INDY SPOKEN HERE

August 28, 1991

Because car racing is my life, I have been asked to provide a simple answer to the No. 1 Question asked by first-time spectators at an Indy-type race:

"What the hell is going on?"

This is usually followed, logically enough, by the No. 2 Question:

"How come the cops pull me over if I do 30.0001 mph on a deserted road at three a.m., but these guys can break the sound barrier on city streets in the middle of the day and the only cops around are the ones assigned to make sure no one bothers them?"

There is a simple explanation for all this confusion: First-time spectators do not know the Jargon used by the people around them, the life-long racing fans who speak Car. Therefore, the first thing would-be Indy fans should do is run out and form a meaningful relationship with someone who does.

It's easy. Just hang around singles bars going "Vroom! Vrrrr-OOM! VRRRRRR-OOOM!"

If a member of the opposite sex responds with "Hi! What's your rpm? Your garage or mine?" you have found your 'enry (or 'enrietta) 'iggins, that Mr. or Ms. Right who will soon have you saying things like "crankshaft", "spoiler" and "I'd like to thank the Good Lord and Molson's" as though you'd grown up in a pit crew.

Or, since time grows short for this particular race, you can simply memorize the following terms:

LAP: Where your engine can wind up if you make a Really Big Mistake. (See: WALL)

BALACLAVA: A street in Kerrisdale. If you live on Balaclava and you see Mario Andretti go by at 200 mph, chances are he has made a wrong turn.

OVERSTEER: A common mistake by rookie drivers, who tend to pig out on steak at the pre-race meal when they should be loading up on carbohydrates.

OVERWATER: Rookie driver, suddenly realizing he's actually going to climb into this thing and race it, attempts to compensate for dry mouth by drinking a quart of liquid. (See: PIT STOP)

POP-OFF VALVE: A safety device surgically implanted behind a driver's left ear. Originally designed for pressure cookers, it allows drivers to let off excess steam without injuring themselves or spectators when a member of the media peers into their two-million-dollar car and asks how come it has no stereo or a set of angora dice hanging from the rear-view mirror.

STAGGER: The difference in circumference between right and left-side tires. Also: common rookie error when pulled over for speeding and asked to step out of the car.

YELLOW FLAG: Flag waved by hooting spectators at drivers who complete the entire race without once hitting a wall, throwing a tire or having one of those Narrow Escapes they paid good money to see.

TIRE: Weariness caused by trying to figure out who's ahead once cars start lapping one another.

BANKING: Monday morning ritual by Really Good Drivers who made weekend prize list.

WITHDRAWING: Monday morning ritual by Really Angry Sponsor whose driver *didn't* make weekend prize list.

DECELERATE: Pronounced DECAL-erate, from the French, meaning "the peeling off of former sponsor's decals". (See: WITHDRAWING)

"ADIOS, OLD PAINT": Traditional prayer of pit crew which must repaint each car after every race. Sometimes called "A horse of a different colour".

"SPEAK UP! I CAN'T HEAR YOU!" Monday morning ritual by spectators who had track-side seats all weekend.

ENOUGH TO CURL YOUR HAIR

March 3, 1991

The first thing I noticed, watching the Canadian women's Eskimo bowling championship, was that, collectively speaking, the participants seemed much younger and much better looking than they were in the misspent days of my youth.

Fortunately a little voice whispered in my inner ear:"Don't write that! The Aunties will get you!"

"The Aunties?" I whispered back.

"You know! The Terrible Twosome: Auntie This and Auntie That!"

He (or possibly she) was right. It could cause trouble. ("Dear sexist pig: You obviously hate older people and any woman who

34

doesn't make it to the *Sports Illustrated* swimsuit issue. You stink and we hate you. Signed: Committee for Rational Unbiased Discussion (CRUD).")

So I won't write that.

Instead, let us consider the development of the game that has progressed from the frozen lakes and rivers of Scotland through the drafty rinks with the pot-bellied stove at one end to winter clubs where the state of the ice ranks second only to the size of the cocktail lounge and on to the heated rinks with the artificial ice where the likes of Victoria's Julie Sutton and New Brunswick's Heidi Hanlon can do battle as they did yesterday in Saskatoon.

BROOMS: The original Scottish curlers used straw brooms yielded with nary a protest by their wives and/or girlfriends. This had two advantages: The wives didn't complain when the men went off to curl because losing the broom gave them a break from housework and the men a chance to go somewhere and drink. Later, the Scots switched to pushbrooms because they were easier to lean on when you were still hammered but had to at least pretend to sweep.

ROCKS: The first curling rocks (also known as STONES) were taken from the Scottish hills because they were free, and matched by watching them as they were rolled down the hills onto passing Englishmen. The move to manufactured stones and peace with England occurred over the protests of old-timers who thought rock 'n' roll was here to stay.

CLOTHING: The early curlers wore rubber overshoes and pre-synthetics sweatpants ("breeks") and sweaters that weighed about 300 pounds and made participants look like matched sets of wheat stooks. This year's move to team jackets is considered a definite step forward. Now instead of stooks they look like touring softball players.

LOUNGE: A rest area developed in Alberta after Humungous Hec Gervais rose to fame and single-handedly blocked all the heat from the pot-bellied stove. The modern lounge is a curling essential in that it provides a comfortable place to pick up a drink or a companion, to watch and to second-guess. Curling remains the only game that could not exist without a liquor licence.

PITFALLS: As Heidi Hanlon can now attest, for all its technological wonders, the sport can be won or lost by picking up a hair from one of the modern miracle pushbrooms. The old Scots never had that problem with their wives' brooms. It was easy to see a piece of straw — or a piece off last night's haggis.

HOIST THE MARTINI, A TALE OF THE SEA

May 3, 1991

As you all know, yachting is my life.

There's nothing like the thrill of climbing up the stairs to the main floor of one of those big shippy things, strolling from the pointy end to the back, then popping downstairs for a spot of grog (or, as we yachtsmen call it, Perrier).

It's a humbling thing, standing alone out there with nothing between you and the briny deep but a solid teak floor and a basement full of about $60,000 worth of navigational and sonar gear to track the fish you may want to kill later, gazing up at the stars you'll soon be counting on to guide you the 30 or 40 yards down the dock to the yacht club.

For years I've been enthralled by the sheer beauty of these vessels as they sit parked by the dock, listening to the colourful language of the sailors who yearn to go down to the sea in ships and will if they can ever get everything working at the same time.

"Aw, Dad, I polished the teak last time! Can't I go play football?"

"Polish the goddamn teak! This is a family outing! Have fun or I'll kill you!"

"Harry, don't you yell at him like that! It isn't enough that we mortgaged the house to buy this thing which we never get to sail because it's always broken and we spend every waking hour trying to fix it. No! You've gotta strut around like some kinda Captain Bligh! You know what you are, Harry? You're nothing but a big... what's the name of that white whale?"

"You mean Moby Dick?"

"Well, I dunno about the Moby part, but you're definitely a..."

But that's the beauty of being a yachting fan: You never have to go out on the water!

Face it, there's nothing to do out there anyway but drink and get seasick. Veteran fans sit in restaurants overlooking the dock, sipping something cool and gazing at the boats of their dreams, because *they* never actually go out to sea, either!

Think about it: Have you ever passed a boat-parking place that isn't jammed? Never! They're never ready (or, as we say, shipshape). They just sit there, supported by the lapping waters and overlapping mortgages.

Not all of them. It is a little-known fact, but some yachts actually get out to sea and race. That's when the excitement really gets out of hand.

Take the weekend Swiftsure Classic race in Juan de Fuca Strait, a body of water so cold a person would have to be terminally dumb to sail on it in anything smaller than the *Queen Mary*.

On Sunday, John Buchan of Seattle was declared the winner in his sloop (a nautical term meaning "really expensive") which he named *Heather*, perhaps because Hang On Sloopy sounded common. Rookie yacht-watchers were not surprised, since Buchan crossed the finish line first, one hour and 44 minutes ahead of his brother, Bill, on board his sloop *Sachem*, named after the late, great New Orleans skipper, Sir Louis of Armstrong.

But wait! The margin of victory was then lowered to eight minutes after figuring in the "ratings", a complex procedure in which factors such as weight, length, height and the number of crew sailing three sheets to the wind are fed into a computer which spews out figures about as simple to read as the Dead Sea Scrolls.

However, John was still the winner.

But wait again! With computers rolling at flank speed it took officials only until Wednesday to discover that the machine had fouled up and *Bill* was the real winner by 11 minutes and 59 seconds. Pending appeal, which can happen any time in the next three weeks.

How fortunate we are that Columbus was a simple sailor. If he'd been a yachtsman, we'd all still be living in Genoa.

CHINESE HAGGIS TO GO

August 14, 1991

Why are they screaming in Scotland over that Chinese historian's claim that the game of golf actually originated in China? You'd think they'd be happy to shift the blame.

Here they've got a country ready to take the blame for centuries of broken marriages, 19th-hole alcoholism, congenital lying, plusfours, exorbitant green fees, wanton waste of prime agricultural land, over-priced sweaters and that idiot who shows up at every major tournament screaming "You're the man!" whenever Jack Nicklaus swings — and they're fighting it.

"Stunned," the wire story calls the Scots. Boy, they've got that right.

Any self-respecting Scot should be hailing the discoveries of Professor Ling Hongling of mighty Northwest Normal University in Lanzhou, who claims golf matches are recorded in Chinese history as far back as AD 943 — or 400 years before that first enraged Scot hit a ball and chased it lest he lose it and have to buy another one.

What an opportunity to get out from under.

Until now the Scots have lived under the cloud of the Enormous Mistake of 1457, when the Scottish military complained that the game was distracting Scots from archery practice. Spurning the obvious solution (have the archers practise on the golfers), Parliament banned the sport forever. Naturally, forever didn't mean forever (See: PAROLE BOARD). By 1754 the Scots were back hitting the old ball (some say the *same* ball), forming the Royal and Ancient and stealing the ball markers of tourists silly enough to use pennies.

In no time at all they'd given the world a game featuring membership fees so high only bank robbers need apply, for the privilege of hitting the ball from the back with an assortment of expensive clubs and driving it to where it must be pursued in order to be hit again.

For some reason the Scots are proud of this. Mind you, these are the people who serve their traditional meal using a sheep's stomach for a casserole dish.

It has never occurred to them that any golfer with brains enough to know that the ball washer is for the game's equipment and not the player's would buy one club, put the ball down in his back yard and hit it on *top* so it lodges in the dirt where he can hit it again whenever he feels like it. No golf cart, no green fees, and if he wants a beer it's a few steps to the kitchen. Perfect.

Then again, what can we expect from the people who formed a committee to invent the flute and emerged with the bagpipes?

But now Professor Hongling has given them a way out. He says golf is actually a Chinese game called "chiuwan" — from the Chinese "chiu" (hitting) and "wan" (ball).

They should grab it while they can. Even the Scots have to admit it would explain one of the game's great unsolved mysteries — why the game's addicts can play 18 holes, and 20 minutes later they want to play again.

ANNIE, YOU DONE ME WRONG

February 6, 1991

I was a kid, maybe nine or ten, hunched by the radio waiting for a secret message to decode with my new Ovaltine Little Orphan Annie Secret Decoder Ring.

The message came. Letter by letter I decoded it:

D-R-I-N-K O-V-A-L-T-I-N-E.

I never did.

Other kids kept telling me how good it was. My mother said it was good for me. Deep down I even wanted to try it. Years later my own children smacked their lips over it. It smelled delicious. I yielded not.

I'd loved Little Orphan Annie. Okay, so she wore the same red dress and never changed those little white socks. Nobody's perfect. She had a neat dog and a rich old man and a turbaned giant to thump on big people who bothered her. What else was there?

So I entrusted her with a major portion of my allowance just so I could be the first in my gang to get that decoder ring, to collect all the secret messages and make my friends crawl to hear them.

What did I get? DRINK OVALTINE.

It scarred me. But out of that moment came three Rules of Life I have never broken:

1. Never drink Ovaltine.
2. Never trust a girl with no pupils in her eyes.
3. Never collect anything.

Collecting had never been a big thing with me. By the time they'd passed through three sets of hands the baseball cards were grubby and dog-eared. You could lay roadbed with the gum. Ace Percival's track-and-field tips were aimed at athletes and even then I was showing all the physical promise of the stumbling clod to come. It was, I thought, a pretty dumb pastime — but at least it was sincere.

Kids collected baseball cards because baseball players were their heroes. Years later, when my own son collected and pasted the NHL Power-Players in the book he got from the service station, it was because he liked collecting and liked hockey players. When he got Bob Plager to finish the book it was a big deal.

I think that's the part that's gone missing.

Card collecting is big business. In publishing Bob Scott's new columns on the subject *The Province* is responding to a volatile market generating millions of dollars. Big companies fight to grab the newest superstars. The cards themselves are multi-coloured, market-packaged wonders.

But I listen to kids swapping cards and they're not using words like "trade" or "swap" or "I'll give you two Mickeys for a Willie". They're less interested in the athlete than in the condition of the card itself. Why? Because the better the condition, the higher the price.

They buy the magazines listing the worth of certain cards. They hold long conversations on "futures", the cards that have the best chance of increasing in value over the next few years. Their cards aren't stuffed in their pockets next to their Kleenex or their frog; they're carefully stashed in individual plastic slipcovers or in some cases embedded in plastic. This isn't fun, this is business.

Maybe it's an offshoot of organized minor sport, where the price of better fields and uniforms and schedules is the magic of choosing up sides and playing until you feel like quitting.

Maybe it's the Hockey Pool Syndrome, in which the scores are now secondary to who did the scoring. Or maybe it's the kids themselves, raised on Michael J. Fox as Alex Keaton, boy priest of the profit margin.

Whatever. The point of collecting used to be the keeping. Now it's the market growth potential. Nothing wrong with that, I suppose, but it's cost the kids one of the really fun games of card collecting: flipping them into a hat.

With a bubble-gum card you could do that. With a practically pristine Eric Lindros that might some day be worth big bucks you wouldn't dare. I find that kind of sad.

THE LONG JOHN SOLUTION

April 15, 1992

One good thing about the NHL strike: It gave me time to save the America's Cup.

You know the America's Cup — the yacht race where gallant men of many nations go down to the sea in ships to cast their fate to the winds, armed with nothing more than strength of heart, mind and body and enough computer technology to launch a Mars probe?

Had not Bob Goodenow seen fit to convince his jockstrapped legions to hit the bricks, there'd have been no reason to stay glued to TSN, not daring to leave the big race lest the network interrupt it for another fireside cry with John Ziegler or some 22-year-old trying to get by on $400,000 a year.

That being the case, there'd have been no opportunity to study the race and come up with the one ingredient that could make it interesting for people besides those guys in the Old Spice commercials and yachtsmen with enough money to buy Newport:

Grapeshot.

Originally, I leaned toward missiles. Conventional, nothing atomic. But grapeshot has all that historical significance going for it: Errol Flynn and Burt Lancaster swashing their buckles on the high seas; Gregory Peck hammuphing his way through Captain Horatio Hornblower, clearing freebooters' decks with shot, ever-careful not to spatter the luscious Virginia Mayo as she panted her way to stardom...

Yeah, grapeshot would do it. Mount one cannon port and starboard on every America's Cup yacht and let them go at it. Get some excitement into it. Or, as Long John Silver would have put it: "Aye, mateys — better to die of shot than boredom, eh?"

At that, the crews can't be as bored as the poor guy in the TV truck directing the show:

"Okay, Camera One, tight shot on the Japanese doing nothing. Now Two, gimme the French doing nothing. Now Three, the Americans doing nothing. Three?...Camera Three! Somebody get out there and wake that man up! Please, God, give me a storm. A typhoon, maybe? Okay, okay, a little storm. We've got viewers dropping like flies. Amen."

I know the yachting fraternity will not heed my suggestion. They're still mad at me for suggesting a decade back that a nationwide, fund-raising drive to build Canada an America's Cup yacht might not exactly wow the farmers in Saskatchewan. And, when they got it built and raced, my plea to cut the thing up into souvenir *Canada I* cuff links and tie clips to get the money back.

But they've got to do *something*. A panoramic shot of these beauties under sail is breathtaking. But you can't show two hours of that. Eventually, the cameras have to show you what is actually happening on the boat. And when there's little or no wind, that appears to be damned little.

What we have here is a major marketing problem. How are spectators supposed to get wrapped up in a race when almost every close-up shot shows one guy holding the wheel as though he's got power steering and a bunch of other guys sitting around waiting for those frenzied few minutes in which two of them pump frantically on two-handed winches and the rest pretend it's fire drill?

Look at the crew and their positions, on which I have done considerable research:

SEWERMAN: You never see this guy. He's downstairs hauling sails in and out. For all we know, it could be Art Carney.

BOWMAN: Attaches jib to forestay, mans foredeck. Possibly shoots arrows at rival yacht.

GRINDERS: Operate winches that trim headsails. Don Cherry's favourite sailors, unless they're European.

TAILERS: Really? On a yacht?

MAINSHEETMAN: See: Tailers.

There are a bunch of other guys like navigator and mastman and skipper and the most important guy of all, the tactician, whose job it is to advise Dennis Conner on which corporate sponsor to hit up for another million or so, and which lawyers to hire when the losers go to court to have the winners disqualified.

I tell you, grapeshot could save the sport. They wouldn't have to use the old-fashioned kind, which ran to rusty nails, chunks of iron and anything else found lying around that would cause pain upon impact. Make an environmental statement: Recycle the used olives from the martinis at the Club.

That way, the winners would have another reason to drink, and the losers could say it was the pits.

Chapter Two

THE SWEET SCIENCE

Professional boxing is the rawest, meanest, dirtiest, crookedest sport on the face of the earth. Maybe that's what makes it so fascinating.

Show me another sport that produces a Don King, who did time for murder and emerged to become a feared and fearsome controller and manipulator of the heavyweight division and its champions. "Only in America!" he crows. God willing, he's right.

Then there is the Wisconsin state licensing department which in May of 1990 allowed a comeback fight for former world junior welterweight champion Aaron Pryor. When someone questioned the prudence of licensing a fighter legally blind in one eye and fresh out of a drug-abuse program, department secretary Marlene Cummings replied that "Handicapped people should not be penalized for their handicaps. They should be allowed to do the same things non-handicapped people can do."

Yet this same sport produces a Runyonesque, live-on-the-fringe promoter named Nick the Matchmaker, who once found himself dead broke in a bar in Alaska and raised his out money by staging an impromptu fight card right there — "Hudson's Bay rules, boys. Hit 'em with everything, but no shivs!" — and the wondrous Archie Moore, who sat with me for two magical hours in Edmonton and told me what it was to be young and black and exploited. "The freeest I ever felt in my life was when I played the slave, Jim, in the Huckleberry Finn movie," he said. "That time my agent got ten per cent and I kept the rest."

On that same day, 36 hours before a bulbous, 41-year-old George Foreman would paw his way past a Canadian trial horse named Ken Lakusta en route to a $12,000,000 payday in a heavyweight title fight with Evander Holyfield, I met a short, bent-nosed story machine named Mouse Strauss, manager of Canadian flyweight Scotty Olson, who bragged that he'd fought 245 times and lost most of them.

"Once I fought twice on the same card," quoth the Mouse. "I'd just been kayoed in one fight, and when I woke up in the locker room I was listening to the main-event fighter coming up cold feet and duckin' out on his fight. I put on a different set of trunks and fought that one as my twin brother. Got knocked out in that one, too — but I got paid twice."

Or, the Mouse on his world record: "I had the world's shortest fight. Eleven seconds. I was gettin' some last-second instructions in my corner, turned around, and woke up in the dressing room. Getting the record was easy enough. The tough part was getting paid for it."

Nick and the Mouse and hundreds like them are the other part of the game, the short-on-bread, long-on-dreams guys with the thousand stories of the times they were this close to hitting it large. The Mouse loves to tell and retell the old stories, which are mostly jokes on himself. But there is a note of pride as he claims the modern-day record for most fights and most times knocked out, and mourns the shortage of old-school fighters who'll go anywhere, fight anybody.

"I am," he laments, "the last of a dead breed."

BIG NOISE IN THE VALLEY

December 18, 1981

Larry Holmes and Gerry Cooney to earn $10 million each for heavyweight title fight. Sugar Ray Leonard and Thomas Hearns guaranteed minimum $12 million each for middleweight title bout. — *The Province*, December 17.

The scribes gathered with the dawn in the tent in the Valley of Elah. For it was here, on the site of the original battle, that promoter Don King would announce details for the greatest rematch in history, the Return of the Bible Belters — David vs Goliath.

Because of what he termed "the enormous religious significance of a fight fans have been awaiting for centuries," King had decided to stage the actual negotiations before the world press. You could sense that time had not cooled the animosity.

DAVID: "Still got your coat of mail, eh, Fatso. Better pull it up over your forehead or you'll go down in one like last time."

GOLIATH: "Sheep lover!"

KING: "Gentlemen! Gentlemen! Let us get down to the issues. First and foremost, the purse split."

DAVID: "I don't lift a sling for less than $20,000,000. I'm the champion. Give him $10,000,000 tops. And I get the closed circuit and all ancillary rights including the T-shirts."

GOLIATH: "No way, Shorty. You get lucky in one fight, and..."

DAVID: "One fight! One fight! That's all I ever hear. Before I decked you last time the beef was that I had no fights. Even Saul was buggin' me about it. Ask the lion I smote when he stole one of my lambs. POW! Right in the mouth! And when the bear got into it I whupped him, too. What about them?"

GOLIATH: "Big deal. The WBA didn't recognize the lion and you hit the bear when he was hibernating. I asked your whole damn Israeli army to come out and fight. You only came out 'cause you lost the draw..."

KING: "Uh, I think we can leave that for the moment, gentlemen. Let us move along to the actual site for the fight."

GOLIATH: "Right here in the valley, same as last time. I'll whip him on his own turf. I'll fight him right now for nuthin! I'm the baddest! I'm..."

DAVID: "You're the *dumbest!* Look at this place. Mountain on one side, mountain on the other side, lousy sight lines. This is AD, man! The 20th century! You think people will pay half a grand to stand on a hill for a fight? No slot machines, no johns...? Nah! It's got to be Caesars. That gives us all the comforts plus maximum advertising potential in the major market areas. You wanna fight in front of two camels and an ox, that's your business. Me, I'm goin' for the shekels."

KING: "I've been handed a question by the scribes. Goliath, what weight do you plan to come in at?"

GOLIATH: "I never worry about my weight. Long as I got my six cubits and a span, I..."

DAVID: "Sure — and your 5,000-shekel coat and your greaves of brass around your legs, and your spear with the shaft like a weaver's beam — you look like a scrap-iron drive, and me with nothing but a robe and a jockstrap. Whyncha come out and fight like a man?"

GOLIATH: "People who throw stones shouldn't knock brass housing, creep. You got in one lucky shot last time and even then I had to be out of shape. I didn't sweat a drop during the whole fight. I think it was my pituitary medicine. All that trying to put on an extra cubit in a hurry left my forehead weak. But this time I'm ready. Say goodbye to your sheep, baby. It's over!"

KING: "Goliath, the scribes note that in the first fight David took your own sword and cut off your head. How do you respond to doctors who say if you fight again you're risking permanent damage?"

GOLIATH: "Listen, for ten million dollars they can cut off whatever they want and I'll come back, fight, and do the anthem as a soprano."

KING: "And for you, David — is there any truth to published reports that God will be in your corner?"

DAVID: "We're workin' on that. We figure He'll be worth four points in the Neilsens. Last time we fought for nothing. This time we're gonna do it right."

A CLASS OPERATION

April 29, 1972

Sixty years ago they'd have come in by wagon, thrown up a big tent on the outskirts of town, sold their fight and their snake oil and fled with the money and the dawn.

But we live in sophisticated times. Now they come in by plane, hitting the hicks with Aliburgers and Chuvaloburgers, on sale at your local drive-in. They flog their name fighter on an open-mouth show with a wrestler, producing 90 minutes that would insult the intelligence of a sponge. They parade a list of visiting celebrities to prove we've really hit it big. They hold giveaways, including some of those $100 tickets they said were sold out weeks ago.

And they sweat a lot. Because so far, the hicks aren't buying. As of last night they'd sold 3,500 tickets. How serious that is depends on whom you believe. For a further report on that we take you now to Fight Control Central...

Down on the third floor, the somewhat abridged version of the celebrated, 96-hour non-party is beginning to move because, what the hell, they ain't fighting and it ain't their dough. So Murray Pezim's a guppy in a piranha pond — it's *their* fault? Easy on the mix, Mac.

46

In room 508 sit Murray Goodman and son Bob, who push both the fight and the closed-circuit TV that just might save Pezim from the worst bath since they dipped the witches at Salem. Goodman Sr. is being optimistic.

"This fight now has a chance," he insists, gesturing with a soggy cigar, "because this fight now has credibility. Chuvalo has a chance!

"Well, okay, not much of a chance," he says as a visitor blinks. "But a chance. And that's what will bring the people in. Ticket sales...well, fight people are late buyers. Forty-two years in the business, it's been my experience that if you take the gate you've got the morning of the fight and triple it, that will be your gate."

He heads for the bar and is replaced by Bob, who says it's been his experience that if you double the gate you've got the morning of the fight, that'll be your gate. In 30 seconds we've lost one-third of the gross.

Out in the hall, Nick the Matchmaker is asked for a scientific analysis of what's gone wrong. "I think," he says judiciously, "the %$&%$ have underestimated the %$%#% intelligence of the $%%$% blue-collar guy carrying the %$&%! lunch bucket into the %$#&! pub. Those are the guys who make your %$#&! fight!"

Earlier, somebody asked Nick about celebrities and he named, among others, Robert Goulet, who blew the anthem in the Ali-Liston fight. Could it be that...

"Nah!" scoffs Nick. "We got him singing in the semi-main. We give him 'O Canada' 'cause we figure it's easier. Murray's bringin' in somebody else for the American anthem."

(Inside, Murray G. is elaborating on the Credibility Theory. "George can win," he says. "You never know what's gonna happen. Lookit Pittsburgh in 1951. They give the old man, Jersey Joe Walcott, a last payday for old times' sake. He gets lucky, catches Ezzard Charles on the jaw and, bingo, we got a new heavyweight champion. Not for long, mind you, but...")

A guy named Shelly hauls out a sheaf of publicity shots of the many celebrities who are to flood our lucky village. There's Yvonne Craig, who played Batgirl on TV and from what I saw could whip both of these stiffs. There's Karen Malouf, somewhat of a sport herself in *Hell's Angels on Wheels* and *Savage Five*. There is Edy Williams of *Return to the Valley of the Dolls*.

"And," Shelly says with justifiable pride, "we've got the star of *Cat Balou*!" He's wrong. They haven't got the drunken horse at all. They've got Michael Callan. Obviously, an expansion fight.

("...and you look at the Buster Mathis fight," Murray G. goes on. "No credibility. He loved Ali. Used to follow him around, laughing at his jokes. We're supposed to sell that? And Mac Foster...no way he could ever beat Ali, so no credibility. But George...")

In the elevator, a bunch of the fight mob are telling each other what a class %$#%$ fight this is gonna be. At the rear stands a stately lady in furs, quietly radiating more class than the rest of the joint combined. Ella Fitzgerald is going to work. Maybe they can get her to do the anthem in scat.

THE USUAL QUART OF BLOOD

May 2, 1972

George Chuvalo went out and did his thing last night. He bled.

He plodded stoically out for 36 minutes against this curious, one-fisted boy-child with the greatest legs since Man O' War and took the pounding everyone knew he must. He accepted the usual amount of punishment and shed the usual amount of blood, and when it was over he said yes, he wanted to do it again.

He was courageous, all right. No one has ever questioned George's courage. But even at the $1,666.66 per minute he got last night it was sad and somehow terribly wrong.

George is a throwback. He shouldn't be fighting a Muhammad Ali. He belongs back there in the 18th century throwing bare knuckles at Jem Mace or Sam "The Bath Butcher" Martin, when a round ended only when one man went down and sometimes there were 30 or 40.

Over 20, he might take an Ali if they gave him time out for transfusions, since pride and a concrete jawbone keep him so unfailingly vertical. But today, cursed with a skin that splits at a piercing glance, he can only stand out there and give.

He was giving again last night, walking steadily forward to meet a left jab thrown with contemptuous arrogance by an Ali who has flaked the rust off some of the old skills. At one point, Ali threw and landed seven straight jabs before Chuvalo got in a punch. Then he threw five more. He is getting in shape for Joe Frazier and, tough fight or not, he had the perfect foil.

George can be hit. He even seems to relish it because to hit him you must get close. But despite all the courage and willingness to bleed for the bucks, we may have been misrepresenting him as a guy

48

who'll take five for the chance of landing one. It becomes a question of whether he has the one.

He had his chances last night, including one in the third when he timed it perfectly, caught Ali bouncing off the ropes, and threw as clean a left as he is ever likely to get. It stung. That's all. Against the good ones, George lacks the firepower. If it isn't there, the bleeding is for nothing.

The crowd wanted Chuvalo to take this one. Sometimes it was deceived into thinking he was making progress as he pinned Ali in a corner. But all he could hit was those rolling shoulders, the gloves, the arms. Seldom the body he had to reach to kill the legs. On three cards he won a total of three rounds, and one of those three gave him none. Ali was in command here as he was in Toronto in 1966, and perhaps more so.

On three occasions last night he lay back against the corner ropes and dared Chuvalo to come in. Once he even stretched his arms out on the top strand. How often will he have to invite Frazier — or has he forgotten the last time he tried?

He dances out every round, scalpel in left hand, mothballs in right. Behind him, a glowering Bundini Brown crouches like some great black buddha, frothing out instructions. ("Be mean! Be mean! Squeeze out some of that beet juice! Work the cut! Work the cut!") and for a while Ali does. But he fights like a man with a short attention span, as though the fun lies in getting his man on the hook, not in landing him.

I doubt anyone will ever understand him entirely. All you can do, really, is appreciate the skills and try to forget that you paid ten dollars to come in and watch another man bleed.

Chuvalo bled. Manny Gonzales bled in a preliminary, and wobbled around the ring in a grotesque, rubber-legged and pathetic dance to prove he wasn't really hurt. "Nobody stops this fight!," the man in his corner yelled after five. "He'll be all right." They never lay a glove on the men in the corner.

Murray Pezim bled, too. The turnstile count, which hasn't been released yet, was 7,498, of which about 300 represented people in on free tickets. Another 368 came through the pass gate, which does Murray no good at all. He — rather, his backers — could drop anywhere from $50,000 to $100,000. "But he might also break even," Murray Goodman, the PR man from New York, says with a shrug. "You know, a lot of virgin promoters have done worse."

But nobody bleeds like Chuvalo, who doesn't seem to mind as long as he's standing at the finish. Somebody asked him how he stayed up. "I dunno," he said. "Maybe it's just a gift the Good Lord dropped on me." If it is, He must have had a better use in mind.

GIANT FOR RENT

May 11, 1976

On size alone he should be scaling the Empire State Building, swatting airplanes and putting the clutch on Fay Wray. But there are bigger plans than that for Andre the Giant, and Frank Valois knows them all.

"My man is the world's biggest athlete and everyone wants to see him," he explains, the words bouncing off the yellow concrete dressing-room walls. "We wrestle all year. All year we get ten days off — at Christmas and New Year's — and we have to beg for them."

He speaks in the royal we — first person plural, definitely possessive. Frank Valois doesn't wrestle, not anymore. He is the manager, interpreter and voice of Andre the Giant, who is shortly to become famous.

Andre the Giant — 7'5", 460-pound native of Grenoble, France. Undefeated, of course. The marketable ones always are. For ten years he's been in dressing rooms like this all over the world. Monday night it was Exhibition Gardens, joining Jimmy somebody in a tag bout with Sieg somebody and John somebody else. Today he was en route to another town, another ring. Only the names change.

On June 25 the name will be Chuck Wepner, and everything will change. Boxing's closed-circuit hucksters, looking for a prelim to the Tokyo wrestlebox between Muhammad Ali and Antonio Inoke, have matched Andre the Giant, a big-screen natural, against Wepner, the walking blood bank.

The rules will be identical for both bouts. "The first thing they make us agree to," says Frank Valois, "is that we don't break no bones."

The fighter wears gloves and must deck the wrestler for a ten count to win. The wrestler wrestles and must pin the boxer for a three count. Once they touch ropes they break and start over. "We sell out Shea Stadium at 50,000 seats, we do an $800,000 gate," Frank Valois says, "and we got a $50,000 guarantee or a gate percentage."

It is, he says, the Giant's biggest payday. "We do maybe $250,000 a year now," he admits, "but the government, it takes so much..."

He shrugs, and obligingly goes into the Andre the Giant story. The plan had been for Andre to tell it himself. Massive in his trunks, he ducked into a room that was suddenly full, extended an enormous hand, grinned and said "Hello." The interview was over. He posed amiably for pictures, turned, and walked out. "Andre," explains Frank Valois, "gets confused in English."

It is no trick for him to do Andre's talking. He's been doing it for ten years, since the night in Paris when the 19-year-old giant approached him at the wrestling matches and said he'd like to try.

"Me, I was just getting out of the game," he says. "I'm from Montreal and I wrestle 25 years, but at the time I'm doin' not bad in the movies and some other things. He was a kid then, only seven feet and maybe 250, but he wants to wrestle.

"He's played soccer four years — he makes all-France at fullback — and rugby for nine months. I mean, he's an athlete. So I take him to Paris and in six months he's ready to go. We wrestle all over Europe and we don't lose. Not ever."

Andre wants to come to the U.S. Valois says no and keeps him in Europe for four years ("I didn't want to come in with just some big clown") until the kid is up to 336 and has learned the rudiments of his trade. Then they make their move.

He is an instant hit. North America is ready for a genuine wrestling giant. The talk shows want him ("We do Mike Douglas and Johnny Carson, then he plays Bigfoot in a *Six Million Dollar Man*"). Carson wants to know how big his father was — he was 5'11", but grandpa was 7'8". Mother was average. Washington Redskins offer him a tryout because George Allen likes big men, but don't want to pay him $50,000.

And then came the Wepner offer.

"We have to think it over because we have lots to lose," says Valois. "We're undefeated for ten years then lose in a thing that isn't even a sport, where are we?"

For $50,000, they agree to take a chance.

"It had to be a big name, though," Valois insists. "First it was Jerry Quarry, which was fine, but that fell through. When they said Wepner we say okay, because he fights Ali once and is known. The publicity for this thing is gonna be worth a lot of money. We didn't want it to be against a nobody."

Is it a fix? He draws back at the suggestion.

"Everybody says that, but I was right there when the New York Boxing Commission warned Wepner that if he fools around he gets suspended for life. That is a very serious commission."

How about training?

"We're gonna take ten days and really work. Maybe bring in a fighter, just like it was a real fight."

How does Andre like it?

"Fine," says Frank Valois.

You remember Toro Moreno in *The Harder They Fall,* and wish you could ask Andre.

Maybe it doesn't matter.

Is he lonesome, this huge, lumbering man of 29, in a country where the language isn't his and the towns change every night?

Maybe that doesn't matter, either. He is Andre the Giant. He is marketable.

THE FOUR-MILLION-DOLLAR CRAB

June 26, 1976

For lying on his back for 45 minutes Antonio Inoke made four million dollars. Barring a claim by Xaviera Hollander, it is a record.

When you think about it, she looms as the next logical contender for Muhammad Ali. They offer the same public service, although the segment of the public they're servicing may differ, and they're both getting away with it. It seems only fitting they should meet.

And don't think the public wouldn't buy it. If Friday's closed-circuit Bore of the Worlds proved anything, it's that there's nothing the pigeons won't buy, even when their money buys them the treatment they themselves reserve for statues.

Because that's what Top Rank and Ali and the rest of the con artists packaged last night: nothing. They quit fooling around pretending to offer legitimate entertainment. They put nothing in a box with gaudy wrapping, tied it with cheap tinsel and sold it as a sports happening.

In Vancouver some 1,500 people paid ten dollars and $12.50 to watch it in the Queen Elizabeth Theatre. Hello, suckers.

Did you like it when the War of the Worlds opened with 60 minutes of wrestling featuring the tag team of The Crusher and Bruiser, who chomped cigars and swore and hit each other in the face to show their fans they were disappointed in their own performance?

Did it grab you when Verne Gagne wrestled Dick Buckwinkle for da woild hevvywait champeenship and it ended in a no contest on accounta the bell rang and it was a curfew bout so's we can switch to da big Wepner fight with Andre the Giant?

Must have been pretty exciting for you after that one when they introduced Rocky Graziano, "former middleweight champ and current auto transmission champ," and Graziano, who is flogging some kind of auto dealership, came on to say 50 or 60 times dat he tot Ali could be in fer trubble.

Did you like the commercials between every round? Didn't tell you about those when they sold you the tickets, did they?

Hell of a fight, though. I especially liked the part at the beginning where Wepner contemptuously threw away his headgear. He could have used it in the third when Andre dropped him carefully over the ropes after standing there for a minute holding him aloft and trying to remember where he was supposed to put him.

And the ending — well, I tell you, when Wepner climbed back into the ring and tried to get at the Giant, and Andre's advisor, Gorilla Monsoon, tried to get at Wepner... wheew! Just the greatest since Mr. Kleen whipped the Great Bolo.

It wasn't until they switched to Tokyo that we found out your money wasn't enough.

The backs of the T-shirts worn by Inoke's handlers had been sold to a Japanese distillery. They let some guy named Medley sing four American patriotic songs over a montage of American scenes and signs pointing out that the songs were from his album, currently available.

But so what? You were there for the martial arts championship of the world, right? Boxing champ vs wrestling and karate expert. Migawd, the blood!

Then they explained the rules governing Inoke: No karate. No kicking except with the side of the foot. No kicking above the waist. And Ali could break any hold by touching — touching! — the ropes.

Inoke met the challenge. In every round he ran out, threw his legs at Ali and his butt at the ground. And he stayed there, inching his way across the canvas on his behind, flailing his feet to pound at Ali's left leg. "It's hemorrhaging!", the announcer screamed. "Ali's corner looks worried!"

Of course they were worried. They were worried that the seat of Inoke's trunks couldn't go fifteen.

53

Ali threw his first punch in the seventh round. He threw his second in the tenth. In the 13th he picked up the pace and threw two. In all he threw six — six punches in 15 rounds, not counting the two times he reached out and grabbed Inoke by the foot.

A couple of times Inoke actually got him to the canvas. Once — for shame! — he kneed him, and Ali climbed through the ropes and threatened to go home. That was after Angelo Dundee demanded that Inoke have the tips of his shoes taped because one of the lace's eyelets was loose and it was cutting Ali's legs. The old jagged eyelet trick. Gets 'em every time.

But what Ali did most was shout "Inoke coward! Inoke no fight!", jump around the ring with his arms dangling, and make gibbering sounds. He looked and acted like an ape. A Six Million Dollar Ape. They'll probably make it a series. And you'll buy it, won't you?

Hello, suckers. Have a good time?

LETTER FROM TAP CITY

August 25, 1977

This time nothing can go wrong. No more ankle express. No more gaspipe. It's champagne in the fridge, opera on the stereo and an elderly-type broad reclining on the bed. This time The Matchmaker has it made.

I have this on the authority of none other than The Matchmaker himself, who has found another hotel that runs a tab and used its stationery to fire off another of his State of the Wallet reports:

Friend Taylor:
This could be a double large deal, just like winning Lotto Canada ticket, this deal will launch my nudest [*sic*] camp its either brick-house or bleep-house because there are plans of printing ten million calendars in 20 languages.
Happy New Year.
Zube.

The letter arrives in a big cardboard tube, and you know right away Nick is serious because it does not come postage due. Also in the tube are four copies of a large poster; one copy of a letter of intent between Nick and W. James Mills Communications Ltd. of Toronto; a document showing that Nick has the posters copyrighted so nobody should muscle his action; and a press release The Matchmaker must have written himself because it says the first posters have already gone to Moscow and Pravda.

Nick Zubray, 56 years on the make, has finally pulled it off.

He told me three years ago it would happen. "I got a collection of pictures of every heavyweight champ who ever was," he said. "Some day I'm gonna find me a kind stranger with a roll, put them all together on one big poster, and him and me are gonna get seriously rich."

I didn't believe him.

After all, it was Nick who booked closed-circuit TV of the Mac Foster-Muhammad Ali fight into the Coliseum at seven dollars a pop, then found out the night before the fight that it was live on home television out of Seattle. He had a simple explanation: "What happened was, somebody made a mistake."

It was Nick who talked Murray Pezim — his bankroll on the closed-circuit caper — into backing an Ali-George Chuvalo heavyweight title fight here. Pezim took a $180,000 bath, Nick said $42,000 of it was his, and thereafter took a lot of interest in Murray's health.

"He gets sick there a while ago, I even go to church a couple times to light candles," he says virtuously. "Because if he croaks, where am I? I got an investment in the guy."

It was Nick whose plan to start a nudist colony outside Edmonton died of the financial shorts. "Couple of lakes and the rest we was gonna leave in bushes so the kids could fool around," he said then. "Sure, the nudist season in Edmonton is kinda short, but how can it miss? You show me a kid in today's younger generation don't wanna run around naked."

It's been Nick who bounced all over western Canada with closed-circuit promotions, sometimes hitting semi-big, sometimes crapping out, sometimes letting his enthusiasm trap him. He once gave away 350 tickets, beamed at the full house, then noticed that the paid gate was 18.

For Nick, defeat is a temporary inconvenience. There is always a stranger around the corner waiting with a roll and an itch to invest it. It's just a matter of staying alive until you find him. "You go by limousine, you go by boxcar, you're still movin'," he shrugs. "And if you can't ride there's always the Ankle Express. The action, that's what counts."

I have known The Matchmaker for years and sometimes suspect that we are friends. He is an old-school hustler who talks like Harry the Horse, runs up enormous hotel tabs when down with the shorts, but stuffs the fridge with champagne, puts pictures of his latest lady on the dresser — "a nice, elderly-type broad," he'll say affectionately — and fills the room with opera from the record collection that travels with him even when he goes by ankle.

If you have some money he'll come for it. If you lose it he'll weep, because his plan was always to make you both rich. The tabs get paid when he hits his next score. Sometimes it takes a while, but I would put his handshake in the bank.

His record hotel bill to date is $10,400, but when he settled, the manager knocked off the $400. Until then he tended to stay in a lot because once he was out they might change the locks.

Now Nick has maybe hit one that will stick. The poster, with every heavyweight champ from John L. Sullivan to Ali, is a first-class, beautifully-conceived little number that could be very big in rec room, bar and gym.

Naturally, Nick is optimistic. He has found his bread man. "We make 100, maybe even 600 big ones out of this," he chortles, "and that ain't even countin' the ash trays and the glasses and stuff. They come later."

His partners no doubt take a more cautious view. But caution is not Nick's bag.

"Listen," he says, "I figure over the years I promoted maybe three million dollars in deals and ended up getting screwed on a lot. But this time I hit big.

"The money...I'll tell ya," says The Matchmaker, "it'll be like shootin' fish with an axe."

I have one of Zube's posters on my wall, beautifully framed in copper, covered with that arm-and-a-leg double-glaze, no-glare glass. He gave it to me one night on the corner of Georgia and Granville when he didn't have two nickels to rub together and there wasn't a mark in sight.

He'd phoned to say he was in town and could I meet him. Now it was ten p.m. and he was standing there in his cracked-but-shiny patent leather shoes and the black suit with the white tie, sausage-sized knuckles bent from too many fights, the ears curled over from slipping too many headlocks in the bad old wrestling days.

Word had come down that Nick had hit hard times. The posters hadn't sold. A couple of other things had gone sour. "He sold his record collection," a guy said, "so you know he's gotta be in tough." But he didn't say anything about it that night on the street corner. For Nick, he didn't say much at all.

"This is for you," he said. "We know each other a long time."

Then he turned and walked into the darkness. It was the last time I saw him.

I was on a road trip when word came that Nick had died. I phoned a friend in Edmonton and asked how the funeral had gone.

"Nick would have loved it," the guy said. "It out-drew his last three promotions."

"HE FOUGHT A HELL OF A FIGHT..."

October 3, 1980

LAS VEGAS — "I went out and did what I had to do," Larry Holmes said later. What he did was batter a legend into submission with the impersonal dispatch of a carpenter pounding a nail.

For ten rounds he watched Muhammad Ali pull every trick out of a grab bag 20 years old. He met them and ignored them and went about the business of defending his world heavyweight boxing championship.

The end came with Ali on the stool in his corner, trainer Angelo Dundee calling it off with corner man Bundini Brown plucking angrily at his shirt and shouting that he couldn't do it, mustn't do it, because the champ could still come back.

But it wasn't Dundee who did it, it was Elijah Muhammad, Ali's long-time manager and spiritual advisor. In the confusion after the tenth, as Ali's corner fought to patch the cuts and reduce the swelling under the eyes, one of the handlers shouted down to Muhammad: "What do you want? What do you want?"

"I want it stopped," Elijah Muhammad said quietly. "He was getting defenceless and I want it stopped."

So did Dundee, the man who's been in Ali's corner from the beginning. Through the ninth and tenth he hunched there, chin in hand. As the tenth ended he looked at the referee and mouthed the words "Next round." But there was to be no more next round. The fight was over and so was a career unmatched by anyone in the annals of his sport, perhaps any sport.

The measure of his impact on the game he dominated for so long came in the final round — a round that ended in eerie silence, the silence of 25,000 people watching a legend die the death of ordinary men.

Midway in the round, as Holmes battered him on the ropes, there was a brief, almost pathetic chant, the old "Ali! Ali!" that's spurred him so many times before. But it died quickly. The message had finally gotten through. It was over.

The 38-year-old body hadn't been trimmed to the 28-year-old man. Time hadn't stopped in this city of no clocks. The waist was trim, but there were stretch marks. The face was taut, but it cut as it had never cut before under a merciless pummelling. The eyes flashed and taunted through the warm-up and early rounds, but in the fifth the light in them went out.

"I did what I had to do," Holmes said in the post-fight conference. "When you fight a friend and a brother you do what you have to do. But you don't get happiness. All I really got out of this was money, and money don't mean anything. I can make money. What I had to do tonight...well, I can't be happy about that."

Unofficially, he had won every round. The damage inflicted on Ali's eye in the ninth — the uppercut or thumb that made him turn away and down and paw at his face like the rawest amateur — was not the turning point in the fight. That came in the eighth, when it became a mathematical certainty that Ali would have to knock him out to win, and a dead certainty that he lacked the tools to do it.

"I held him up a few times, yes," Holmes admitted. "I told him 'Don't keep taking it!' "

He was almost as savage in his defence of Ali as he'd been in destroying him.

"Those people who'd say that Ali's nuthin', that he didn't fight, let them jump in the ring. Let's see them go through what athletes go through for two months, sitting there in your room, running every day, boxing in the gym, watchin' what you eat, no sex, no nuthin', and you go in the ring and some guy looks at you and says 'I'm gonna kick your butt!'

"I fought the greatest heavyweight in the world, and he fought a hell of a fight."

It was a gracious gesture by a generous man, but it was charitable. Like so many others, Ali had answered the bell once too often, and fallen to the time he'd held back for so long.

"HONEY, IT WAS LIKE THIS..."

January 18, 1981

Leon Spinks says he was struck on the head outside a Detroit bar Wednesday and woke up in a hotel room 13 hours later, naked and minus $45,000 worth of jewellery, including his partial plate.

Sounds reasonable to me.

Mind you, there are conflicting reports. Spinks says he was hit outside Spears Bar. The manager of the Last Chance Bar, two miles down the road, says he doesn't quite see how, since Spinks was drinking in *his* bar at the time he supposedly was smitten upon the noggin — and had been for about ten hours. "I usually walk him to his car when he leaves," says Tom Tappelletti, "but when I looked up at about two a.m. he was gone."

Poor Leon. Although they later found his upper plate with the gold fillings, his full-length blue fox coat is gone and now he's the centre of an argument between bartenders over where he prefers to get stiff.

Worse yet, Mr. T must be gone, too.

Mr. T was Leon's bodyguard. I say "was" because he couldn't have been Wednesday night or they'd have known the bar where Spinks was attacked by the bodies stacked on the sidewalk.

I first met Mr. T last October in Las Vegas, where Spinks was fighting the immortal Bernardo Mercado on the undercard of the Muhammad Ali-Larry Holmes title bout. Mr. T was about 6'2" — and that was across the shoulders.

He stood about 6'1" and went about 230 and you could see bony ridges on the back of his skull because he wore his hair in a Mohawk. Where he walked, the crowd parted like the Red Sea.

It was whispered that he had black belts in every form of unarmed combat that existed, and that he clanked if you touched him because his tuxedo had enough holsters to hold an arsenal. On one of those TV participation shows he'd won the world bouncer championship by, among other things, hurling a drinker-actor farther and faster than was deemed possible.

I don't know his full name, but I was there when someone asked.

We were lined up for press credentials.

"Name?" the girl asked.

"Mr. T."

"That's T for what?"

59

"Just T. Mr. T."

"I'm sorry, but I'll need more than..."

"*Look under T!*"

The girl looked under T. Quickly. And there it was — a press card made out to Mr. T.

"Thank you," said Mr. T.

"Oh, thank *you!*" she said, sounding like the governor had just signed the pardon.

Mr. T was just one of the lovely people swarming around the fight. There were loud guys and tough guys and guys who looked like they ate motorcycles. They shoved their way through crowds, but they walked around Mr. T.

So I don't think he's Leon's bodyguard anymore. Maybe he just turns up for the fights and lets Leon train in his own inimitable fashion for bouts to come.

Leon Spinks, remember, is the man who took the heavyweight title from an unwary Muhammad Ali and held it for seven months until Ali took it back. The best thing you can say about his reign is that he made it eventful.

Most of it was car trouble. He ran his $13,000 silver Corvette through a fence near Cleveland, had his Cadillac stolen, got the Corvette back and wrecked it, was stopped twice for driving without a licence and once for possession of tiny amounts of cocaine and marijuana. The drug charges were later dropped — leaving him with the landlord suing him for back rent and the paternity suit involving one woman and three children.

And now this, which might be his biggest problem of all. Leon, you see, is married. He has a home in Detroit. Try this on your wife or husband and let me know how it comes out:

"Look, honey, there was a *reason* I was gone all night. I was standing outside this bar, see, and all of a sudden everything went black. Thirteen hours later I woke up naked in this hotel room, and..."

Me, I'd sooner face Mr. T.

NO YESTERDAYS FOR SALE

December 6, 1981

NASSAU, Bahamas — The Drama in Bahama T-Shirts look as tired and washed-out as the ladies flogging them. The card table bearing the shoe box full of money wobbles under the responsibility.

"Three dollars," the lady says, ripping a ticket from a roll. "Three dollars to watch Muhammad Ali train..."

Twenty feet from where she sits the casino regulars are feeding the machines. Behind her in Le Cabaret, the dining room that explodes nightly with the sparkle and sound of a mini-Vegas show, the stage is cleared to bare boards, the backdrops hoisted to the ceiling. Like the man now stepping to centre ring they are best viewed from a distance, where you can't see that the silver is aluminum foil and all the glitter is sham.

"Ladies and gentlemen," a man addresses the 100 or so who've filled the shoe box for today's show. "As you know, Muhammad Ali is in serious training for his upcoming fight with Trevor Berbick. It would be appreciated if you did not call out or do anything to break his concentration."

The room goes respectfully silent. Muhammad Ali, the larded legend of days well past, begins to shadowbox.

He wears the look of a man in mindless ritual — jab, hook, jab, dance, move — backward, always backward, bobbing and weaving against an opponent only he can see. The feet shuffle and slide, the breath snorts through the nose. There is no other sound.

After the third round he leans against the ropes in his corner, his back to the crowd, waiting while they hook up the heavy bag.

"I have returned! I have returned! I have returned!"

He hasn't turned his head or moved anything but his lips. It is as though he's reading cue cards on the canvas at his feet. "There's gonna be a *miracle*! Be among those who dare to dare!"

There was a time when he could do it and make the world sit up and beg for more, a time that ended last October in Las Vegas when Larry Holmes exposed him as a tired, used-up old man. The lines are still there, but the magic is missing. He is 40 years old, and the show has run too long.

Chances are he'll be in better shape for Berbick than he was for Holmes. He seems less frantic about shedding the pounds this time, saying he'll step into the ring Wednesday at 231 rather than at the 217 he hit in Vegas. He has pared off considerable weight. A week ago a member of his own entourage was asked how he looked. He shook his head sadly and made balloon motions around his stomach. Now the balloon has shrunk to a pleasant paunch befitting a man of his years — unless that man plans to step into a ring for what might be a fight for his life. Now the heavy bag work is over. Ali does a stiff-legged, slow-motion, stilted impression of the way he says Berbick moves, then pulls a chair to the ring apron, slips on a white robe, and addresses his flock.

"This is the time of evening...uh, day...when I talk to my fans. Questions? Any questions?"

He breaks the silence himself.

"I've got all these suckers where I want them," he says in that husky, slightly hesitant speech pattern he's taken on of late. "You will see a *miracle*! Berbick, Mike Weaver, then the winner of Holmes-Cooney. Gerry Cooney wins that one, the Ku Klux Klan will sell tickets to see him fight me...

"The press has spread all kinds of rumours. I'm too old, I'm fat, I've got brain damage...well, I'll tell you, I've got brain damage enough to take ten million dollars out of this town. I've got my speed, I've got my power...

"Questions!" he demands. "Any questions?"

From the stage one of his hangers-on does a Howard Cosell impression. Ali puts him down. The tourists are in on it now, asking the old, tired questions. ("Who was the greatest fighter you ever saw?" "Why do you keep fighting?") and getting the same tired answers.

Fifteen minutes. Ali gets up, waves good-bye and leaves. Once it was fun. Now it's part of the job.

Outside, a lady begins packing the T-shirts.

"Sell many?" a guy asks.

"Maybe tomorrow," she shrugs. "Maybe tomorrow..."

A DAY AT THE OFFICE

March 5, 1982

NANAIMO — His name is Arnold Sam. It's stitched in white across the back of the bomber jacket he strips off for the weigh-in: Arnold Sam, Indian Heavyweight.

He's from California or Reno, Nevada. No one seems to know or care which. When he steps on the scales his obsidian eyes gaze through the weights and the people out of a flat moon face that seems as old as time. In a few hours he will give away 46 pounds to a large-bellied, droop-chested 274-pound ex-linebacker named Harold Rice, spend about 17 minutes absorbing what punishment Harold can dispense, then plod wearily out of the ring, loser by a technical knockout, to collect payment on his pound of flesh.

It will come to about $800 — more than he's received on other nights on other cards in other forgotten towns, because this time he's on the undercard of a championship fight. He's fought in a lot of towns, has Arnold Sam, and he'll fight in more until the offers or the body run dry. He's a fighter, and this is Nanaimo, and it's Friday...

His name is Francisco Roche — "The Cuban" Roche, it says on the fight card — a junior welterweight thrown in against Sanford Ricks, a Halifax kid said to be of some promise. Roche is from Carson City by way of Seattle, where he's training in matchmaker Dick McDonald's gym. Ricks beats him unimpressively, but for Francisco Roche, who dreams big and perhaps futile dreams, it means a minor payday and perhaps a more comfortable bed.

"You know where he's been sleeping the past few weeks?" McDonald asks. "In the back of an abandoned car..."

Gord Racette was there for the weigh-in. He saw the impassivity of an Arnold Sam headed down a too-familiar road to nowhere. One look at Harold Rice's hulking form ("For God's sake, Harold," a fan would plead during his pawing match with Arnold Sam, "wear a brassiere!") should have told him this is no profession for anyone not totally prepared and utterly committed. Francisco Roche's housing arrangements offer mute testimony that even preparation and commitment carry no guarantee.

Today, as the soreness eases in a face pounded hamburger red and the swelling leaves a battered right eye and the aches and stiffness make sudden movement risky, he should be thinking about all those things and checking his hole card. Because it may be time for Gord Racette to put his dreams in a box and store them unfulfilled.

He dreams of being a champion. So do thousands of fighters all over North America who had 15 years' experience before he ever laced on a glove. Sanford Ricks has been fighting since he was eight years old. Laurie Mann, his professional career just starting, is a six-time Canadian amateur champion at 21. Racette is 27, and barely underway.

It isn't that he lacks potential, it's that he lacks time to achieve it. He has fought two men who have been at or around the upper echelons of the trade. An out-of-shape Jimmy Young stopped him and Friday night Trevor Berbick chased and battered and pounded him for 11 rounds and looked capable of ending it any time after four.

He should at least read the warning signs implied. Then he must decide: stay on a crash course of an education where fees are paid in blood and battered tissue, or grab a couple of fast minor paydays in Europe against men of his own skill level, then tell manager Tony Dowling it's all over.

He is a nice, big, carefree and handsome kid, but the nose is bent now and there are spidery white lines around the eyebrows. How many more are waiting down the road?

His backers take a more optimistic view.

"Gordie showed me something," Dowling says. "He's never been hit. Let's face it, he's been brought along so he wouldn't be. But he took it, and he showed me a heart as big as outdoors."

He said it as though heart were all that mattered. Racette should get a second opinion from Arnold Sam.

"THE TIMES, MY FRIEND, THE TIMES..."

September 5, 1982

Mostly they are kids in their 20s, out of work and willing to risk a beating for a shot at a few bucks. Some of them don't have bus fare to get to the doctor for their medicals, so Jack McLaughlin leaves his temporary office in the back room of the video movie store on East Hastings street, picks them up and delivers them personally. That way, he gets to see for himself if a kid has let his desperation get in the way of his common sense and steer him in another direction if he has.

"It's the times, my friend," the old fight promoter says. "It's the times. When you can't get a job and your UIC's run out and you're not the type to mug a guy and take his wallet, it's always been the same: first you hit the pool rooms, and then you hit the gym."

The times are the reason McLaughlin has changed the name and scaled down the house for his latest "So You Wanna Fight?" card Thursday night at Queens Park Arena. Now it's called "Hard Times Promotions", tickets down to $12 and eight dollars from the old $15 and ten. "You've got to let the people know that you know the times are hard," he says. "So far, they're going like a hot damn."

Not that everyone on the card will be a hungry kid desperate for money. As usual, it will be laced with street types who figure they might as well check their chains at the door and do in the ring for money what they do in the pubs for free. But some will be throwbacks to Depression days when some men pounded one another in the ring and others roamed the continent in box cars, stopping wherever there was a town with a tough guy, squeezing out a living on the side bets.

They, too, had "managers", guys who'd open the scam in the bars with "You people got a guy who thinks he can fight? Fifty bucks says my man here can take him." And off they'd go to back alley or barn to battle bare-knuckled and fully clothed. Win or lose they were on the next train out, nursing their cuts and bruises en route to the next town, the next fight for the next meal.

Times like those produce good fighters. ("Some of them were lucky," McLaughlin says. "Jimmy McLarnin had a great manager named Pop Foster who not only knew the game, he could also make a great stew. When him and Jimmy went to California to fight, Pop would make a big pot of stew and they'd live on it for a week.") In 1979 the "So You Wanna Fight?" fad in Vancouver spawned Gordie Racette and Jerry Reddick, the one they called Mack Truck.

"Oh, the Truck," McLaughlin recalls. "He could bang. He could bang like hell. He had a lot of raw ability — more than Racette, lots more. I had it set up with Angelo Dundee for him to go to Angie's camp for a couple of weeks so he could win the Canadian. But he got headstrong. He could think, the Truck could. He thought himself right out of the ring."

McLaughlin, lifelong fight fan, 26-year owner of logging camps, 63 come October and not long on gold himself, is hoping another Reddick or Racette will surface Thursday, but it isn't necessary. "Some people come out looking for good fighters," he concedes, "but let's face it, a lot more just want to see a bunch of guys knock the crap out of each other."

Come Thursday they'll crawl into the ring two by two for three two-minute rounds or less, winners to fight again later, twice if they reach the final. For some it will be a lot tougher than they figured. "I been hit with clubs, bats, chains, guns, you name it," a biker named Schnoz said last year. "But I never been hit that hard. This guy hits me once, I think I'm gonna have a cardiac. So I think 'To hell with this', and I leave."

For him it wasn't important. For some it will be. The $1,000 top prize may be out of reach. They may get badly whipped. But bruises heal, and for just getting into the ring you get $50. In hard times, it beats having no job at all.

"WE'RE TALKIN' OSCAR HERE..."

March 20, 1986

I have neither met nor ogled Billie-Jo "Flash" Finlay, the exotic dancer who's given up her career as a pro boxer because the medical bills were too high, but I think she's being a bit hasty.

There's got to be a movie in there somewhere.

Has she talked to Sylvester Stallone? How about Stephen J. Cannell, the guy who produces *A-Team* and all those other car-through-a-supermarket brain-testers? You think people so short of material they make a hit show out of a smartass talking automobile wouldn't jump at the chance to do a life story like hers? I can almost hear the agent making the pitch:

"Sly, baby, I tell ya it can't miss. We got a dame here who's an exotic dancer, see, and one of the guys stops watchin' and starts grabbin', so she decks him. She *decks* him, Sly — one punch and he's taps.

"And it turns out the guy is a boxer himself, see, and the guy he's with hands her a card, and it turns out he's a *trainer*! He tells her she could be a pro! Well, okay, we'd have to re-phrase that a little. Big deal. That's why we got writers.

"She thinks about it. Lotsa good footage there, Sly. We could pan in and have her furrowin' her brow as she dances. That way we get the dance past the censors 'cause it advances the plot and has whatchacall your socially redeeming quality.

"Finally she says yes. She gets a room over the gym so she can live upstairs and train downstairs. Can you picture it? Upbeat theme music, shot of her risin' with the dawn, tossin' off a Carnation breakfast, puttin' on her make-up while she's still half asleep? It's *Rocky* all over again only better, 'cause when she skips rope she jiggles.

"What? Hey, listen, this is all legit stuff! It was right there in Wednesday's mornin' paper up in Vancouver where you filmed the big fight in *Rocky IV*. If it's inna mornin' paper it's gotta be serious, 'cause those people don't fool around.

"Oh, we'd hafta fiddle the story a bit. This Billie-Jo says she was unbeaten in about 40 fights and ended most of them early. Only she quit because it was costin' her more to get her nose reset than she was takin' outa the ring. We could maybe change it to build up to a title fight with Big Momma Mayhem, and she needs the money to get her boyfriend his hernia operation, only the mob has got her kid sister and says if she doesn't dump the fight they'll

66

send the kid home in three manila envelopes. Like you always say, Sly, heart stuff sells.

"I figure we get Streep to play the girl, with maybe Della Reese as Big Momma. The trainer with the heart of gold is a toughie, though. Is Barry Fitzgerald really dead, or is that just street talk?

"It's a show about a girl from Vancouver who goes to Seattle to learn to fight, so naturally we shoot on location in Toronto, and throw in a bit where she does a celebrity shot on a quiz show and wins a main event at Madison Square in New York. And she doesn't quit because of the medical bills, she wins the fight and falls in love with a nose-and-throat man who gives her a group rate.

"And it ain't just the flick. We also flog the novelties like Billie-Jo eyepatches and paste-on blood blotches. The marketing guys want to call them Sticky-Hickeys. They say we could hit large. And speakin' of names, I've got the title aced. Think about it, Sly. Think: Rockette 1..."

You think about it, too, Billie-Jo. You could be big. Trust me.

NEW LINK, OLD CHAIN

January 24, 1988

He sat there at ringside in Atlantic City, heavy dark glasses covering his eyes, his puffy face frozen into immobility.

All around him the Beautiful People gossiped and chirped and waved at the TV camera — Kirk Douglas, Cheryl Tiegs, John McEnroe and Tatum O'Neal, billionaire Donald Trump, Don Johnson with a proprietary arm around Barbra Steisand, all there to see and to be seen. But Muhammad Ali, with them yet curiously alone, stared straight ahead in silence.

Once he would have stolen their spotlight and matched them quip for quip. Once he would have bounced around the ring during pre-fight introductions, giving it the Ali Shuffle or the Rope-a-Dope. Nobody ever played a crowd like Ali. This man, this stranger, looked out into the blackness above them as he briefly touched his fingers to his lips and allowed himself to be led first to Larry Holmes' corner, then to Mike Tyson's. Only there did those lips move ever so slightly.

Holmes ignored him. Tyson nodded briefly, a man with other things on his mind. Then they cut to commercial, and Muhammad Ali was gone.

67

Did he know where he was? Did he understand that these men were about to fight for the heavyweight boxing title he'd held three times? Was there life in the eyes behind those glasses? Doctors have suggested that the cumulative years and the punches took their toll on his brain as they'd coarsened and slowed his speech. Did it cross his mind, I wonder, that he'd become another link in the chain...?

October 1, 1980, Las Vegas. Ali is there to fight Holmes. But now he is leaning over the wheelchair of Joe Louis. He's refused to have his picture taken with this stroke-ridden caricature of the former great champion — not out of arrogance but out of respect for the champion that was. Now he whispers into Joe's ear:

"Does it hurt, champ?" he asks softly. "Does it hurt bad?"

Louis croaks an indecipherable reply. The following night, sitting in his chair at ringside, he stares fixedly at a spot off in one corner of the Caesars Palace parking lot as the fight begins. An attendant leans over and gently turns his head toward the ring.

"How did it happen?" Ali asks reporters, staring at the withered wreck in the chair. "Why did he come back that time? How did they let it happen?"

"Make you wonder if maybe you shouldn't be trying *this* come-back?" a guy asks.

Muhammad Ali, age 37, slips into the shuffle. "You're gonna see a miracle!" he chants. "A miracle...!"

October 2, 1980. Larry Holmes is discussing the Ali that was as opposed to the man he would face that night.

"No chance," he says. "The man's got no chance. He's 37! His brain is making appointments his legs can't keep. Why's he wanna come back? Why?"

January 22, 1988. Larry Holmes, 38, is clubbed to the canvas three times in the fourth round before it's mercifully over. "He's the greatest fighter in history," says 22-year-old Mike Tyson. "If he'd been like he was I would never have stood a chance."

At ringside, Muhammad Ali stares fixedly into nothingness as another link is forged in the chain.

THE DONALD, IVANA AND ME

April 26, 1990

ATLANTIC CITY — Dear Mom: Twenty-four hours I've been living in the Trump Taj Mahal, and Ivana Trump hasn't phoned, she hasn't written, she hasn't even sent a fruit basket.

I guess we'll have to scratch Plan A, wherein she and I have a brief, torrid affair, I threaten to sue her for alienation of affections and The Donald (that's what the papers call Donald Trump here: The Donald) shuts me up with a few million out of petty cash.

Pity. I had such high hopes after reading Wednesday's New York *Post*.

"SAFE SEX" the headline screamed in that typeface we used to save for world war outbreaks. "DON & IVANA SIGN 60-DAY PACT TO PLAY THE FIELD."

Inside, it details a signed agreement which, according to "a source close to Trump" means that "anything that would normally permit you to get a divorce, such as adultery or sex, will not be a claim. Technically, they can have sex with other partners and nobody can run and say 'You are guilty of adultery'. Ivana" (who the source claims pushed for the deal) "basically is saying 'I don't want a divorce and I don't want to become a nun'."

But Ivana hasn't gotten in touch, even though I left the safety chain off my door all night. Neither has Marla Maples, the Other Woman, despite the fact that she's apparently dateless for her scheduled Saturday appearance at the White House Correspondents Dinner in Washington. (She probably knew I'd be busy here that night, covering the Michael Olajide-Thomas Hearns fight, a.k.a The Barrage at the Taj.)

How's the fight look? Not as good as the hotel. The Taj makes The Mirage in Las Vegas look like a mud hut on Gilligan's Island.

It's got 1,250 rooms, ten restaurants, the world's biggest casino, 4 1/2 times more steel in it than there is in the Eiffel Tower and, says the press release, "if laid end-to-end, the building's support pilings would stretch the 62 miles from Atlantic City to Philadelphia." Fortunately they didn't do that, or the building would fall down.

How successful is it? The other day they had to close it for a few hours because they couldn't clear the coins out of the 3,000 slot machines quickly enough.

The room decor leans to pale pink and grey and the service is — well, I mentioned to a porter that there was no wastebasket in my room. He turned pale, took off at a gallop, raced back, screeched to a halt so dramatically that static flew from the carpet, and triumphantly handed me a crinkled glass job that looked like it would sell for big bucks at Birks.

Lunch time in the Bombay Cafe I was served by two waiters and a hostess. In 45 minutes they asked me 11 times if everything was all right. If I'd said no, I think they'd have thrown themselves on a shish kebab. Seemed a lot of fuss over a club sandwich.

This place has everything, including, I think, a zoo. People in the elevators are always saying "I just come from Gnu Yak. You ever seen Gnu Yak?" But the best zoo is in the casino.

There's this guy stands 12 feet tall, wears a turban and a long, black, silk outfit, wandering the lobby having his picture taken with tourists. One of the Gnu Yakers saw through him right away. He leaned over to his wife and whispered:

"Honey, I think he's wearin' stilts."

"O-o-o-h!" she said admiringly, "I bet he is, at that!"

Oh, yeah: the fight.

Well, there's this 5,300-seat stadium inside the hotel. But Hearns and Olajide don't spar there. They train by the light of two $250,000 chandeliers in one of the smaller ballrooms — Tiara 3 — which probably doesn't seat more than Nat Bailey Stadium.

"Two chandeliers worth half a mil," marvelled Olajide's trainer, Angie Dundee, who's spent a lifetime building champions in smoke-filled, cold-water gyms. "No wonder they didn't want me to swing on 'em."

Hearns makes $1.6 mil for the fight, Olajide $250,000. In this joint, they clear that before lunch. I think I'll go donate a quarter.

Luv.

The Jim.

MONGOOSE MEMORIES

July 31, 1990

EDMONTON — The Ol' Mongoose wears a knitted pillbox cap, the blue as bright as the memories that flash in his eyes as he obligingly sends his mind back over the years.

"The last time I fought? Well, now, I guess that would be about 1963. I was on my way home to San Diego after fighting somebody in the east and I stopped in Dallas, where I saw there was a wrestling card that night. Well, there was this truck I wanted to buy, but it cost $4,000, which I didn't happen to have. So I phoned the promoter and said 'This is Archie Moore. Can you use me on the card?' He said sure, I could fight the main event. 'Not unless he puts gloves on,' I said, which is what he did, and I boxed this wrestler fella and got the $4,000 and bought the truck."

He stops, thinks about it a bit, and a sly little grin creeps across his face.

" 'Course I was in trouble then because I couldn't drive the truck, which was one of those big 16-gear things, so I had to have a boy who worked for me take the night coach out and drive it back for me."

Archie Moore is 72, 74 or 77 — probably the latter, since his mother always said he was born in 1913, not four years later as he claimed back in the days when he bothered with approximations. He is here as George Foreman's assistant trainer for tonight's bout with Ken Lakusta, a title that is far more than honorary. If a fighter wants to cheat time, who better to have in his corner than the legend who simply ignored it?

Archie Moore fought 228 times in 29 years and the only mistake he ever made was being so damned good people wouldn't fight him. He turned pro in 1936 as a welterweight. Seven years later he'd worked his way up to fifth-ranking middleweight — and was washing dishes at four dollars a day on a train between Oakland and Ogden, Utah. Even then, nobody wanted a piece of the Mongoose.

He was 39 when he finally won the light-heavyweight crown from Joey Maxim, 49 when he fought a young man named Cassius Clay. ("He laid a trap for a tiger," Archie chuckles, "and all he caught was a mangy old fox. He stopped me in four and danced around my ancient carcass.")

Four years earlier he'd had his celebrated war with Yvon Durelle, in which he was floored four times but came back to win.

"Durelle was maybe the hardest puncher I ever fought," he says. "With Marciano it was a cumulative effect of his punches. They dead-end you like you were hit with a sack of cement. With George [Foreman] it's like a jolt of electricity going through you. Right now he might be the hardest puncher ever. Durelle, though, he could take you out with one shot."

"Yeah," a listener objected. "But that was all he could do."

"Perhaps," said the Mongoose. "But he was most adept at it."

If there was a sadness to his career it is that his youth was gone before he got his real chances. He fought in the final years on guile and memories and the art of making do. "Give him a ball of steel wool," it was written, "and he'll knit you a stove."

Today he writes poetry, runs the boys' boxing club he's operated for years in his personal war against drug use, makes up scrap-books of copies of press clippings and photos from his ring days to give to friends or auction for charity and occasionally, as he did here Tuesday, steps up to the heavy bag and shows them, in a brief spurt, how it should be done.

"Would you like a scrap-book?" he asks a couple of visiting writers. "Excuse me, I'll just go on up to the room and get them."

He rises from the couch in one fluid motion and disappears into the elevator, to return with two books.

"You know," he says, "that fight with the wrestler? It may not have been *exactly* my last fight, because it seems to me I had a couple more when I got home..."

The scrap-book cover is a pencil sketch of the Mongoose as champion, *circa* 1960. He is sitting on a stool, hands taped, robe over the shoulders, gazing dead ahead at whatever Time would bring. Mr. Foreman, you're in good hands.

BELLY UP TO THE TILL

April 17, 1991

ATLANTIC CITY — The Battle of the Ages — George Foreman vs Evander Holyfield, Friday night, closed-circuit (Run, do not walk, to your phone and get tickets because God forbid you should miss it) — is about:

God.

Money.

God.

Pay-per-view TV.

God.

Disadvantaged kids.

God.

Dreams.

Oh, yes: and the heavyweight boxing championship of the known universe (World Boxing Council and World Boxing Federation divisions).

I know this because I had lunch Tuesday at the absolutely, positively final pre-fight press conference in the Trump Plaza theatre where The Donald himself sat under a sign that said "King of Beers" and somehow managed to block out the "of Beers" part.

("Never believe what you read," he told the media about rumours that his next book will begin with Chapter 11. "Even though most of you folks are the ones who write it.")

George was there, of course, resplendent in new grey jacket, shiny dome and the Belly That Ate Houston. He will weigh roughly 250 at the opening bell, approximately 35 pounds more than Holyfield, who was also there although hardly anyone seemed to notice.

Co-promoters Bob Arum (Top Rank, which represents Foreman) and Dan Duva (Championship Bouts, the Holyfield reps) were there with people like Archie Moore, the Old Mongoose — originator of the famed Armadillo Defence in which you cross your arms in front of your head — who says he is teaching George the art of defence including "escapeology, trickology and breathology". Also the legendary Angelo Dundee, handler of champions and cut-and-cornerman supreme, a late and key addition to the Foreman entourage who'll be in George's corner come Friday.

Holyfield had some people there, too. You remember him. Undefeated (25-0) heavyweight champion? Conqueror of the immortal hiccup-in-history, Buster Douglas? Not that it mattered. This is Foreman's show, as it is every time the 43-year-old Punching Preacher takes the stage.

George, you see, says he had a religious experience in the dressing room after the final fight of his previous career when he lost to Jimmy Young in Puerto Rico on St. Patrick's Day, 1977.

He says he died and his spirit briefly left his body. Others blame heat prostration, but George took it as a sign, shaved his head to shed himself of the old mean image and turned to preaching, never to return until 1987, when the need for money to fund his youth centre and his appetite brought him back to the ring.

Holyfield, a good, honest, deeply religious man himself, cannot fight a schtick like that, not even in dedicating the fight "to disadvantaged kids." Okay, so they both had big dreams of winning the title.

In the land of megahype, how can "I believe in prayer, hard work and dedication" stand up to "After I'm champ I'm gonna grab me legs of chicken! Roasts of beef! Porks of chop!"

So what we had was a slick video presentation featuring Foreman being Foreman; Holyfield reciting ad agency lines "Something big's coming down April 19 — George Foreman!"; clips of their various fights (including that blast from the past, Howard Cosell on mike); a commercial for the new Burger King 59¢ Buddy Burger ("Evander Holyfield, would you pop a buddy in the mouth for 59¢?") and a clip from comedian Billy Crystal: "Evander, forget about it. It's over. You've never fought a man with a prostate problem."

The important stuff, the *raison d'être* was delivered by Arum:

It will be the biggest grossing fight in history, maybe as high as $100,000,000, the biggest ever pay-per-view, maybe 18,000,000 viewers including two million home subscriptions at $34.95 and up. The live gate, tickets from $100 to $1,000? Chicken feed.

These records will stand for eternity or until Mike Tyson fights Friday's winner. That won't happen until after February 11, the day Tyson's contract with estranged manager Bill Cayton runs out and he no longer gets the 20% from all Tyson's fights, which he shares with the widow of his ex-partner, Jimmy Jones.

Who's next for the nice-but-dull Holyfield should he keep the crown? I thought you'd never ask:

Who else but Tommy "Duke" Morrison, a suspect 26-0 who fights an even-more-suspect Soviet, Yuri Vaulin, on the undercard. The Duke has everything going for him. He is pleasingly Caucasian, co-star of *Rocky V* and — wait for it — John Wayne's nephew!! Did I mention this was about money?

COMMANDER EVANDER MEETS THE BLIMP
April 18, 1991

ATLANTIC CITY — "Well, shame on me!" George Foreman said, stepping off the scale at the official weigh-in. "Only 257? I thought I'd come in about 265! 'Course, I ain't had dinner yet," he conceded.

Minutes earlier Evander Holyfield had checked in at 208. Asked if he was concerned about being that light he gazed sincerely into the TV camera and said:

"No. The fight is not in the weight. The fight is in the individual."

"Thank you, Evander," sighed the man on the mike. "And now, the former heavyweight champion of the world, GEORGE FORE-MAN...!"

Evander the Commander had done it again: allowed himself to be caught in the riptide that is Foreman and washed up on the media beach like a log waiting for Bruno Gerussi.

He, not Foreman, is the heavyweight champion of the world. He, not Foreman, likely will enter the ring as betting favourite. While it is true that the main event will be settled inside the ring, it is just as true that Foreman has won every preliminary.

If this week was refereed it would have been stopped on Wednesday and awarded to Foreman. Richard Steele, who stopped the Tyson-Ruddock fight because he thought he saw a glaze in the Razor's eye, might never have let it start.

It is this as much as anything that has the boxing crowd going nuts.

Foreman, 42 or 43, depending upon which of the two birth years he acknowledges (the official tale of the tape, taking no chances, lists his age at 42 but his birthdate as January 22, 1948, which would make him 43) has engulfed this fight the way he ingests cheeseburgers.

His age, his size, the personality transplant that turned him from the surly champ of a dozen years ago to a laughing, poetry-spouting overblown Ali ("Float like a bowling ball; sting like a SCUD") have made him the clear winner before they even don the gloves.

"This fight," a guy said yesterday as he watched Foreman clown his way through a workout before a couple of hundred adoring fans, "is about George Foreman, the heavyweight title and Evander Holyfield — in that order!"

Which is all very well but for one tiny detail: No one knows yet whether Foreman can really fight.

The 24 victims in his undefeated comeback were guys who could do guest shots as the Unknown Soldier. He can hit. People like Angelo Dundee and even Dan Duva, the unofficial boss of the Holyfield camp, concede that old George might pack the most lethal punch the game has ever seen. But it's like watching that big black wrecking ball swing down and punch holes in old Comiskey Park. How effective would it be if the building could move?

Evander Holyfield has beaten every fighter he's faced. What it's won him is the heavyweight crown and $8,000,000 for taking it from Buster Douglas; an estimated $20,000,000 (Foreman gets $12,000,000) for whatever happens Friday night, and a no-verdict decision from a boxing world that still can't decide whether he's a legitimate champ or an overblown light-heavyweight with the luck of good timing.

If it's possible to call a multi-millionaire poor, Evander the Commander is Poor Holly. Part of it is the high-tech manner of his training methods. He has a weight trainer, a conditioning coach, two co-advisors, two trainers, two personal assistants, and an ex-ballerina named Marya Kennett who awakens him each morning and is in charge of his flexibility.

Obviously it's worked. The man is 25-0 and 14 (or 15) years younger than an opponent who's really proved nothing except that when it comes to grabbing the public imagination no one in the game, not even Ali, has ever done it better.

Holyfield is what you see: dedicated, motivated, church-going, socially-conscious and publicly about as exciting as soil erosion. Foreman is — what?

A clown? Ali was a clown given no chance against the glowering hulk named Sonny Liston. A hypester? A big, people-talking jokester who's laughed his way into the biggest fight gross in the history of boxing, knowing he's overmatched but willing to swap a few lumps for a few million?

Or could it be that he is what he's selling — an age-defying man-mountain with thunder in each hand who just might be laughing even louder when it's over and he contemplates an even bigger pay-day for meeting Mike Tyson as the new heavyweight champion of the world?

"My, my," said old George, stepping off the stage. "Only 257! Well, it's revenge in the restaurants tonight!"

On the other side of the room, the champion of the world stood quietly, watching the crowd go the other way. There's no business like show business.

Chapter Three

THE PUCK STOPS HERE

If hockey is the national religion, then *Hockey Night In Canada* is church and Don Cherry is the high priest, or maybe the bouncer. Maybe you didn't grow up listening to Foster Hewitt (if everyone who claims to have flopped on the floors of prairie farmhouses staring at the radio and listening to Foster do the Maple Leaf games had actually done it, the prairies would be one big farmhouse floor), but you've spent years of Saturday nights and Stanley Cup playoffs in front of the TV listening to Danny and Dick and Brian and Bob and Ron and Harry and the rest of the *HNIC* mob.

And you've done something else. I know you have: You've sat there watching the intermission on a hockey telecast, turned to the guy next to you and said:

"Hey, I could do that! What's so tough? Some guy sits down on a stool next to you, wipes his face with a towel, sweats all over your network blazer, which you don't even have to buy, because all the sports networks have got contra deals with Ugly Blazers Inc. ('If It's Tacky, It's Ours!').

"You say, 'Well, Fred, I guess it's a big thrill for you getting a chance to play in the NHL and get rich, considering that your other employment opportunities would involve a shovel and a lot of heavy lifting.'

"He isn't even listening, but he doesn't have to because he's only programmed for one answer: 'Yeah, I sure am. This is a great team and a great bunch of guys and I'm just here to give it 110% and help the team any way I can.'

" 'Thanks, Fred, and good luck in the coming season,' you say. The network shows ten commercials of bar girls being ogled by guys so dumb they're always pouring the stuff but never once do you see them taking even a sip, and you say 'Now, back upstairs to Bob and Harry.'

"Then you watch the rest of the game for free from the best seats in the house. And that's it — another tough day at the office. Yeah, I could do that. No problem!"

Well, I tried it.

As an extension of a weekly TV show with my friend and fellow jock-watcher, Greg Douglas (called, cleverly enough, *Douglas and Taylor Live*) he and I did the colour commentary of a 1990 pre-season game between the Vancouver Canucks and the Detroit Red Wings, live from Seattle.

Let me tell you how easy it is:

During some outdoor pre-taping, a guy in a floppy hat and long hair drives the world's noisiest fork-lift past the camera. About 16 tries later, we get it taped.

The scripts are printed in big letters on huge cue cards (did I mention that the teleprompter, which performs this service automatically, didn't work?) held up by Rose the Makeup Lady, who is almost as tall as the cards. Just as the director points his finger at me to start, the first card drops from her hand. Just like that, I'm on Page 2.

All week we've been planning to interview the coaches in the designated Interview Room, safe from noise, crowd and distraction. Naturally, we interview the coaches at rink-side lest we risk straining the arm of the fan hurling crushed paper cups from the stands or deprive the man on the PA of the thrill of playing heavy metal music as we speak.

We each have a receiver thing stuck in our ear. This is vital, for how else can the director whisper "Straighten your tie!" or "Your fly's open!" while you're trying to listen to your guest?

I interview Detroit rookie Keith Primeau, who leaves during a commercial break. The Plan says I'm to move to that chair and Douglas is to replace me in my chair so we can talk. We have 30 seconds before we're live on camera.

I stand up, thereby disconnecting the wire to my clip-on microphone. Douglas' earpiece jerks from his ear, knocking his glasses to the floor, where a lens pops out.

The floor man is yelling "Fifteen seconds! Ten seconds!" while trying to jam back the lens, without which Douglas cannot see more than six inches. Another guy is re-connecting my mike. There are now four of us on the set when there should be only two.

"Three! Two! One!" yells the floor man. He dives one way, the mike repair man dives the other, just as the little red light on the camera says we're live.

"Welcome back!" Douglas says — and no one out in TV land has any idea what's just happened. Show biz. It's my life.

THE ACCORD ACCORDING TO FRED

May 25, 1990

Word that the country might be splitting in two has not gone unnoticed in the Coquitlam home of Fred and Martha Schwartz.

"Fred," Martha said over breakfast, "I'm afraid we could lose the Accord."

The sports pages rustled impatiently.

"It ain't an Accord," Fred said. "It's a Nash Metropolitan. And it ain't lost. It's in the garage."

"Not the car, Fred. I'm talking about the country. Meech Lake! Constitutional reform! We're teetering on the edge of disaster. Mr. Mulroney says so."

"Who'd he ever beat?" Fred asked.

"Pardon?"

"Who'd he ever beat?" Fred repeated impatiently. "Joe Clark in the semi-main when Clark's fighting miles out of his weight class. Then John Turner. Big deal, John Turner."

"But..."

"But nothin'! I should get excited because some Irishman with his feet in Ontario and his heart in Quebec tells me B.C.'s gotta do what he says or we're all going to hell in a bucket? You wanna talk problems, I'll tell you problems: I took the Bruins in six."

"But, Fred, every day the paper is full of stories saying we have to pass Meech Lake or Quebec will pull out of the country. And then what will we have?"

Fred gave it some thought, counting on his fingers.

"A 19-team NHL," he said triumphantly. "But it's no big deal. San Jose's coming' in next season, and maybe Seattle and Milwaukee after that. Lose two, gain three. Where's the problem?"

"But, Meech Lake..."

"Will you knock it off about Meech Lake? Eighteen months ago, who heard of it? I don't see it in any fishing guides. Name me one team from Meech Lake. You can't! Nobody can! You could watch network sports all year and never hear one damned thing about how the Meech Lake Whatevers are doin'..."

Fred was shifting into high.

"... but a bunch of guys we pay to run the country got a problem and what do they do? They go to the lake for the weekend, probably drawing overtime, and they come away without one damned thing settled! You think I could get away with that at Public Works? I should maybe go tell the foreman that sewer line is blocked so I'm goin' to the lake for the weekend to figure out how to unplug it? He'd kick my butt off the truck!"

"But, Fred, if we lose Quebec, we lose..."

"What?" Fred roared. "A lousy hockey team in Quebec City. A baseball team TV keeps telling us is Canadian and we all should pull for it. Hell, *Montreal* ignores it! Montreal ignores everything. It ignored Canadian football. Now it's got a team in some dumb NFL farm league that's gonna play in the spring and go head-to-head with the Stanley Cup playoffs. Whoopee!"

"But your hockey team, the one you always pull for. You'd lose them, too..."

"We lost them years ago. The Flying Frenchmen, my butt. The Flying United Nations is more like it. Used to be they had all those great French-Canadian players. Richard... Beliveau... Cournoyer... Geoffrion. Now a guy's gotta have four languages just to read the lineup."

"But surely, Fred... surely there must be something in Quebec worth saving."

He thought for a long time.

"Danny Gallivan," he said finally. "I wouldn't wanna lose Danny Gallivan. The rest I would say what my old coach used to say to guys who got big-headed."

"What was that, Fred?"

"'Hey, I'd love you to stay. But get on the team or get off the bus.'"

80

WEEP NOT FOR PELLE

December 5, 1985

There was great news from two hospitals Wednesday. Kathylean McNeal and Edward Parvin seem to be doing fine. The nurse at John F. Kennedy Hospital in Stratford, N.J., says McNeal, who was listed in only stable condition when they brought her in 25 days ago, has been at home for a week. The University Medical Centre at Cooper Hospital in Camden, N.J., didn't know exactly where Parvin was at the moment — possibly at a trauma hospital for further treatment — but he was released from their unit Tuesday, and the problems of the skull fracture that had him on the critical list apparently are under control.

Perhaps you've forgotten Kathylean McNeal and Edward Parvin. They don't get their names in the paper much anymore. Bit players in a tragedy seldom do. Even the night it happened they were deemed worthy of only a couple of paragraphs in the wire story.

Kathylean McNeal, 22, and Edward Parvin, 28 — the other two people in Pelle Lindbergh's turbocharged Porsche 930 at 5:41 a.m. on Sunday, November 10, when the Philadelphia Flyers' goalkeeper lost control and slammed it into a wall.

Lindbergh was declared brain dead in hospital. Two days later, his parents made the agonizing decision to turn off the life-support system and have his vital organs removed for use as transplants. A doctor suggested that we think of it in terms of Pelle's ultimate save being the saving of lives.

There was a 22-minute memorial service at centre ice prior to the Flyers' next home game, including a prayer by a priest who finished by pointing out to the Lord that in addition to the sorrow of the loss of Lindbergh, who were the Flyers' "guests" (opponents) tonight but the Stanley Cup champion Edmonton Oilers.

I did not hear any mention of Kathylean McNeal or Edward Parvin, the two friends of Lindbergh who'd squeezed into that front seat with him and somehow escaped with their lives. Perhaps it would have been out of place. *Sports Illustrated* managed a five-page colour spread on the Flyers and the accident without so much as mentioning that anyone else was in the car.

And Pelle Lindbergh is leading the fan poll as goalkeeper for the Wales Conference team in the NHL All-Star game February 4 in Hartford.

Many — but not all — of those votes would have been cast before the accident. But he will get more, in a gesture from people who'll view it as a final tribute to a fine athlete killed at age 26, just when he'd been fitted for the mantle of superstar. We do that with our athletic heroes and our entertainment greats, ignoring the fact that they were just people with the usual mixture of virtues and faults.

Pelle Lindbergh's death was a tragedy — one of thousands of such tragedies every year. Doctors say his blood alcohol reading was .24, three times the legal limit in Canada and well over the .10 limit set by the state of New Jersey. By any standards he was incapable of driving when he climbed behind the wheel of a car described as the closest thing to a racing car available for the streets.

It cost him his life. It could have cost the lives of Kathylean McNeal and Edward Parvin. But there would have been no public eulogies for them, no moments of silence all over North America. They would have been two statistics buried in a million more. But Pelle Lindbergh was an athlete, and somehow that makes it different.

"The saddest part," Brad Marsh of the Flyers says at the conclusion of the *Sports Illustrated* article, "is that we're going to go on and win a couple of cups, and Pelle's going to miss it."

No. The saddest part is that a 26-year-old with the world at his feet essentially took his own life, and could have taken two others, because in the end he made himself just another drinking driver not lucky enough to get caught. When we weep for Pelle Lindbergh, weep first for that.

THE OLD SIX HOLE

December 6, 1985

Mr. Howie Meeker,
CTV Hockey Analyst,
Vancouver, B.C.
Dear Howie:

As you know, hockey is my life. Yessir, just give me a cold beer and the Kings and Maple Leafs on the tube and I'm good for ten, maybe 15 minutes.

Naturally, I have tried to imbue friends and colleagues with my enthusiasm for the game. Much of my technique involves instructing them to listen to your analyses on Canuck telecasts — a process that has met with limited success. (Mr. Anthony Eberts, our outdoors writer, has no sympathy for any Canuck who cannot get the puck out of his own end, pointing out that he shouldn't have sat on the damned thing in the first place.)

But that is not the big problem. The one that's driving me nuts is the matter of the Old Five Hole. Because the Old Five Hole isn't the Old Five Hole at all. It isn't even the Old Five-Thirty Hole in your beloved Newfoundland. All these years you have been perpetuating a fraud.

Thousands of kids who hang on your every word and telecast have grown up believing that the Old Five Hole is the space between a goalkeeper's legs where shooters put the puck so they can score and you can make the goalkeeper look stupid.

"Right through the Old Five Hole," you chortle, and all over the telecast area little kids giggle and make plans to aim for the Old Five Hole every practice so they can go to the NHL and go around a defenceman like a hoop around a barrel to put the puck in the hole you've made the most famous in hockey.

And it's not the Old Five Hole. It's the Old Six Hole.

Think of a clock, Howie. Think of a goalkeeper's legs as the hands of that clock. If his legs are spread slightly to create an opening, the clock reads 7.25 or 5.35. Where is the six? Exactly: At the very bottom.

Now, where is the five? That's right, Howie: Off to the right and slightly above the six along the circumference of the clock. Hey — you're getting good at this!

Therefore, if a shooter puts the puck between a goalie's legs he is not shooting it into the Old Five Hole at all. He is shooting it into the Old Six Hole. (You can always tell when he puts it really high in the six hole. The goalie curses in a high soprano.)

Where, then, is the Old Five Hole? Surely the clock proves it is in the right corner a few inches above the ice surface, between the goalie's left skate and the post. Similarly, the Old Seven Hole would be at the same spot in the lower left corner, between the post and his right skate.

Given these loci, it is possible to conclude with reasonable assurance that the Old One Hole is the area above the goalie's left shoulder, the Old Eleven Hole is between his head and his right shoulder, the Old Three Hole is waist high to his left and the Old Nine Hole waist high to his right.

We will resist the temptation to discuss the half-hour holes. There aren't five guys in the league who could read them, let alone hit them. All I ask, in the interests of all those kids out there, is that you give the Old Six Hole the credit it deserves.

After all, once they learn to tell time they'll figure it out for themselves. And you wouldn't want them thinking you'd stopped too many in the Old Twelve Hole.

THE RIVER GAME

September 16, 1987

HAMILTON — Before there could be champagne, there had to be beer.

Before Mario Lemieux and Wayne Gretzky, the Dom Perignon of the Canada Cup tournament, could make the play that beat the Soviet Union 6-5, there had to be the lunch-bucket, steelworker guys with the shovels and the hardhats, digging in to give them the chance. Because, more than anything, this one was for the diggers.

A moment, though, for Lemieux's winner with 86 seconds to play. This is the kid, remember, who came here with the reputation of a guy who worked when he felt like it, sulked when he didn't. So here he was on the boards just outside his own blue line, winning a battle for the puck with a Soviet point man, shoving it ahead to Gretzky, and on sheer effort turning it into a three-on-one break with Gretzky and Larry Murphy. After that, it was showtime: Gretzky drawing the defenceman over and over, then sliding the puck across to Lemieux as Murphy played the human screen. And this time, after a hatful of missed opportunities earlier, shots he'd been putting away all week, Lemieux gave it vintage Mario. Pow — Game 6-5, series 3-2. It was a typical Lemieux or Jari Kurri goal on the play that Gretzky has made his own. But as they sat in the dressing room with the champagne flying, Gretzky put it into perspective.

"Hawerchuk and Tocchet," he said. "Before the game, Messier said we'd need someone to come through big. They were the guys — them and Sutter. We get down 3-0 and Tocchet scores the first goal and sets up the second. In the second period Hawerchuk sets up Sutter and scores the one to put us ahead 5-4. They just kept digging and digging."

Somebody asked if Team Canada was worried, three goals down after eight minutes. "Other teams, maybe. Not this one. I don't know how to describe this team. It's ... special is all I can think of. Special." Hawerchuk, who rarely got to play the centre ice position he dominates with the Winnipeg Jets, had said all through the tournament that he had to school himself to be patient, to accept the limited ice time and wait his chance. It came last night and my, did he cash in.

But then, there were so many stars. Grant Fuhr, the one they call Cocoa, letting in the occasional soft goal, but coming through with two successive big saves to open the third period without which it would have been 5-2 and over. "He's the best big-play goalie there is," Gretzky says reverently. "When the chips are down, Grant just slams the door."

Or how about Leon Rochefort, the prototype defensive defenceman? General manager Serge Savard insisted over considerable objections that Rochefort be on this team. He'd seen him play too often, and knew that somewhere in this champagne set of puck-carrying defencemen there had to be a guy who'd stay home and mash. Speaking of mash, there was the ever-malevolent Messier, intimidation on skates. And Crossman and Gilmour and so many more.

And in the end, what does it all prove, this incredible series in which every game ended 6-5 and two of them required overtime to settle?

Not much. It wasn't vindication for one type of hockey over another, no victory for the Canadian system over the Soviet. Maybe the best thing about it was that we have outgrown that. This was a series in which the greatest hockey talent in the world took the puck out onto the river and played. There was no Them vs Us in the sense that there had been in 1972 when the whole thing started. This was a series between national teams, not ideologies, a series in which the overriding emotions were pride and mutual respect.

"Now, Wayne," a radio guy said, poking a microphone into the Great One's face, "now, how about the Olympics?"

"No thank you," Gretzky said. "This was the Olympics for me." That said it all. Five days from now when the telephones ring and general managers beckon, they'll be Rangers and Oilers and Jets and Nordiques and Islanders again. But last night, as the champagne and beer mixed along with the laughter and the tears, they were Team Canada, and they'd carried their country to the top. And beer or champagne, it doesn't get any better than that.

WEDDING 99

July 15, 1988

"What kind of shorts is Wayne Gretzky wearing on his wedding night?" asked the Ms. from the land of the Living section.

"Huh?"

"His underwear, or pyjamas or English Leather or whatever. What's he wearing? *The Edmonton Sun* ran an interview with the salesgirl who sold Janet Jones the lingerie *she's* going to wear, so it's only fair that we get the same inside information on him. I mean, does he go for the jockey shorts, which are tight and according to some medical studies thus generate more heat which, you know...or does he play it safe and go for the boxer type? Our readers want to *know*."

This is the same Ms. person who once asked "If boxers wear metal cups to protect their groins but don't wear anything to protect their heads, does this mean they're more concerned with their testicles than with their brains?" You'd have a better chance ignoring a typhoon.

"I don't know."

"Will you try to find out?"

"No."

"Balanced reporting," she sniffed. "Ha!"

There is no balance to coverage of Saturday's Wayne Gretzky-Janet Jones wedding in Edmonton. Balance went out the window shortly after sanity. Nine weeks ago I told him my wedding present was going to be an aluminum extension ladder, directions to Janet's window, and a road map out of town. He laughed. I bet he's not laughing now.

In Edmonton the wedding has turned into a circulation war between the rival *Journal* and *Sun*. No detail is too trivial, no guess too wild to make a headline. A month ago, each paper carried a two-page full-colour spread on the wedding plans. There have been stories almost every day since. Some idiot called it "Canada's Royal Wedding," and it stuck: Wayne and Janet as Chuck and Di. It is to barf.

Wednesday night I received a call from the *Journal*. Some poor reporter had been ordered to phone people on the guest list and ask them two questions.

"What are you bringing as a wedding present for Janet and Wayne?"

"None of your business," I said pleasantly.

"Oh. Well, the next question is, if you could offer Wayne one piece of advice for the first year of his married life, what would it be?"

"Beat Mario," I said.

"Excuse me?"

"Beat Mario Lemieux. Win back the scoring championship and the Hart Trophy."

"But... what's that got to do with the first year?"

"Well, I don't know what it will do for his year," I said. "But it will do a hell of a lot for mine. See, I'm a big fan and I always take him in the hockey pool, and..."

"Thank you," he said faintly.

It had to be a big wedding. There were too many commitments, too many friends and business associates for it to be anything else. But neither Gretzky nor Jones had any idea it would get this crazy — and guess who'll get blamed for the overkill?

Is there really a millionaire who's providing his yacht for their honeymoon? No — but it made a hell of a story. Did the ring set really cost $250,000? No — but it sure made a splash, didn't it? And that's all that counts, right?

As usual, it was left for Wayne's dad, Walter, to put things in perspective. He still owns the little house in Brantford, still works at the phone company, although right now he's on strike, and still has both feet firmly rooted in reality. The other day a reporter asked him what he'd be wearing to the wedding.

"I dunno," Wally answered. "Clothes, I guess."

Nobody asked about his underwear.

WEDDING 99 (Continued)

July 19, 1988

After much thought over the weekend, the coveted Jimmy Awards for outstanding achievement and excellence at the Gretzky Wedding. The envelopes, if you please:

Best Ad Lib Performance Under Pressure: Mark Messier, Edmonton Oilers.

As a member of the wedding party, Messier got to escort and sit down with one of the more luscious of the many gorgeous bridesmaids, a young lady he favoured with the kind of loving gaze Popeye reserves for spinach.

87

The fourth or fifth time the reception crowd tapped spoons to glasses to call for the bride and groom to kiss, Messier grabbed the girl by the hand, hauled her to her feet, and laid one on her that probably registered on the Richter. Then, as the crowd roared, he looked up, gave it the old surprised and apologetic "Oh, you didn't mean me?" and sat down. To date, the lady has not pressed charges.

Fastest Answer to Dumbest Question: Gordie Howe.

As he checked into the hotel, a reporter womanperson ran over and gushed, "Are you here for the wedding?"

"No," Howe replied, straight-faced. "It's our anniversary."

Worst Line, One Table: John Short, *Edmonton Journal,* upon learning that Gretzky's best man, Eddie Mio, was there on his own.

"Oh. Solo Mio."

Best Line, Head Table: Kim Gretzky.

The groom's sister, upon being told she looked stunning in her bridesmaid's gown, smiled demurely and said "If I can just kick off these damned shoes and get into sweats, I'll be fine."

Most Dazzling Figure (Bride's Aside): 1,900.

That's the number of hours designer Pari Malek of Los Angeles estimates it took her and her staff to produce the bogglingly beautiful wedding gown. "Plus 90 hours apiece for each of the 11 bridesmaids' gowns," she added. Of course.

Best Mock Telegram: Alan Thicke, MC.

Allegedly reading one sent by Dr. Jerry Buss, jillionaire former owner of the Los Angeles Kings and current owner of the Los Angeles Lakers, who has a reputation for dating girls young enough to be his daughter:

"If your firstborn is a girl, I'd like draft rights to date her."

Most Appreciate Audience: The crowd gathered outside the church awaiting the arrival of the wedding party, which gave the bride and groom of the previous wedding a standing ovation as they left.

Most Daring Fashion Statement (Male): (Tie) Dave Semenko and me.

Ex-Oiler Semenko wore a tuxedo and no socks. Your faithful columnist's ordinary grey suit was nicely set off by the blue simulated leather strap of his genuine Wayne Gretzky wrist watch.

Best Performance (Continuing Series): (14-way tie).

"Wayne is married now," Mio said in concluding his toast to the groom, "and there are too many missing keys to that penthouse. I want them all, right now."

One of the loveliest girls in the room stood up, walked to the podium, and handed him a key. After a slight pause, another honey stood up and did the same — and another, and another, until Mio was holding 12 keys.

The 13th key was handed over by Gordie Howe. Normally, that would have been the show-stopper. But Dalyce Barnett, wife of Gretzky's agent, Michael Barnett, topped him. She, too, strode to the podium to hand over a key, gorgeous, dark-eyed, poker-faced — and obviously pregnant.

BABE PRATT
December 18, 1988

Damnit, Babe, you weren't supposed to go yet. Six of us had tickets for *Cabaret*! You know how hard those things were to get?

We were supposed to go together — you and Floss and Greg and Diane Douglas and Deb and I — and at those prices you were our insurance policy: Joel Grey could fall flat on his prat, but we knew ours would be strictly Tony Award. When it came to revivals and memories and stories of the times and games that were, nobody did it better than you.

Did you know that, Babe? Did you have any idea, standing up at those hundreds of head tables at everything from black tie bashes in posh hotels to minor hockey fund-raisers in drafty rinks all over the province, just how well you did it, or the respect in which you were held?

"These jokes are old," you told me once, "but what the hell — so am I." Then you'd kind of wander up to the mike and start in with the "At my age I don't buy long-playing records" (pause, two-three) "I don't even buy green bananas" schtick, and the big shooters who had to follow you would start looking at each other and wondering why the hell they were there.

I'm a little ticked off at you, Babe. *Cabaret* was going to be the first night we'd ever be together on a purely social basis — no banquets, no press conferences, no post-game shows, no hockey games. At some point in the evening I wanted to tell you how much I enjoyed your work and the way you never alibied for the Canucks in the mostly bad years; how you could absolutely trash them when you felt they deserved it, yet do it in a way that never disguised the fact that this was and would remain your team, playing the best it could in the game you loved.

And there were some stories I wanted to check.

That time in July 1956, when the Mounties caught you speeding on the Barnett Highway, did you really beat the rap by telling the judge that radar was unreliable because the *Andrea Doria* and the *Stockholm* had collided in the North Sea the day before and what good did their radar do them?

Did you mean it, that night you watched one of the Western League Canucks shy away from a corner and sniffed, "How'd you like to have a heart transplant and get his?"

Or how about the night Hugh Watson, the old Canucks' PR man, borrowed a microphone and did a phony between-periods interview with the head of a Seattle Totems' Fan Club? When the guy (who thought you were really on the air) was finished offering his opinions of the first period and Watson put the microphone in front of you as the local colour man, did you really look at the guy and say, "Sir, you're full of shit!"?

In the old days when Lester Patrick was running the Rangers on the cheap and kept the team on the trains overnight rather than pay for hotel rooms, did he really stay up all night huddled under a blanket, waiting for you to sneak in from a party? And did he fine you $1,000 — mammoth in those days — and say the only way you could get the money back was if you promised to quit drinking?

And is it true that you tried, and by Christmas you were playing so badly that the rest of the team took up a collection, gave you back the $1,000 and told you to go back to doing it your way?

There were a lot of things I wanted to ask you, Babe, and now you've ducked out. And you know what gets me about that? Of all the things that could have gone wrong, the heart was the last I'd have bet on. I always figured yours was big enough to survive anything.

GRANNIE GOALIE

December 14, 1988

Paul Reinhart would have been 11 years old when Mary Gretzky leaned over the boards at the Brantford Arena and smacked him over the head with her purse.

He was playing defence for an Atom League team called the Kitchener Krauts and pinning her grandson against the boards in a manner that everyone in the rink deemed legal except Mary. She didn't hesitate. "Let him go!" she yelled, and began flailing away at Reinhart with her purse.

"Grandma," Wayne Gretzky says fondly, "was a competitor."

She was also a friend, a confidante, and the first goalie Gretzky ever faced, bouncing rubber balls off her legs as she sat in the big chair in the farmhouse by the Nith River where, two months shy of his third birthday, he took his first, hesitant step on skates. When she died Saturday at 85, No. 99 lost his No. 1 fan.

I met her first in 1983, out on the farm near Canning, Ontario, where her five children were born and raised and where Wayne and his sister and brothers did much of their growing up. We'd driven the 12 miles out from Brantford after lunch, but she insisted we sit down and have a little something, which turned out to be a huge bowl of homemade soup so thick with vegetables the spoon all but stood on its own.

"I don't think I can ..."

"Eat," she said.

We ate, and watched the pickup game in the yard — tennis ball, tennis racquet, over the trailer is out and into her vegetable garden, you deal with Grandma. The Gretzky kids played, and guests in town for the Celebrity Tennis Tournament, and Mary shook her head and told me stories about the way it was.

She always knew Wayne would be rich. "Hairy arms," she said, with a finality steeped in Polish folklore. "I told him, 'Hairy arms mean you be rich someday.' And in the mornings he would come and ask me if he had any more hair."

The farm was where Gretzky built the high jump pit after practising by jumping over the wire fence to feed her chickens. It was the place he first learned to fish and, in later years, the sanctuary that was always there when the pressure of being Wayne Gretzky grew too severe.

It had been a working farm, and Mary kept her part of it that way to the end. Walter would bring her home from a hospital session she'd spent battling a heart problem or stroke, full of doctor's warnings to take it easy. She'd nod yes, and the next day she'd be in the garden harvesting potatoes. "This is my life," she said. "What else would I do?"

The other part of her life was watching Wayne. Once Frank Mahovlich had been her hero. Now it was the WHL, the Wayne Hockey League, and there was only one player in it. For years she squirrelled money away, bit by bit, against the day she'd be able to buy him a car. When he turned pro at 17 and bought one of his own, her first reaction was, "Now what will I do with the $4,000?"

She was in Edmonton when Wayne married Janet Jones, making the trip with a nurse by her side. "Nice," she said, looking around the hotel ballroom. Then she looked at Wayne and Janet. "Very nice," she beamed.

A couple of years ago technology came to the farmhouse on the Nith: a satellite dish so she and her daughter, Ellen — a Down's Syndrome victim — could watch more of Wayne's games, there in the room where he'd crouched on the floor beside her, watching Toronto Maple Leafs. "So many games," she mused. "So many things..."

Today the Gretzkys say good-bye to Grandma. Then Wayne jumps a plane for Pittsburgh to join the LA Kings for another showdown with Mario Lemieux. Maybe, somewhere, she'll be watching. It's one she'd have hated to miss.

GOOD ON YOU, MR. ASSELSTINE

January 31, 1989

Deep down I've found myself pulling a little for the athlete who goes into the stands after some clown who figures the right to hurl beer and epithets comes with the price of admission.

Not that I want to see the jerk hurt. Usually he's some beer-swilling twit without an athletic bone in his body, or a sagging, over-40 ex-jock who wasn't nearly as talented as he now recalls. Hitting him would be unfair — but he deserves that moment of stark, bladder-clearing terror as he sees a large, sweaty and enraged athlete bearing down upon him with malice aforethought.

The down side has always been that in getting to the twit, the athlete can inadvertently injure or frighten spectators unfortunate enough to be in his flight path. To me that's the only reason the practice should not be condoned — nay, encouraged — by the league involved: The potential risk to the innocent makes it too risky to contemplate.

Now a young Bostonian has chosen to eliminate that risk.

One Frank Baro, 22, climbed the glass in Boston Gardens Saturday afternoon during the Bruins' 4-3 loss to the Winnipeg Jets and headed for referee Bill McCreary, presumably to offer his opinions on McCreary's officiating.

Before he could get to McCreary, linesman Ron Asselstine came flying in from behind with a good head of steam and drove Mr. Baro into the boards with enough force to rattle the foundations of the Gardens and certainly those of Mr. Baro.

A large number of people seem upset about this.

"He could have been hurt," they said. "He could have broken his neck!"

That's true. He also could have stayed in the stands where he belonged.

"Asselstine didn't have to slam him that hard! He could have just grabbed him by the arm and held him back!"

Sure. And what if he'd had a knife or a gun?

We're not talking about some overweight conventioneer drunk out of his gourd and shoving someone in a bar. We're talking about a young, seemingly fit individual enraged or bagged enough to scale the glass in front of 15,000 people and take out after an official.

What if he'd had more than invective on his mind? How could Asselstine know what was running through his mind or nestling in his pocket? In a world where clowns with criminal records can buy machine pistols and spray a school yard, or take potshots at passing cars on the freeway, who's prepared to write off a potential physical assault as something that will be no worse than a shouting match?

"Well, you don't see linesmen jumping in and smashing players around like that."

No, you don't, for a couple of valid reasons. Except in the rare instances the sticks are dropped, the fight is little more than a hug-and-headbutt contest, and they can be reasonably certain that neither man will pull a knife.

Until they issue linesmen with tins of MACE and orders to give the combatants a 20-second warning before firing (to me, a solution long overdue) the best way to stop a hockey fight is to let them go until they fall down or get tired.

Asselstine wasn't dealing with a hockey fight. He was dealing with a potentially dangerous situation, and he defused it as quickly as he could. It was McCreary who appeared to be at risk; McCreary who belonged there, not Baro.

Baro could have kept his butt in his seat. If it had wound up in a sling, he'd have no one to blame but himself.

HE/SHE SHOOTS! HE/SHE SCORES!

February 7, 1990

I am worried about Jim Robson, the practically peerless play-by-play person. (His wife won't let me call him peerless, because he gets his shoes dirty scuffing his toe in the ground and going "Aw, shucks!")

Judging from the document in my hand, Robson's life is about to get complicated. It's from the Canadian Association of Broadcasters, and every radio and TV station in the country has a copy. Subject: GUIDELINES FOR NON-SEXIST LANGUAGE.

In brief, it lists once-acceptable words that can no longer be used because they can be taken to contain sexist overtones, particularly by those who devote their every waking hour to straining to hear them.

There are NO lists (foreman, mankind, gentlemen's agreement) and alternative YES lists (site supervisor, humanity, informal agreement) plus warnings about using the dreaded third-person pronoun in the male sense ("best way HE can increase", "HIS new car") rather than ("TO increase", "THE new car").

And you thought your tax dollars were being wasted!

Now, there is no reference to sports broadcasting per se, but the painted talons of the femalewomenpersons of WOE (Women Opposed to Everything) grow longer by the day. In his position as the aforepersoned PPPPP Robson can hardly avoid a gently scratched reminder — or having his throat torn out if he refuses.

And I can't help but wonder how he'll handle it...

"Well, Tom — which I hasten to add could be short for Tomasina — the Vancouver Canucks are in a bind tonight, but if these persons can come up with the kind of all-out effort they showed Sunday against the New Jersey Devils and/or Witches, they could move a little closer to the Los Angeles Monarchs."

"You're absolutely right, Jim. But these people have a person-sized job cut out for themselves tonight, particularly in their own zone, where the defenceindividuals have had trouble lately giving goalie Kirk McLean the kind of protection an individual with the nether-area reproductive equipment to play that position truly deserves."

"That's right — and you'd be hard pressed to find a position more deman — oops! — challenging than goaltender. But he — that is, Kirk, — has to be pleased by the support he's had lately from defenceperson Garth Butcher."

"Couldn't agree with you more, Jim. Garth's become a real police officer back there. It's taken a few years, but Garth's finally come into his or her own."

"Of course, there's much speculation these days on the job security of coach Bob McCamcitizen. Bob came here with a unisexdate to get this team into the playoffs, and person-oh-person, it's been tough."

"Yes, but don't forget, Jim, Bob's from the old school. Still remembers those Saturday nights on the prairies, the entire McCamhuman family lying there on the farmhouse floor listening to Foster Hewitt shout 'They shoot! They score!' "

"And some of the youngsters from the farm are starting to show signs. Rob Murphy, for instance, can really carry the letters, and based on the New Jersey game it could be that Dave Capuano is the point-individual who can run the power play."

"Tonight also marks the unveiling of the Canucks' new uniforms, Jim. What do you think: will the slacks catch on?"

"I'm more worried about the new shoulder pads, Tom. I don't care how good they looked on Barbara Stanwyck, they should do more than make the arms of the sweaters hang straight."

"You've got a point there, Jim, and it's one we'll raise right now with the general manager of the Vancouver Canucks, who has joined us at the microphone.

"Tell me, Patricia Quinn..."

GO (SNORE) SENATORS, GO!

December 7, 1990

NHL expansion intelligence test. Select the best answer from the following multiple-choice questions:

The Ottawa entry in 1992-93 will be called the Senators because:

(a) Ottawa was one of the original NHL members in 1917-18 with a team called the Senators.

(b) The way the current NHL clubs will rig the expansion draft, the only players left for Ottawa will be aged, doddering and basically useless.

(c) What else would you call a team that's elected today but doesn't have to attend a game for two years?

Phil Esposito, backed by Japanese money, is front man for Ottawa's new traditional rival, Tampa Bay. He won't last because:

(a) He thinks Domo Arigato is a head waiter.

(b) He'll try to trade Tampa for Sault Ste. Marie.

(c) At his first press conference with his Japanese backers he'll sit down at the piano and attempt to play "Chopsticks".

The best way to get a spot on the Senators' roster is to:

(a) Know Brian Mulroney personally.

(b) Do a Conservative a big favour.

(c) Catch a Conservative doing someone else a big favour.

If you answered (c) to the above, you can best secure your position as a Senator by:

(a) Developing your skating.

(b) Developing your shooting.

(c) Developing your negatives.

NHL franchises traditionally attract big tourist dollars from visitors who come to see the game and stay to spend money. From the following list, name Ottawa's No. 1 tourist attraction:

(a) The House of Commons.

(b) The house of Russ Jackson.

(c) The bridge to Hull, Quebec.

Plans to build a new rink in Ottawa have been delayed because the site is part of the agricultural land bank. Select the most likely ending to the impasse:

(a) Franchise owners come to B.C. and take land re-zoning lessons.

(b) Conservatives designate land as Senatorial burial ground and arena as crypt to hold 18,000.

(c) Disgruntled Hamiltonians plant two nests full of baby birds on property and phone the animal-rights people.

Hamilton has a rink and commitments for a minimum 10,000 season tickets. Ottawa has no rink, no land and no commitment. Ottawa gets franchise because:

(a) When Tim Horton Donuts backed the Hamilton bid, NHL president John Ziegler said "DUH! Donuts have holes. Pucks don't have holes. They must be thinking of ringette."

(b) It cuts down travel time for the Ottawa lobbyists using the free tickets they get for pressuring the NHL into awarding a Canadian franchise.

(c) If Hamilton got an NHL franchise, Toronto would want one.

99 MEMORIES

January 25, 1991

It's not fair, Wayne Gretzky turning 30. If Gretzky is 30 that means I'm (Ahem! Cough! Cough!) and his father is, too. That can't be right. We're both 35. Ask anybody.

But the record book says Wayne turns 30 tomorrow. *Sports Illustrated* has a big weekend piece, the wire services are at the ready and we may soon be awash with stories and legends of the man who was a star almost before he was a kid. Here are a few personal ones they might miss:

* The Bob Krieger cartoon on my wall, me sitting on the blade of Gretzky's hockey stick, notebook in hand, him beaming out from under his considerable nose. Incredibly, the normally reliable Krieger has failed to capture my sunny smile. I look like the blade is about two feet up my butt and I've just swallowed a prune.

It's autographed and dated January 26, 1982 — his 21st birthday, four days after I'd met him for the first time, and followed him all over town for a day-in-the-life profile the cartoon was used to illustrate. The day began at the CBC, where he was doggedly rehearsing a parody of "The Devil Came Down to Georgia." ("The Devil came down to Showdown/He was lookin' for a soul to steal...") for a segment of the Paul Anka TV show.

"Tired? Yeah, sometimes," he said. "But being tired is a part of living..."

In four days he'd be 21, and tired was a part of living.

* The autographed picture of Cheryl Tiegs leaning up against a rock that looked ready to melt. "To Jim, with warm thoughts of Jamaica. Lots of love. XXX Cheryl."

July 12, 1983. I was in Brantford to meet Walter Gretzky for the first time. Cheryl was there for the Gretzky tennis tournament. Instead of coming to the room to introduce himself, Walter sent Cheryl.

I opened the door, and there she was.

"Mr. Gretzky would like to see you," she said sweetly.

"Uh, would you do me a favour?" I gasped. "Would you take two steps forward?"

"Why?" she asked.

"Because before I die, I want to be able to tell my friends that I asked Cheryl Tiegs to come to my hotel room, and she did."

* The Gretzky house in Brantford, that same week. I've been pumping Walter and Wayne, researching a book Wally and I were writing on No. 99.

"Turn on the satellite dish and we'll catch a ball game."

I push the button and set it on scan. The channels blur past too quickly to register.

"Stop," Wayne says. "Two channels back. Cleveland's playing."

"You saw the Indians in there?" I asked.

"Yeah, and it's a home game. I could tell by their uniforms."

"Horse feces," I scoffed, and pushed the button. The Indians were playing — in Cleveland.

"His eyes have always been pretty good," Wally said.

* Breakfast in the new penthouse apartment in Edmonton. The night before, Wayne has scored three times on his old teammate and friend, Eddie Mio, in a pre-season game.

"Isn't this apartment great!" he said. "The security is super. My name's not on the mailbox or anywhere. Nobody knows I'm here!"

I get the paper from the front door. On the wrapper it says "Great game last night, Wayne! Your paper boy, Dave."

* We are talking about the pressures of being Wayne Gretzky, the pressures he's always accepted as being part of the game. There is a moment of silence. Then:

"You know the only place I can get away from it during the season?" he asks. "The only place I can totally relax? On the ice. The ice is where I get away. You have this one thing to do and that's all. It's great.

"The games," he says softly, "are always the best part."

* So many games, so many records, so many moments of pure magic. Why is it, then, that the conversation I remember best is the one in which he recalled coming in from play on the backyard rink with toes so cold he cried.

"Chillblains," he said. "Every kid who stays out in the cold then comes into a warm house gets them. When your feet warm up it hurts and itches like mad.

"But I don't remember the crying. I remember the hot chocolate, and my Dad's big, strong hands holding the toes to make the cold go away..."

Watch him play. Thirty years old, but inside the helmet the little kid still skates on the river, lost in the joy of the playing, the taste of hot chocolate already on his tongue.

DEAR DIANA: SEND MONEY

May 15, 1991

Mr. Paul Anka,
c/o Ottawa Senators Hockey Club,
Ottawa, Ont.

Dear Paul: Sorry to hear about your accidental purchase of part of the Ottawa Senators NHL franchise. At least, I'm assuming it was accidental, since no one in his right mind would do it on purpose.

Truly, it is a marriage made in heaven, the kind that's been known to launch dynasties: You have money, they need money. Who could ask for anything more?

> "You're so rich and we're so broke,
> Oh, Paul Anka, what a joke
> We don't care just what they say,
> Long as you can pay and pay..."

I gather this is the honeymoon phase, when you and your new partners get all cutesy-poo and blushy at the mention of each other's names, just thinking of the wonderful life ahead with all the really neat people who run the NHL. They'll all love you, too, (You really DO have a lot of money, don't you?) — more than you'll love them once you understand the way things work when it comes to welcoming new teams to the lodge.

> "And they call it puppy training,
> Except the owners pee on you..."

Mind you, things will get better once they actually have your money. (You're sure, now? You can cover the $22,500,000 (U.S.) due in June, just like your partner, Bruce Firestone said? Or, at least, I assume that's what he meant from that quote in the paper that now the Senators can stop worrying about that money due in June.) Before you know it you'll be involved in the expansion draft where your new NHL partners sell you some of their very own players to get you started.

> "Put your hand on my shoulder,
> I can't stand up un-aided,
> It's been years since I've skated,
> Hold me, tell me where I sign..."

The important thing at that point is not to panic. Out-of-shape Senators have always been big in Ottawa, although you may have trouble actually getting them out to games. Then again, in the tradition of Senators through the years they won't get much accomplished when they do show up, so it all kind of evens out.

True, there will always be unforeseen operating expenses (Have they mentioned that you don't have a rink? Or a place to build one?), like jars for the false teeth, individual prune-juice glasses and a prostate-removal clause in the team medical plan, but think what you'll save doing the anthem yourself and maybe writing a team fight song:

> "We've got the fight!
> We've got the fizz!
> Let's go, Senators!
> Zzzzzzzzzz....."

Okay, so it will take time to build a winner. What's 30 or 40 years when you're having fun? Just think what it could do for your creative juices, trying to write hit songs fast enough to break even.

And if you don't, if you lose your shirt, well, you've already sort of written a great exit...

> "And now, the end is near, I've got this team, no hope of winning.
>
> My friends, I'll make it clear: They're fat and slow, they're double-chinning.
>
> The league, it drained my poke, I got sucked in, yes, in a square way.
>
> And now, I sit stone broke, I did it their way..."

ERIC THE READ

July 10, 1991

Eric Lindros has published his biography. He is 18 years old. I guess he figured time was running out.

Maybe you saw the picture in Tuesday's *Province*: Eric the Better-Be-Great, signing an autograph for nine-year-old Jordon Lovig at a booksellers' conference in Toronto where he was pushing his book (Eric's, not Jordon's) *Fire On Ice*.

We don't know whether Jordon bought a copy — but then, why would he? He's already half as old as Eric. He probably rushed home and began his own autobiog: ("It seems like only yesterday I was in the fourth grade. In fact, it was.")

But a lot of people will buy the Lindros book. He is the hot-ticket item in hockey these days, not bad for a guy who hasn't got a team or a league and has yet to shoot a puck as a pro. Marketing being what it is, it should be at least a Canadian sports best-seller. In no time we'll have to start calling him Eric the Read.

I just wonder what could possibly be in it.

The kid is 18. I think we can safely assume nothing much happened before he hit six. That leaves 12 years' worth of living to fill an entire book. Since he did not go to war, smuggle dope, date Marla Maples or have an ongoing affair with Yolanda Ballard, you'd think subject matter would grow a tad sparse around Chapter Three.

Since my free review copy has yet to arrive I can only guess at how Eric has broken his life into chapters...

FOREWORD: In the Beginning, there was Me. And my Crayolas, the very ones I'm using to write this book.

I was going to do the whole thing in red and white, the Team Canada colours, but the white doesn't show up too well on the white paper. So do I change to coloured paper, or what? I guess I've got one of those writer's blocks.

I asked my Mom how I should write this. She says the important thing is to print without going over the lines.

THE PAMPERS YEARS: I remember the first time Dad dressed me in my hockey gear. It took him half an hour. By the time he finished I had to go to the bathroom. He took it all off again. "Mother!" he yelled. I thought that was pretty funny. She wasn't even in the rink.

BORN TO SCORE: I can't remember when I wasn't playing hockey, but I remember the day I knew I could be a star. It was after a game where I scored 23 goals. I stood 5'11" and weighed 160 pounds. I was eight years old. "Dad," I said, "this is my game."

TO JUNIOR WITH LOVE: My parents were never pushy. Mom waited until I was 18 months old before she put me on skates. And Dad? Where would I be today without his support and advice?

I'll never forget what he said to me the day I went to Oshawa to play Junior "A". "Son," he said, "This is the first step toward the pros. NHL scouts will be watching your every move. So remember: When you pull on that uniform, make sure you've gone to the bathroom first."

101

MIDLIFE CRISIS: I was 15 when it happened. I looked in the mirror and there it was: a zit!

BORN TO SCORE (II): Two weeks later, a bunch of girls were waiting outside the rink. It had been a good game. I'd scored 46 goals, set up 23 and agreed to run for mayor.

"Wanna party?" they asked.

I guess the guys were right: Girls do work better than Clearasil.

A VERY GOOD YEAR: Well, the Crayolas are down to stubs, my Walkman has run out of tape and if I don't get to bed in a hurry Mom is going to kill me.

Tomorrow is a big day. I've got to decide which way to get rich — sign with Quebec, stay in junior, go to the Continental League, join the Olympic program or just stay home and write another book.

Dad offered to help, but I'm old enough now to stand on my own two feet and lift the seat before I go. Besides, I've got an older friend to advise me, a guy who's faced the same problems and knows the responsibilities of turning pro.

Before I print my name on anything, I talk with Rocket Ismail.

EXCUSE ME — IS THIS PART OF YOUR BRAIN??
April 12, 1991

He was large and loutish, standing safely on the concourse behind the LA Kings bench, bravely hurling insults at a bunch of hockey players he knew could not strike back.

Oh, but he was a bold one, jerking away from PNE ushers 30 years and more his senior, jabbing his finger at the Kings, putting on a show for the handful of mental midgets there to urge him on.

"I must write to that man," I thought. "I must attempt to discover why he would do something like that, and tell him what he looked like from up in the press box and to the 16,000 or so others in the Pacific Coliseum."

Dear Jerk:

This is a letter to you from me. It is also to the other people like you who threw golf balls and other things at the Kings to show what great hockey fans you are. I will try to keep the words short so you can understand them.

I would like to know how you get ready to go to a hockey game.

Do you stand in front of the mirror practising your swear words and your scary looks?

Do you check your pockets before you go to make sure you have your golf balls or your whiffle ball with the tape on it so it will fly better and hurt more if it hits someone?

Do you giggle a lot about how mad you're gonna make the hockey players?

Do you get all excited, thinking about how the big people in the stands are going to be watching you, and how maybe you'll even get on TV?

Boy, that would be neat, wouldn't it? Right there on TV where your friends at home can see you! And maybe, if you time it just right, you could even wave. You'd really be a big man then, wouldn't you? People would notice you.

Do you have any idea what you really look like? You look like you're either coming from or going to your lobotomy.

Oh, I'm sorry. I used a long word. I know what a strain that is on your lips. A lobotomy is like a brain operation where they cut away the parts that aren't working right. But I guess you couldn't have one. The doctor wouldn't know where to stop.

Besides, you're just having fun, right? Hey, you're a Canuck fan, supporting your team! So you swear at the other team! So you throw things on the ice where guys might trip over them! You're just having a little fun.

I'll tell you a story that will really make you laugh.

Years ago at a junior lacrosse game, someone just like you threw some pennies out onto the floor. One of the players slipped on one and went head-first into the boards. Isn't that funny?

I wrote a story about him. He'd broken his spine and was paralyzed from the neck down for the rest of his life. He was 15. When he cried, his parents had to wipe away the tears.

But you're different, right? Never happen with you. You're just a Canuck fan having a few laughs.

Of course, they don't want you there. I guess the PNE people feel sorry for you, because the police never come. But no one wants you there. Not the Canucks, not the Kings, not any of the 16,000 people who came out to watch the game.

You know what's really funny? You think doing these things makes you part of the crowd, when all it does is show everyone how much you're really alone. I guess the real joke's on you.

Chapter Four

JOCK AND JILL

I've always considered sex a participant sport. I'll worry about my sex life, you worry about yours, and neither of us need worry about the other's unless we happen to be together at the time.

Until the 1980s, sports fans took pretty much the same attitude. If their heroes and heroines had a sex life that didn't involve marriage — or, for that matter, drank anything that didn't come from cows — they didn't know and didn't want to know.

Babe Ruth, a beer-swilling womanizer? No way! He was the Bambino, the Sultan of Swat, the barrel-chested, toothpick-legged legend who hit 60 homers in 1927 and made Yankee Stadium "The House That Ruth Built". Bobby Layne, a quarterback whose off-field legend was as big as the one he built in the National Football League? Hey, could the guy throw, or what? Layne's explanation of how he could burn the candle at both ends ("I sleep fast!") was good enough for them.

Television changed all that. TV, the growth of kiss-and-tell journalism (and make-it-up tabloids) made sex a spectator sport. Throw in the steroid scandals and out-of-the-closet admissions by sport's gay underground, and suddenly we had a whole new ball game — some of it funny, some of it sad.

Maybe, in the process, we've grown up a little.

Maybe.

THE OLD SKIN GAME

February 14, 1991

Sure I'm shocked by the *Sports Illustrated* swimsuit edition. Some years I've been shocked for hours at a time.

Just yesterday I was expressing my shock and outrage over the 1991 edition, its cover featuring the gorgeously pneumatic Ashley Montana. When this edition hit the streets, it bounced.

"Look at this," I said, thrusting the colour layout at my wife. "Will you look at the prices on those suits? Sixty-two bucks for a bikini you could use for three cocktail coasters? It's outrageous. I am shocked and disappointed."

Actually, that's not why I'm shocked and disappointed. The real reason is that every time *SI* does this the next three editions are full of letters from women bitching about it:

"I'm hiding this from my husband because it degrades and shames women and I'm afraid my son will grow hair on his palms and go blind. Cancel our subscription."

And:

"You continually portray women as slaves and sex objects when every thinking woman knows we should be running the country and besides, I could probably look that good if I didn't have to raise six children and could afford the implants."

This wastes valuable space that might otherwise be used to explain the complexities of the run-and-shoot offence, the zone press or Pete Rose's income-tax form. And all they're proving is that they're not bright enough to realize they're being had.

SI runs the swimsuit edition because it makes more money than any other edition. It makes more money because it generates more comment, mostly from women complaining about how degrading it is. Sales and ad lineage jump not merely for one issue but for the next two as buyers rush to chortle over the apoplectic reaction. *SI* doesn't care. *SI* just counts the money.

As for the girls in the skimpy suits... well, speaking as your average soon-to-be-54, slightly overweight, bald, happily-married man I would like to say they certainly are gorgeous and young and yummy and built and utterly unattainable.

They have as much relationship to reality as Rocky has to boxing or Rosanne to Weight Watchers. They pose on tropical beaches in suits that wouldn't last ten metres if they ever actually swam in them.

They generate nothing but harmless sighs, and for a few moments at least they burn away the February chill.

They do not look upset. I have not noticed handcuffs or leg irons, and God knows I've looked closely enough. Sex objects, maybe, but if a six-figure income is slavery, where do I sign?

In the same edition of *SI*, just before the swimsuits, eight colour pages are devoted to a young and handsome surfer named Kelly Slater. He is wearing less than Elle MacPherson. There's also a full-page, naked-to-the-waist portrait of Benito Santiago and others devoted to muscular basketball players in shorts.

Do you hear me bitching? Did men rise up in protest when Joe Namath posed in pantyhose or Jim Palmer in nothing but Fruit of the Looms? No! 'Enry 'iggins had it right: By and large, we ARE a marvellous sex.

PECS BY THE BUSHEL

August 16, 1985

"If the jelly buns put me down," she says, "I'll show them this." Panting then points to her sinewy buttocks. "It doesn't get any tighter than that." — *MVP Magazine*.

Deanna Panting is a 20-year-old from Winnipeg who says she wants to be the female Arnold Schwarzenegger. Judging from the pictures, she's off to a hell of a start.

Not that she isn't pretty. No indeed. Ms. Panting ("Canada's Sexy Savage" says *MVP*, the Canadian *Sports Illustrated*) has tawny blonde hair, great eyes and a lovely face — all perched on a body that could kick-start a locomotive.

There is no doubt we're talking girl here, but it's so thickly covered with muscle you find yourself wondering: girl what? There should be a zipper somewhere, or maybe a seam. Crack it, she splits down the middle and out steps Annette Funicello.

Ah, Annette... now there was a girl. If she wanted to be anybody, it was Betty Crocker. If she pumped iron it was to do Frankie Avalon's shirts.

But the old order changeth, boys, and I'm not sure we're going to like it. Women are into body-building, flexing their oiled little buns off, performing under hot lights like Sally Rand on steroids for titles both amateur and pro.

Ms. Panting finished fourth at the world pro championships in Toronto last April and can hardly wait for the Miss Olympia contest November 30 in New York. Vancouver's Donna Lea is just back from the World Games in London, an amateur event in which she finished third in her class. They've worked hard to get that far and will work as hard as it takes to get better and they'll deserve any success that comes their way.

But...

("Aha! Here it comes, Martha: the Sexist Pig stuff. No place for a woman in a man's game. Why isn't she staying home having babies...")

No, indeed. If there was ever a sport dumb enough to handle both sexes, body-building is it. Not physical fitness — although that is a natural and desirable byproduct. Body-building. Pectoral show-and-tell. Oil and flex and stand there like a Roman statue waiting for the pigeons.

I never minded guys doing it, although sometimes I wondered which had the greater density, the barbell or the head of the guy who was lifting it. And it's always fun going to Conan movies to watch Schwarzenegger's never-ending battle with the two-syllable word.

But girls ... Can you imagine taking a body-builder to the senior prom? You wouldn't know whether to give her a corsage or a stilson wrench. You want we should drive over in the car, honey, or would you rather carry it with you for later?

Here, as described in *MVP* is Ms. Panting, getting ready for her date with destiny in Toronto:

"Rested, her body is clean-shaven, deeply 'tanned' from the application of a chemical lotion and 'dried out' from a reduction of water intake, a process that renders the skin covering the muscles thinner, tighter and more 'transparent' — making the muscles appear more defined and thus more impressive."

Wonderful. And after the hop we can all go over to Arnold's for a wheat-germ shake.

Ms. Panting thought she might win in Toronto. The crowd loved her, but some judges said she needed more muscle in the back. (That's the first thing you look for in your dates, right?) So it's back to the old fitness centre, and with work the muscle will be there for New York.

Good luck, Ms. Panting. But frankly, you'll never look like Arnold Schwarzenegger. He's taller.

GUNILLA MAKES THE CUT

December 16, 1987

Gunilla Axen, 22, a member of the Swedish national women's soccer team, says she had her breasts surgically reduced to improve her athletic performance. I trust she was not in her cups at the time.

Ms. Axen says the decision had nothing to do with her looks. She was simply too well endowed to give her all in the games, so she gave part of herself on the operating table. *Sic transit gloria booby*.

Naturally, the world will be watching her performance with more than a passing interest. The implications of her re-definition of the term "giving a little bit extra" are potentially staggering, and not just among women athletes in other sports who feel pressured into following her example.

What about the husbands and boyfriends who admire their lover's figure, and face the prospect of watching it deflate like a soccer ball with a slow leak? What about male athletes? Did she ever think of what it could cost them?

No longer can a baseball player take a week off because he has a bwister on his wittle fingy. "Pop it, drain it and tape it, you wimp!" his coach will snap. "You call that a bump? That Axen dame gave up ten times that much before the doctor even got to the other side of the table."

No more will a Refrigerator Perry be able to come to camp weighing more than the dressing room, and protest that weight loss is too great a task. "Uh, William, just lie down here on this table. This is Gunilla Axen's physician. Go ahead, doc. Trim the drumsticks, flatten the butt, and if he gives you any trouble, nip off the jockstrap, contents included."

And yet, we cannot blame Ms. Axen for the chaos she hath wrought. Hers was a decision based on pure logic. If weightlifters and others in sports requiring strength are stupid enough to use steroids to bulk up, what's wrong with a woman who feels the weight of two worlds on her chest being wise enough to pare down?

Besides, it's a decision that could prolong the competitive life of women athletes, and one that should have been made long ago. For was it not Shane Gould's swimming coach, back in the 1970s, who watched his young watersprite blossom as her freestyle times declined and sighed "Once they develop like that you've got two choices: Retire 'em, or turn 'em over and make 'em backstrokers."

Not all sports would require such radical trimming. Surely a sprinter straining to breast the tape is better off with the maximum in natural equipment to get the job done. And I'm not certain how the cutback will improve Ms. Axen's performance in soccer, where the rules allow women to chest a ball down with the arms crossed over said chest for the same reason male players are seen with hands covering their nether regions while forming the wall defending a free kick.

The lady obviously feels she'll play better a size smaller — but her solution to the problem does not mean that other athletically inclined young women should follow suit. Only time and performance will give us the true picture. Until then, ladies, please do not adjust your sets.

COVERING KATARINA

December 1, 1988

International Skating Union orders female skaters to wear skirts that hide their hips and bottoms and do not expose bare stomachs — News item.

I've always been into equipment watching, myself. "Look at the equipment on that broad," I'd say. That was in my sexist days. By the Calgary Olympics I was far more mature. Years of rigid discipline had brought me to the point where I could watch Katarina Witt for, oh, 30 or 40 seconds before I felt moved to point out that the female womanperson unit representing East Germany had a great set of skates on those long, long, l-o-o-n-n-g lower appendages.

Now the ISU is going to take all that away, and about time, too.

What male in his right mind would want to watch the newest Katarina gliding across the ice in something feathered and dazzling and cut up to here and down to there when he could see that same wonderful creature in, say, shoulder-to-ankle coveralls?

"We aim to remind skaters and the public that we're a competitive sport," sniffs Brian Wright, chairman of the ISU technical committee. "We don't want further growth of exhibition-style attire in championships."

Amen, brother. Competitive sport is what it's all about. The never-to-be-forgotten thrill of victory, the agony of defeat as the judges battle nose-to-nose and promise-to-promise to win their skaters additional support next year or the year after or whenever it's their turn.

Who will ever forget that moving moment at the Calgary Olympics in February when Peter Dunfield, coach of Canadian silver medallist Elizabeth Manley, accused Katarina of being too sexy? "We're here to skate in a dress, not in a G-string," he hissed. "The costumes are getting wilder and wilder."

Amen again. They certainly are: low necklines, sequins, flowers down the front, skin-tight around the butt — and that's on the men. The girls' costumes are even wilder. Watching some of the pairs in action, you didn't know whether to applaud or run out and throw water over them.

Who needs that, really, when what counts is the suspense of watching skater after skater execute compulsory figures, and the judges peering down at the tracings and muttering in five languages that Freida's eight is better than Betty's, and Angela would have been better off trying for it the hard way with a pair of fours.

And the freestyle. What right had Katarina to skate around like that, fogging up the glasses of every male in the rink? How dumb are these ice-show people anyway, signing her for big money to wear those same outrageous costumes and float around the ice with those same sensuous, lovely, incredibly sexy movements of those long, long, l-o-o-o-n-g ...

But I digress.

Cover the navel. Cover the hips. Let no word leak out that they even *have* bottoms. The world cries out for sexless skating. After all, it worked for the Miss Grey Cup pageant.

When Mrs. Karen Harrison of Ottawa beat out that 74-year-old lady for the Miss Grey Cup title with a stirring address on what the CFL meant to her, I never once noticed that she was a toothsome morsel indeed.

"Boy," I sighed, "does that womanperson know her zone defences."

It'll be the same way with figure skating, you watch. And do let me know how it comes out. I'll be at the ice show, checking to see whether Katarina has repented. It's a dirty job, but...

TAIL STORY TIME

September 12, 1990

Due to the weekend football bother I was unable to dash off the cinch No. 1 letter in love columnist Kathy Tait's Sunday hot-damn, you-tell-me-yours, I'll-tell-you-mine personal sexpose contest.

I admit there were pretty steamy contenders in there from people like Mrs. X and Ms. Slocan Valley and Thoroughly Satisfied. (Funny name for a kid, Thoroughly. I can just see the parents sitting around with the Baby Name Book and Daddy shouts: "I've got it! Let's call her Thoroughly!")

Admittedly, when it comes to Doing It on a parachute drop, in a traffic jam or an airliner rest room I am more than somewhat lacking in experience.

In fact, unless you count the time in the B.C. Place end zone during the third quarter of the B.C.-Edmonton game (we used the Eskimo end zone because we knew there'd be no Lions running around in there to disturb us) when passions were really running high and we thrilled to the possibility that Lui Passaglia might put one through the uprights above us at the Crucial Moment, and the referee came running over and threw a flag at my wife for unsportsmanlike conduct and Murray Pezim rushed up offering to pay the fine and marry her...

Aw, you don't believe me.

Well, it was worth a shot.

My problem is that I view sex as a participant sport. I've never figured the kick in making love, then rushing to the word processor to tell someone about it or reading an instructional book on how we should have Done It. Sex has been around a lot longer than books. If the pre-book people were doing it so badly, how come we've got a population explosion?

If it was a spectator sport, it long since would have been franchised. Think of the advantages of a Canadian Sex League:

Small rosters (in most cases, two, although the possibilities in offensive and defensive units are intriguing).

Low equipment costs. A condom here, a pill there, maybe a few aspirin and a pack of post-game cigarettes.

Minimal field maintenance. Just throw a water bed on the 55-yard line and stand back.

Guaranteed mixed teams (at least, we certainly hope so).

No Little League. (Show me one set of pushy parents who'd demand that 12-year-old Johnny play with 11-year-old Jane.)

Great slow motion, stop-action replays and expert analysis. ("See, Kathy, he starts out pretty well — good position, elbows flexed — but then on the downswing it kinda gets away from him...") There are drawbacks. It would have to be a judgmental sport, with a panel of officials holding up scorecards awarding points for compulsory figures and freestyle. And sure as hell the judges would trade off to get better position for their own competitors.

No doubt about it. In its formative years the CSL would not be without kinks. But then, based on Sunday's letters, there's a lot of that going around.

TRICK QUESTION

September 27, 1990

"How would *you* like it," my wife asked, "if you were covering a women's team and you went into the locker room and some naked girls came over and stood really close and dared *you* to touch their private parts?"

Inside my headbone, alarm bells sounded.

"This is a trick question, right? One of those where if I say I wouldn't like it you say 'Oh, sure!' and if I say I'd like it just fine, you smack me upside my head."

"It is not a trick question. It says right here on your sports pages that some players for the New England Patriots did that to a Boston *Herald* sports writer named Lisa Olson when she was in the dressing room getting an interview and they were coming out of the shower.

"And one of them said 'Is this what you want,' which she says was one of his tamer comments, and the team owner, that Victor Kiam electric shaver person, called her 'A classic bitch!' and her paper was considering a sexual-harassment lawsuit but Kiam and the team have apologized and some players have been fined, and I was just wondering how you'd feel if the shoe was on the other foot."

Dance, Jim. Dance!

"You mean, I've just finished covering the women's professional tennis tour, and I'm in the dressing room interviewing, say, Martina Navratilova, and Gabriela Sabatini is coming out of the shower, and she walks over to me wearing only soapsuds and a smile and says....Naah!"

"What do you mean, naah? You're saying Gabriela Sabatini, who you've only been slobbering all over the TV screen about since she was 17, is standing there starkers, making suggestive suggestions, and you don't even react? Oh, sure!"

"No, I mean..."

"*No?* What do you mean, no? Thirty years I give you, and the first time some little 20-year-old comes swishing by mother naked, you go chasing after offering to towel her down?"

"Wait! I don't mean no, I don't react. I mean, no, it would never be a problem because the offer would never be made! What does Gabriela Sabatini need with a 53-year-old, out-of-shape bald guy? She's gorgeous and stinking rich."

"Then why doesn't she have her own shower room? Why does she need to come parading around after you?"

"Hey, don't blame me! I'm just standing here interviewing Martina Navratilova!"

She paused to regroup.

"All I want to know," she said, dangerously quiet, "is how you would feel as a reporter if you were treated that way in a women's team dressing room."

Bob and weave. Bob and weave...

"What happened in New England is that Ms. Olson — a qualified reporter who deserved equal treatment — made a rookie mistake in the way she used her assets. What she should have done when the guy made that crack was show a little leg."

"A little *leg*! Why, you..."

"Yeah, a little leg — right up to the knee, just before she brought it up into the guy's crotch. Then she could have said 'No, it's not what I want. And for the next few days you're not gonna want it, either.'

"See, football players are always telling male media guys to stick this and stuff that and perform those physical impossibilities upon themselves, and there's nothing much we can do about it because one swing and we'd wind up in traction. But if a female reporter hauls off and belts some guy who insults her, what's he gonna do — hit her back?"

"All right, but you still haven't told me how you'd handle Gabriela Sabatini."

"I don't know, dear. And you know the sad part? I'll never get the chance to find out."

"FOR WANT OF A BATHROBE..."

November 28, 1990

In a decade or so, when Lisa Olson's name is the answer on the back of a Trivial Pursuit card, the question on the front will go something like this:

"Name the female sports reporter who gave the world a new definition of the term 'Much ado about nothing'."

"Omigod, Martha, there he goes again, that no-good sexist pig, making light of one of the great feminist issues of the day! I move we file a complaint with somebody, study the case dispassionately from all sides, then hang him."

No, no, no.

I'm all for NFL commissioner Paul Tagliabu coming down hard, as he did Tuesday, on the New England Patriots and the players involved in the harassment of Ms. Olson on that fateful day she entered the dressing room to do her job as a reporter for the Boston *Herald*.

Zeke Mowatt, the principal offender, was hit with a $12,500 fine. Teammates Michael Timpson and Robert Perryman have to cough up $5,000 each and the Patriots themselves — meaning Victor "The Razor King" Kiam — have to pay $50,000. Wonderful. Justice is served. I myself will rest easily, the danger of a retaliatory strike by SWAT teams from the LPGA or the pro tennis tour seemingly averted. (Not that I'd be allowed in the dressing room, assuming I wanted to go. In that particular facet of the equality-of-access issue, sauce for the goose definitely is not sauce for the gander.)

But, circus aside, it was no big deal.

Women have been covering NFL teams since the days of Phyllis George. They've been on NHL and NBA beats for years. The I-cracked-the-team-dressing-room-and-all-men-are-not-created-equal story has gone the way of the dinosaur. But one incident occurs in one dressing room to one woman reporter, and everything hits the fan.

Suddenly, Lisa Olson was a talk-show celeb. Kiam, who apparently acted like an ill-mannered lout in the dressing room, then bailed out and threw the blame on team officials, took out full-page newspaper ads for a public apology. A women's group called for a national boycott of Remington razors.

And why? Because three football players got out of line and made lewd suggestions to a working reporter of the female persuasion.

Here's what should have happened.

Ms. Olson should have marched from the dressing room to the office of general-manager Pat Sullivan and demanded an apology and punishment of the players in question. Sullivan should have acted immediately with fines so heavy Mowatt, Perryman and Timpson would have played three games for nothing. Ms. Olson's newspaper should have filed a protest with the commissioner's office. It would have ended right there with justice for all and a warning to other teams that such conduct would not be tolerated.

Instead, the reporter became the story. And a simply-solved, two-pronged problem — Neanderthal mentality of a few and the honest discomfort of a few others for a female presence in the dressing room when players were wandering to and from the showers in various stages of undress — became an international issue.

Ms. Olson is alive and well and covering the NHL and NBA. Her point has been made. The guilty have been punished. But it's been a big-league fuss over a little-league problem, and even at the finish the silliness rolled on.

Half of the Patriots' $50,000 fine was for failing to pursue the issue in the first place. The other half is to provide "counselling on how to deal with the media."

That's easy, Victor. Buy a set of bathrobes.

BUBBY TAKES THE BUSS

January 8, 1991

Several alert readers phoned on the weekend to discuss the latest NFL sexual harassment case. You could hear the shock and outrage in their voices.

It was pretty horrible — worse in a way than the overblown Lisa Olson case in the New England Patriots' dressing room. Ms. Olson, a Boston reporter, was subjected only to lewd gestures and suggestions by naked players as she attempted to conduct an interview. In this latest shocker, something Actually Happened.

That's right. A sexual advance was made without so much as a by-your-leave, a what's-your-sign? or even a your-place-or-mine? In the month that has passed since the incident, not a finger has been raised in protest.

It seems that Ms. Shari Warren, a reporter for KSLA-TV in Shreveport, Louisiana, had just finished interviewing Pittsburgh quarterback Bubby Brister in the Steelers' locker room. Brister, it should be added, was fully clothed and co-operative.

As another reporter asked Brister a question, Ms. Warren said "Bye!", leaned over and *kissed* him. Just flat laid one on him right out there before God and the rest of the Steelers. Worse yet, she has made no attempt to deny the assault. Instead, she has attempted to write it off as a harmless joke.

"I've known him since he was in high school," she said. "We were teasing around. That's what we've always done. I hugged him like I would an old friend."

Oh, sure. A man trying to do his job as an athlete and co-operate with the media has no protection even in the privacy of his own locker room. Instead, he is left at the mercy of any pair of hungry lips that happens by.

Perhaps it was the speed of the attack and the hurried departure. I like to think that's it — that given a second's warning the Steelers would have rallied behind their quarterback, perhaps scaring off his assailant with outraged screams:

"Hey, over here!"

"Second!"

"Thirdsies! I get thirdsies!"

"You got a sister?"

But no. Ms. Warren was able to kiss and bolt. And today, a month later, not one story has been written, not one investigation launched, to help Brister repair his life and make certain such a thing will never happen again.

The TV station has not suspended her. She has not been required to obtain counselling. NFL commissioner Paul Tagliabu has not stepped forward as he did so quickly in defence of Ms. Olson.

When Ms. Olson suffered the verbal assault by some of the Patriots, women's groups organized a boycott of products produced by team owner Victor Kiam. Sales of Lady Remington razors dropped dramatically over Christmas.

But Bubby Brister was actually kissed! Did you hear of any protests in Pittsburgh? Did the women of Shreveport turn their TV dials from KSLA-TV? Did sponsors look elsewhere?

No. Bubby Brister was left to suffer alone.

He'll be back on the field next season, quarterbacking the Steelers and trying to forget. Whether he'll be able to return to the locker room, only time will tell. Sometimes, the scars are too deeply burned.

ARRIVIDERCI, AMORE

May 9, 1990

"No sex until the tournament ends July 8," says Italy's World Cup soccer coach. In Italy's quest for a fourth world title, he wants nothing stiffening but a grim resolve.

"Chastity of players prior and during a major competition has been a long-debated but unsolved problem," quoth Azeglio Vicini. So, at the end of next weekend, his players will be expected to shake hands goodnight with wives and sweethearts and put the hormones on hold until ultimate victory or, God forbid, ignominious defeat.

Videotapes, that's the entertainment ticket for the next month or so, with perhaps the occasional madcap excursion out of the training centre to a movie or a museum, with the coaches on full alert to make certain that every passing female buttock escapes unpinched.

In Italy, he's asking this. Of Italians. He'd have a better chance appealing to the patriotism of Italian women: "Give your all for the team: Refuse to give your all for the team!"

We are not talking here about hockey season in Siberia or Saskatoon, where post-game activities begin with the removal of ten layers of clothing before you're even sure you're dealing with the opposite sex. We are talking hot-weather, summertime Italy, the country that produced Sophia Loren and Gina Lolobriggadigga; the land where World Cup players are gods and scoring is a way of life.

And Azeglio Vicini, himself a former player, wants his players to spurn their ladies fair and convince them that abstinence makes the heart grow fonder? Good bloody luck.

It might be different if there was any evidence that in the field of competitive sport monkishness has an edge over monkey business. But the argument has raged for generations with no clear winner except the athletes, weary or refreshed, who sneak out of bedroom, car or drive-in wearing little but a smug look.

The Bible tells us that the bridegroom emerges from the bed-chamber like a runner to a race, which proves only that the Apostles weren't heavily into honeymoons. Babe Ruth, on the other hand, rollicked through life with but a single instruction for road-trip desk clerks: "Tell her to come up."

I've watched a coach park a chair in a hallway and spend the entire night with his eyes glued to two doors: the rooms of one male and one female athlete.

"I know they're in one of them," he said. "Eventually, they have to come out."

They did — and didn't look nearly as exhausted as he did.

Some shooters have claimed that a little pre-competition sex settles their nerves, sharpens their eye and takes the twitch from their trigger fingers. In the days when you could say such things without triggering court action by WOE (Women Opposed to Everything), a British golfer once said he saw no reason why, when the putts were dropping, the girls shouldn't follow suit. Asked if he thought it best to be true to one woman, Spain's Sevvy Ballesteros replied:

"No, that would be like playing the same golf course every round."

You'll hear some coaches claim that many an athlete has left his game in the bedroom. Vince Lombardi, the football legend, had another theory: "It's not the sex that tires them out," he said. "It's the staying up all night looking for it."

Casey Stengel, pleading with his New York Yankees, put it another way: "You gotta learn that if you don't get it by midnight, chances are you ain't gonna get it; and if you do, it ain't worth it."

Good luck in the Cup, Azeglio, but you're barking up the wrong libidos.

NO SEX, PLEASE, WE'RE SPORTS FANS

January 16, 1990

I've always considered sex a participant sport, sort of like touch football with a lot of holding. Not everyone agrees. To some — to many, judging from the Monday pub ads on our sports pages — it is also a spectator sport, incomplete without rimshots, bump-and-grind music and a guy on the microphone saying "How about a big hand for Miss Truck Stop 1987 — Jugs O'Beer!"

I have no argument with this. We live in a democracy and should defend to the death man's right to snort, whistle, pant, drool, hoot, sweat or sit in the shadows wearing nothing but a raincoat and a glazed look. And if girls want to dance, strip, wriggle, and simultaneously rotate tassels in opposite directions, surely it is but another manifestation of that right for which they've battled so long: control over their own bodies.

But get them the hell off my sports pages.

Put them on the business pages. The girls are there to earn money. So are the people who pay them. This isn't about love or even lust. It's about beer.

Throw some on the Living pages. Drop them into a story on how Florence of Arabia colour co-ordinates the veils she drops three, four times a night. ("I tell ya, Renee, when you're up there with all these like, *eyes* burnin' holes in ya, well, you gotta have stuff that even when you're peelin', it makes a fashion statement, y'know?")

Put one or two a week on the editorial page. The folks at WOE (Women Opposed to Everything) could use a fresh target. Feed a couple into the comic pages. See how well Mary Worth runs the motel when guys keep asking if they can rent by the hour.

Just stop flogging them all off on us.

It's not the newspaper's fault (he said, sucking up to the managing editor). The pub owners *demand* that their material runs on the sports pages. And because newspapers live on advertising revenue, they go along with it — after judiciously editing copy that would otherwise have to be printed on asbestos.

Why do they want the sports pages? Because men read them, and men drink beer, and pub wisdom says what could be more fun for a real sports-minded, beer-drinkin' guy with his fits-all-sizes tractor cap turned sideways to "Lock" position than to sit around starin' at semi-naked dames while discussin' important stuff like the two-point conversion and how to beat the spread?

What we have here is an image problem. Sports fans are not all beer-swigging dolts bent on proving that once you've seen two you *haven't* seen 'em all.

Sports-page readership probably covers a broader spectrum than any other section of the newspaper. Most of our readers feel God made ping-pong balls and pool cues for playing ping-pong and shooting pool. They resent being lumped in with the strip-pub crowd, most of whom watch the girls for the same reason they watch the other professional sports: they can dream of how well they'd perform if they had the chance — but they know they'll never have to prove it.

The ads are nothing to cause alarm. We survived the lingerie illustrations of the old Eaton's catalogue, once the staple of every outhouse. Kids browsing the sports pages will survive these.

But they're taking up valuable space we could otherwise use for good stuff about Joe Montana and John Elway and Wayne Gretzky and Mario Lemieux and Magic Johnson and Michael Jordan and athletes male and female who've got moves that make the pub shakers look like poorly-strung puppets. Say what you want about the Super Bowl. It doesn't go three shows nightly, and the videotape replays aren't rated XXX.

FAMILY TRAGEDIES
November 10, 1991

I was on an airline bus in Hamilton when the Magic Johnson story broke. The local radio station interrupted regular programming to carry the press conference live from Los Angeles.

Hamilton has no NBA franchise. Odds are there aren't a dozen people in the city who've ever seen, met or spoken to him. But the bus driver pounded his fist into the steering wheel in a kind of helpless, unspoken grief.

"Magic? The AIDS virus?" he said. "That's not fair..."

A few miles down the road in Brantford, Ontario, Walter Gretzky's daughter, Kim, contemplates a mountain of mail from all over North America.

There's a personal note from the prime minister, letters and telegrams from celebrities in and out of sport. Mostly, though, they are just get-well wishes and prayers, some accompanied by flowers, for her father, currently fighting back in Hamilton General Hospital from surgery to repair a brain aneurysm.

Most of them are from people who've never met Walter Gretzky or his famous son, Wayne, and are never likely to. But they feel they know him, as they feel they know Magic Johnson, and in these times of crisis they want to reach out somehow and say, "We're here, and we care."

The sad truth about our sense of tragedy is that it can be dulled by sheer numbers. The AIDS virus is cutting through this world like an invisible scythe, felling thousands. We read, and shudder and give our children all the safe-sex warnings — but we cannot grasp the enormity of it.

Aneurysms — ruptures of a weakened blood-vessel wall — claim victims daily and can exact a terrible toll. "The brain is jungle country," a doctor told me once, "and we don't know where all the tigers are."

In a sense the numbers are our shelter, our pain-killer — impersonal news of something that's always happening to unknown people in unknown places, and never to us or ours.

120

Then, suddenly, there is a face on it — a Magic Johnson, a Walter Gretzky — and the battle and the grief become personal.

That's Magic Johnson, standing there in front of a microphone at God knows what emotional price, telling the world he has tested positive for the AIDS virus and must leave the game he has dominated for a decade. Magic, the king of the look-away pass, the high-dribbling wonder who at 6'8" could play tall guard or short pivot. Magic, with the smile that could melt your heart.

And Walter Gretzky, the little Everyman from the phone company, who raised five kids and never let it matter that one of them happened to become the greatest hockey player in the world. The guy in the Coke commercials, handing his son a soft drink and patting him on the shoulder after a tough game or practice the way dads do in rinks and dugouts and gyms all over the continent.

We know these people. We've seen them on TV, read about them in the papers. We know about Wayne's wedding and Wally's grandchildren, and Magic's wedding and the baby on the way.

A few days ago they were like distant friends. But not any more. Tragedy has changed all that. Today, we are talking family.

THE STILT COMES TO PLAY

November 14, 1991

Wilt Chamberlain says he has slept with almost 20,000 women, which works out to about 1.2 per day since he was 15 and doesn't even allow for the nights he had a headache. No wonder they called him The Stilt.

Mind you, he never liked that nickname. He preferred the one he gave himself, The Big Dipper, which until now I'd always assumed was based on his ability to stuff a basketball into a hoop. But The Stilt was the one that stuck, it being difficult to campaign for a change from a prone position.

I don't know about you, but I find the information on Wilt's sexual prowess — in chapter 11 of his autobiography, *A View From Above,* which he wouldn't be terribly upset if you rushed out and bought a copy to find out if he goes into (slobber, pant, pant) *details* — absolutely fascinating. Not for the sex, for the logistics.

Think about it.

Here's a guy about 7'2" tall, travelling from city to city through the National Basketball Association, seldom spending more than one night — two, maximum — in one place. One of those nights he's not free until the game ends about ten p.m. Then he has to shower — no quick task, given the area to be covered — and that's not even considering the cost of body cologne, which he'd have to buy by the vat.

So let's say he's in the bar or disco by 11 p.m. Allowing time for ice-breaking ("No, I don't play basketball, I work at the zoo washing giraffes") and foreplay ("You got a room, babe?", "My car or yours?") he's probably not in Operational Mode until midnight.

Now, then: If The Dipper's mathematics are sound, in order to achieve that average 1.2 conquests per day he would have to make love to *two* women one day out of every five. (I have checked with the rules committee on this: making love to the same woman twice in the same evening does not count.)

This would necessitate a whole new approach to foreplay ("You two babes got a room?") and all but eliminate the car gambit. (I have a picture in my mind of the teenage Wilt, a tad of 6'10", trying to make out at a drive-in movie. It ends with a chiropractor and the Jaws of Life.)

Assuming Wilt, the dedicated professional, overcomes all these hurdles, ignores the headaches, maintains his average and still manages to get up, morning after morning, to make the plane for the next town, the next game, the next bar and the next 1.2, we are left with the real burning question of the whole issue:

How does he live with the pressure?

What about those nights when the team has won a big game and the boys want to kick back with a few brew and play a few hands of poker? The rest of them can do it, no problem. But not Wilt. As they're dealing he's thinking:

"Jeez! It's Saturday night! It's 11:30! Thirty minutes from the start of a new week and I haven't had my 1.2 night! I skip tonight, that means sometime between now and next Saturday I've got to 1.2 twice or 2.4 once just to catch up! Damn, those doubleheaders wear on a guy late in the season. First thing you know it's Christmas and you've got nothing left to give."

It must have been awful for him, all those years. No doubt it's all explained in his book, which I certainly plan to read if they ever send me a free review copy. He must have had phenomenal endurance. Only a dedicated professional and superbly conditioned athlete could have survived.

Then again, he may be lying in his teeth.

KEN, THE CLOSET KEWPIE

November 28, 1991

Mattel survey says 64% of adults want Ken to stay with Barbie.
— News item.

I don't know about you, but I'm shocked.

Wilt Chamberlain sells a jillion copies of his autobiography, mainly on the strength of a claim that he's slept with more than 20,000 women.

Women line up to claim they're the ones who passed the HIV virus to Magic Johnson. Magic fights suggestions that he is (a) a party-mad, irresponsible, sex-crazed fool, (b) gay or (c) both.

Martina Navratilova says she would never have received the sympathetic press Magic's been getting because fans, sponsors and advertisers would say "She's gay. She deserves it."

All of these stories are followed pant-by-pant and slobber-by-slobber in newspapers and on radio, TV and supermarket counters all over the world.

But no one challenges Ken.

Not one viewer-with-alarm or guardian-of-morality sees anything suspicious about a guy who hangs out for 30 years with the same girl, has no visible means of support, yet has the money and equipment to take her skiing, scuba diving, flying or driving around in a fancy sports car, wearing his own line of clothing which you can buy at any toy store providing you're eligible for a second mortgage.

Well, I think it's time someone stood up to be counted. I don't care what the survey said, I think Mattel should give Ken the boot. They wouldn't have to kill him. Just pull his head off and use his body for G.I. Joe dolls the way they do when a particular model doesn't catch on.

Why, you ask? What has this got to do with sport?

Merely everything.

This guy is an insult to all beer league and amateur athletes who have to make do with borrowed equipment and car pool it to the rink or playing field whenever they can get ice or field time — not to mention time off work — and then hang around pubs in TV commercials hoisting beer that must taste like it's been distilled through a horse because you never see them drink it.

123

Never once have you seen a Ken doll on the phone begging for a tee time that doesn't require wearing a miner's helmet with a flashlight on top. For Ken, every day is sunshine. He's out there on the green in co-ordinated golf gear, or at the wheel of his sailboat with Barbie clinging to one arm in her own direct-from-Paris Barbie sailor suit. How can you not hate a guy like that?

Besides, he's probably gay.

Hey, don't get antsy. Any rumour good enough to be pinned without supporting evidence on Magic is good enough for some little plastic guy who can't even hold a job.

Either that, or Barbie's gay.

Look at the evidence. Thirty years they've been going together. Has anyone seen them so much as kiss? Have they ever announced wedding plans?

And what about Barbie's girl friend, Midge? She's been hanging around for at least 25 years, and doesn't appear to have a job, either. What's her angle? Has she got the hots for Barbie, or something going on the side with Ken? How does she keep bread on the table? Who buys her clothes?

I really think we should look into this. If the sex lives of famous people are going to be subject to public scrutiny, it's only fair that famous dolls get the same treatment. Even if they do lack the equipment to be anything more than friends.

PICK-UP 1,209

December 24, 1991

When Wilt Chamberlain claimed in his autobiography that he has slept with 20,000 women, I speculated here on the sheer logistics involved.

Allowing for a start at age 15, I said, that would work out to 1.2 women per night, meaning that he'd have to sleep with two women one night in every five just to break even, and that's not even allowing for nights he had a headache. How, I wondered, could he keep it up?

The column was picked up by a Calgary paper, and brought the following response from a woman on the other end of the equation:

"My credentials are born from mistakes made in my past, more naive days," she writes. "By no means do I consider myself a bimbo, as even a level-headed brunette with a university degree can fall prey

124

to the deceiving words of a 'professional'. So allow me to explain how Mr. Chamberlain accomplished that 1.2-per-day average...

A DAY IN THE LIFE OF A PROFESSIONAL ATHLETE

6 p.m. Arrive at stadium for pre-game warm-up.

6:20 Casual locker room talk with home team. Find the hot spot for the evening. Get lowdown on groupies, etc.

6:30 Pre-game warm-up. Opportunity to 'scout' the audience for the potential 1.2 of the evening.

7:30 Game time. Gossip on bench about previous night's conquest(s). Only Michael Jordan really pays attention to the game.

10:15 Shower, shave and (oops!) just about forgot to take wedding ring off.

10:30 Short trip back to hotel. Call home to chat with kids. Tells wife he's going out for late dinner with the team.

11 p.m. Group of at least four (there's safety in numbers, you know!) players saunter into designated club of evening.

11:10 Group of at least four (there's no such thing as safety in numbers!) groupies saunter in. Right on time, as usual.

11:15 Visiting team huddles with home team and finds out what — and I stress what, not who — is off limits and what is free game. There isn't much that is off limits to a professional athlete.

11:30 Athlete approaches groupie. She smiles and blushes (to convey innocence). He buys her a drink (let it not be said he wasn't a gentleman).

11:40 Tells her he has an early flight, and will she be driving him home. If she's lucky she'll get another drink and maybe even a dance.

11:50 She drives him back to hotel. He doesn't have to give her directions. He invites her up for an early breakfast.

12 a.m. Typical small talk. 'I may be an athlete, but I'm different.' Funny how they always neglect to mention the wife and kids...

12:30 Wife calls to check up on him. He carries on a monosyllabic conversation while his night guest pretends to watch *A Current Affair* (how appropriate). He ends conversation with 'Yah, me too.'

12:35 What's-her-name becomes No. 2,146.

6:01 She sneaks out with pantyhose in purse.

7 a.m. Four athletes sleep very deeply on flight to next city.

Of course, there is the occasional night when he just wants to stay at the hotel and kick back a few Jack Daniels with the boys.

Those are the nights a girl will get the 2 a.m. wake-up call. (That's how you get the .2.)

For every Wilt Chamberlain there is a woman willing to be No. 2,146.

PS: I hope you will print this letter so young women who have gotten caught up in the game will stop and reflect.

Each of these girls believes she is the one to make a difference; that she is special. But let me leave you with these enlightening words I heard one athlete whisper to another after an altercation (in a nightclub) with one of these girls:

'I don't know what she expects. I love my wife. I ain't tryin' to build a home here...'

Signed:

Probably No. 1,209 in Calgary."

Chapter Five

BEN, BENNIES — AND BILLY GAULD

By 1988, when Ben Johnson flunked the urine test after an apparently spectacular Olympic Games victory over Carl Lewis in the 100-metre dash, they were called "performance-enhancing drugs", and amateur sports officials were setting world hand-wringing records trying to fight a battle that was already lost, a crisis they'd condoned for years by pretending it didn't exist.

In earlier, simpler times they were called Bennies, as in Benzedrine, then Greenies because most of them were that colour. (You cannot fool a professional athlete.) The generic term was Uppers because that's what they were supposed to do: get you "up" for the big game or the big exam. Anabolic steroids were there — *True* magazine ran an article on them headlined "The Pill That Could Kill Sports" back in 1954 when their use wasn't illegal — but no one worried. So the athletes got bigger, stronger and faster — wasn't that what they were supposed to do? What could go wrong?

Only everything.

In the wake of the Olympic scandal, coaches of other disciplines quietly admitted they'd known something was wrong. One coach told me he'd gone to Canadian Olympic Association officials and told them there had to be something wrong with Ben, that the yellowish colour to his eyes was a sure sign that he was on something.

"I was told to mind my own business and look after my own team," he said. "Nobody wanted to see it. All they could see was the shot at the gold medal."

Pogo, the philosopher possum, said it best: "We have seen the enemy, and he is us."

Maybe the athletes wouldn't be so anxious to take the drugs if we didn't put such a premium on winning. Maybe if we praised our try-ers as much as we do our winners, our athletes wouldn't feel so much pressure to excel at any cost.

Maybe, if we stopped equating athletic prowess with national supe-riority, some of them would be less inclined to feel that running, jump-ing, and hoisting heavy weights ranks right up there with searching for cancer cures. Maybe some of the air would exit through the ears of our badgers, our athletes and our politicians who are with them, win or tie.

A nice dream, that. But this is the reality:

Athletes cheat, and justify their cheating with the old child's cop-out that everybody else is doing it. Doctors issue warnings, bleeding hearts cry over the plight of the poor cheaters unlucky enough to get caught, and the same officials who ignored the problem before Ben got caught now boast that we're leading the world in making our sports drug-free.

It's too late. We've opened Pandora's pill bottle. We'll never get the lid screwed down again.

WEEP FOR PETER SCHNUGG

January 27, 1980

"We are being sacrificed because we are front page news. The whole world is watching, and you know this is a political year." — Peter S. Schnugg, San Francisco water polo player.

In the hills of Afghanistan, where the rebels reload guns so old they may explode in their faces and aim them at Soviet armour, they're probably thinking a lot about Peter S. Schnugg and his chances of winning an Olympic water polo medal. In the cities, where knots of Afghans watch as Soviet tanks roll through their streets, there will be but one topic of conversation today:

"Psst! Peter Schnugg might not get to play water polo in Moscow! Pass it on!"

"Nine years he's been playing, and now the president's telling him to clear the pool. No free trip to Moscow to play games!"

And the shock waves will roll down the streets in the wake of the tanks, jarring people's minds away from the minor irritation that they are no longer free...

It's not difficult to be cynical about the Olympic Games boycott. The very design of the threat lends itself to cynicism.

In the United States, President Carter gives the Soviets until February 20 to pull troops out of Afghanistan or face an American boycott of the Summer Olympics. He does not mention the Winter Olympics, which open in Lake Placid eight days before his deadline and will be attended by Soviet athletes. Translation: "We'll screw up your Olympics by not attending, but there's no sense screwing up ours by making you stay home."

In Canada, Prime Minister Joe Clark plays follow-the-leader: If Soviet troops aren't out of Afghanistan by February 20, Canadians won't go to Moscow, either. Originally he said he favoured moving the Games, but not a boycott. Then Pierre Elliott Trudeau announced that he didn't want any part of a boycott. Now Clark does. And the deadline is set two days after a federal election that could make it meaningless if Mr. Trudeau means what he says.

So I can forgive the Peter S. Schnuggs of the world their cynicism. But I cannot forgive their tunnel-visioned fatheadedness.

It will hurt to give up a target that's been shining out there in front of them for years, the chance to represent their country against the best in the world. But there are different ways to represent your country. The hill rebels are representing theirs. When the game is over there'll be no shaking hands and swapping sweatsuits. For many, their badge will be an unmarked grave.

Peter S. Schnugg is not being asked to pack a rifle and go to a foreign country and die, as were the best and the fittest of generations past. At worst he is being told he'll have to play his water polo in a different pool. How tough is that, really?

There are world championships now in virtually every Olympic event. They draw the same group of athletes. The Olympics are one major step on the tour. How big a sacrifice is it, really, for an athlete to stand up and say:

"I do not compete in countries whose leaders send troops and tanks through the streets of free people. I live in a free country. I will not compete in a country that denies others that freedom."

Somehow, that sounds better than "To hell with somebody else's freedom. To hell with tanks over the border. Clear the pool. It's time for the water polo finals."

Because that is the issue. Sport is not above politics. Sooner or later the people in it have to drop their discus or their track shoes and say, as

Sebastian Coe said the other day "An athlete cannot stick his head in the sand. This is a decision I'll have to make as a human being."

Certainly the issue is political. Certainly it is easy to say that if this wasn't an election year and if the country being invaded wasn't cheek-on-jowl with the country that produces a large part of the world's oil, perhaps President Carter wouldn't have been so quick to jump, or Joe Clark so anxious to follow. But does that make it any easier for the Afghans?

The posturing of the International, U.S. and Canadian Olympic Committees is ludicrous. They are penny-ante players in a game turned table stakes. Let the world turn into a radioactive slag heap and once the air cleared you'd find two guys in blazers organizing the Geiger Counter Games.

The IOC says the Games "can't" be postponed. The USOC says it doesn't know whether it will go along with the boycott or not. The COA says it will think about it. The president and the prime minister admit they cannot flat-out order the Olympians into line. And Peter S. Schnugg says he wants to play water polo, and that the whole world is watching to see whether he can.

The athletes are upset and understandably so. But there is something they should consider: There will be no lifting of passports, no troops stopping them as they board the plane. The country might withdraw its financial support, but in the end the individual athlete will be free to go to Moscow if he or she chooses.

It is called freedom of choice. Nobody asked the Afghans if they wanted the tanks.

HEY, DOC: BUILD US A 76 LARGE

August 25-26, 1983

"You don't understand," insisted Dieter Stamm, president of the B.C. Weight Lifting Association. "Steroids are simply the next step in the development of sport. There will come a day when only athletes who've been under scientific treatment will compete at the international level."

He sounded like he could hardly wait. What was this, a press conference or a sneak preview of *Frankenstein II*?

Guy Greavette was there to tell his side of the Pan-Am Games scandal in which he was among 11 lifters and a cyclist who tinkled into a beaker and had the machine holler "Bingo!", thereby losing his three medals and possibly his place on Canada's 1984 Olympic Games team.

He handled it well, facing a forest of cameras and microphones and fielding each question with neither dodge nor flinch. But there was a curious sadness to it, because when it was over, all you were left with was a sense of waste. If high-level competitive sport dies, the tag on the big toe will read "Cause of death: tunnel vision".

The answers went round and round and never touched down on reality. Everything was based on frustration: frustration that he'd been caught when so many others get away with using steroids; frustration because "the coaches didn't warn us" about the testing before they left for Caracas; frustration because athletes from other countries apparently know how to beat the tests and ours don't.

I didn't hear much about how the use of steroids is against the rules, or how solid medical evidence indicates that using them in the amounts some athletes do in search of instant muscles can do serious harm to the system in later life and could be a factor in causing cancer and liver damage. None of that seemed to matter.

"I don't want to take steroids," said Guy Greavette. "It's not something I want to do. It's something I have to do."

It was *Alice in Wonderland*. Greavette's father and coach, Ron, says he "didn't take kindly" to Wednesday's column here branding the steroid users as cheaters. He looks ready to punch out my lights. A dark and glowering chunk of muscle in a sweatsuit interjects to suggest I should "try walking a mile in another man's moccasins". Heavy, man. And Stamm is holding forth on what athletic wonders man can perform once the doctors are through rebuilding him.

They have the technology. Quick, Igor, get them a brain.

In theory you could use anabolic steroids to build the world's biggest football team. They might die young but what the hell, you could always build some more.

There would be certain limits. As many a player has discovered, the steroids that develop his upper body do not provide proportional strength for the knees that must hold it all up.

But let's not look at the down side. Any team or sports organization worthy of the name would have a farm system, a chain of young players popping the pills, taking the injections or knocking stuff back in liquid form. There'd be no shortage. There's always some kid you can sell on the money, the stardom or the groupies wall-to-wall for as long as that sort of thing interests him. If you're dealing in volume, who cares if the shelf life of some of the goods isn't as long as advertised? In any mass-production situation you have to allow for a certain amount of spoilage.

Besides, this is the age of science and specialization. Anabolic steroids may simply be a drug whose time has arrived. Team steroids with some of that DNA and gene-splicing research the labs are so heavily into now and we could have the biggest sports-medicine breakthrough since the East Germans figured a way to beat the urine test.

"Hello, doc? Listen, Sandusky's popped a knee. We've got engineering working on a brace that will hold 475 pounds with only a three per cent loss of mobility, but we're playing the Stompers tomorrow and we need somebody who can block that Billy-Bob whatzhisname — you know, the guy with his eyes set to the side like a horse's to improve his peripheral vision? So send me over something in a 76 large, okay?

"What's that? Yeah, maybe you're right. We'll have him delivered. The last guy you sent by himself forgot to stop walking and drowned off Saltspring Island. I wish you guys could do something about side-effects. I know the cheerleaders and female reporters are safe now, but limiting the playbook to 'Go That Way' and 'Go This Way' is playing hob with our offence.

"No, defence is still fine, thanks. They hear 'Kill!', they tee off just like always, and we've improved the reaction time on fumble recoveries by teaching them 'Fetch!'. Anyhow, we'll send the truck over for the kid right now. And if there's ever a breakthrough on those extra-long arms, you call me, y'hear?"

Yes, we could do all that, eventually, in every sport, pro or amateur, individual or team. Science has barely scratched the surface. Steroids are the mere tip of the hypo.

When we get there we could call it something catchy, like The Master Race.

LETTER TO OUR KIDS

September 29, 1988

Dear Kids:

All over this country today the big people are asking each other what they should be telling you about the Ben Johnson steroid scandal. Forgive them. They're silly, but their intentions are good.

They're worried, you see, that you'll be crushed under the weight of a fallen idol. They know the importance of giving you good role models. They discuss that a lot over cigarettes or martini breaks.

"They *loved* Ben Johnson and now it turns out that he cheated," they wail. "What will this *do* to them? What can we *say*?"

Try to look sad when they bring up the subject. You could score an extra dessert or a therapeutic trip to McDonald's.

Personally, I don't see why they have to say anything. If you're over ten years old you know about drugs, you've been warned about drugs, you've been offered drugs, and some of you have been stupid enough to try drugs. By now, you must have it figured out that trying drugs even once is about as dumb as throwing yourself off a skyscraper to see how high you'll bounce.

If it was up to me, I'd tell you this:

Sixteen years ago yesterday, before most of you were born, I sat in the Palace of Sport in Moscow and watched a hockey player named Paul Henderson score a goal with 34 seconds remaining to beat the Soviet Union 6-5 in the deciding game of the first Team Canada-Russia series. The Canadians had to win the last three games, all in Moscow. Paul Henderson scored the winning goal in all three.

Six months earlier I'd watched a Canadian girl named Karen Magnussen, a bronze medal safely in her grasp, go for broke in the figure-skating final in Sapporo, Japan, in the Winter Olympics, and come away with silver. Last March, in Calgary, I saw another Canadian girl named Elizabeth Manley do the same thing.

In 1973 I watched Karen whip them all to win the world championship in Bratislava, Czechoslovakia. Before the year ended I watched a Canadian named Bruce Robertson swim to gold at the first Aquatic Games in Belgrade.

Two years later, in Cali, Colombia, I watched a 13-year-old wisp of a Canadian named Nancy Garapick break the world record in the 200-metre backstroke at the second Aquatic Games — and finish second to East Germany's Birgit Treiber.

As she tried to brush away the tears, coach Nigel Kemp scooped her up and said, "Hello, Sunshine. You did just fine." In those six words, he said everything about what sport is really all about.

I've been lucky. I've seen all those people. I was there when Rick Hansen crossed Canada in his wheelchair — pausing outside Windsor, Ontario, to gaze up at the statue of his friend, Terry Fox. I've come to know Wayne Gretzky, and watched him and Mario Lemieux and a bunch of other Canadians beat the Soviet Union two games to one in the last Canada Cup series, maybe the greatest hockey ever played.

I guess what I'm trying to say, kids, is that sport is no different from anything else in life. It has its tryers and its criers, its workers and its loafers, its heroes and its cheats.

All your life you'll be making choices, some of them between right and wrong. Ben Johnson was on the road to the top of the world, and threw it away trying a crooked shortcut. That was his choice, and that's sad.

But don't forget Ben Johnson, or hate him. Don't feel cheated. *Learn* from his mistake. And whatever you do, don't give up on heroes. Hold your heads up and be proud: You live in a country where they'll never be in short supply.

JAMAICA FAREWELL

August 2, 1989

Ben Johnson says he wants to run for Jamaica when his two-year ban for using steroids is over. All together, now:

> Take 'im to Jamaica where de rum come from,
> De rum come from, de rum come from.
> Take 'im to Jamaica where de rum come from,
> We don't need no medal dat bad.

Better still, let's fly Harry Belafonte in and celebrate:

> Yay-O! Yay-ay-ay-O!
> When Ben can run, he wan' go home!
> Yay-O! Yay-ay-ay-O!
> When Ben can run, let's send 'im on home!

Oh, but that quote from the *Jamaica Record* in Kingston is beautiful:

"If I am clean, then I should be able to run for Jamaica because I am a Jamaican."

I love it. It fits so nicely with that famous tear-jerking exchange between Johnson and his lawyer, Ed Futerman, at the Dubin inquiry:

Q: Do you wish to run again?
A: Every second.
Q: Do you wish to compete in the 1992 Olympics?
A: Yes, sir.

Q: What country do you wish to run for?

A: My own. Canada.

It certainly brought a lump to my throat. The last time I laughed that hard, J.R. had been shot, *Dallas* fans were in shock and I was pulling for the bullet.

Of course Ben wanted to run again. He's one of the best in the world at it, even if he has to race stock instead of modified. Running put the big car in the garage in the big house and brought the endorsements that built the big bank account. The man has no other trade. What's he supposed to do, line up at Manpower and look for something under Unskilled Labour?

Properly phrased, the exchange on the stand at the Dubin inquiry should have gone like this:

Q: Ben, would you like to continue making big money and travelling the world at other people's expense?

A: Every second.

Q: Do you want to run in the 1992 Olympics, where a medal could get back some of the endorsements you've lost over this mess?

A: You kidding? Of course I do.

Q: What country do you wish to run for?

A: The one that can get the suspension lifted fastest.

Competing athletically for more than one country is nothing new. Years ago, another sprinter named Mike Agostini ran for Trinidad, then for Canada. There were no big endorsements then. What money there was came under the table or in the form of gifts like wrist watches. "I've left wrist watches in every pawn shop in the world," Agostini said.

But Ben cheated and got caught. He admitted it, too, just as soon as there was no other option. And the cry for understanding seemingly was so poignant that a cross-Canada survey said a majority of Canadians wanted to give him another chance.

But Ben has dropped another spiked shoe on his foot. Jamaica says it doesn't want him to run as a Jamaican. By his own words he's made Canada a second choice at best.

Ah, well, we'll struggle on somehow. Probably a lot more easily than will Gentle Ben.

HORSE OF A DIFFERENT COLOUR

January 9, 1991

Mr. Taylor, we would like your opinion on the question that is dividing the nation. To wit: Should Ben be allowed to compete for Canada again?

Absolutely — providing, of course, that he can do it without using prohibited drugs, not that I think he ever would. In fact, considering the adversity he has faced in the last couple of years, seeing him in world-class competition again would make me proud to be a Canadian.

But does this not represent an about-face on your part considering all the nasty things you've written about him in the past?

Me? I wrote nasty things about Ben? You're crazy enough to work for Sport Canada. I've been a Ben fan from the beginning. The way he clears those jumps, the way he bounced back from that first colic attack, and now he's pulled through the surgery after the second bout ... I tell you, that is one hell of a horse!

Horse?

Yeah, horse — Big Ben, Ian Millar's horse. Best damned champion this country has ever had, four-legged or two, although I suppose you could make a case for Northern Dancer. But when you consider that the Dancer only had to run flat out and Ben had all those jumps to contend with ...

Uh, Mr. Taylor? We're not talking about Big Ben the horse, we're talking about Ben Johnson, the runner, who begins his comeback Friday in a meet in Hamilton and the whole world is waiting to see how he'll do as a drug-free competitor. What do you think about that?

As little as possible.

I beg your pardon?

I think about him as little as possible. In fact, with the possible exception of Pete Rose, who is now out of jail selling autographed baseballs again and being mobbed by people who want to pay him $10,000 a shot for speaking engagements, I can't think of anyone I want to think about less. Big Ben now, that's a horse of a different colour.

But surely you can't compare Ben the man with Ben the horse?

It is a bit unfair, at that. Ben the man won an Olympic gold medal for as long as it took to get his test results back. Ben the horse won the World Cup equestrian competition in 1988 and 1989 — the first time it's ever been done in consecutive years by the same horse-and-rider combination — and if either he or Millar had to go tinkle into a bottle the results weren't considered worth mentioning.

So you're right: Ben the man doesn't rate mention in the same breath with Ben the horse.

But Ben Johnson is a world-class athlete. People are going to pay millions to watch him run. Surely that proves *something*!

Yes, it does, just as it does with Pete Rose: It purely shoots hell out of the theory that cheaters never prosper. Besides, who says Big Ben isn't a world-class athlete? He trains just as hard for a whole lot less reward. Ben the runner gets the big house and the big cars and the fancy clothes. On a really good day, Ben the horse has a warm stall with fresh straw and maybe a little extra oats in the nose bag.

So you're saying you hope Ben loses Friday's race?

No, I'm saying I hope he gets on with his life and can put the last two years behind him. One important thing, though...

Yes?

Let's not get confused about which Ben is the real Canadian hero.

WHO'LL TELL THE DUKE TO GO WEE-WEE?

July 5, 1989

Alberta SPCA wants chuckwagon drivers to face random drug testing — News item.

The world's greatest chuckwagon drivers are dead or doddering. Everybody knows that. And if anybody'd ever asked them to pee in a bottle they'd have slapped 'em silly.

You take your John Wayne, for instance. How'd you like to be the SPCA guy who walked up to the Duke and said:

"Mr. Wayne, I represent the random and mandatory drug testing body of the Alberta SPCA, and if you're going to drive in this Calgary Stampede you're going to have to take this bottle into that tent and make water.

"Not yet, though. First we have to find a qualified official to watch you do it."

How deep do you figure old John would have shoved that bottle?

Andy Devine, Gabby Hayes, Randolph Scott, Slim Pickens — even that wimp, Guy Madison, who played Wild Bill Hickok in maybe the worst TV western series ever made — none of them would have stood for this nonsense. On the great races for new land, what would have happened to an SPCA guy standing in the middle of the road with his hand up, yelling "Stop! It's your turn for the drug test"?

Mind you, they didn't know much about drugs. Grass was what you fed the horses. Heroin was the local school marm. (Nice girl, but she tended to swoon and say "Oh, Roy!" — or Dick, or Rex or Gene — a lot.) Hash was served by Becky Sue down at the cafe.

Whiskey, now, that was different. They knocked 'er back pretty good, but never enough to get nasty with women folks, or desert 'em, or throw 'em through walls or fool around on 'em, or any of those other current participation sports. They drank, they got hangovers, and they got on with their drivin'. And nobody, except maybe the crabby boss at the Wells Fargo, ever gave 'em any lip, because people knew they'd get the job done.

Oh, yeah: they loved their horses. Kissed 'em, even, in the last reel when it was either the horse or Miss Becky. Nobody said they were brilliant. But they didn't mistreat the horses. Fact is, they beat the bejaysus out of villains who did (who were usually teamsters until they got organized).

Which is why I think this Alberta SPCA thing is a pile of horse pucks. Not that the people don't mean well. They probably just figure that if thoroughbred horse racing can have drug testing, chuckwagon racing should have, too. A pride thing, if you will. But cowboys are special. Willie Nelson says so. And they have to stay special.

I can stand knowing that Ben Johnson cheated and that the people who run international sport in this country have spent years sticking their heads in the sand lest they see anything that might spoil their pursuit of gold, silver, bronze and a new blazer.

So Pete Rose is a jerk who gambles. Tough. So Joe DiMaggio pushes Mr. Coffee and baseball's heroes charge for autographs. So fights are circuses and the sports pages look like rap sheets. I can live with all of that.

But don't suggest to me that cowboys do drugs. Don't you go spitting on the one great North American folk hero we've got left. We're not leaving our kids much to dream on these days. Let's not kill this one, too.

BULK BEEFCAKE MEETS THE STEROID CHALLENGE
July 17, 1991

World Wrestling Federation announces crackdown on use of anabolic steroids — News item.

Bulk Beefcake, world wrestling champion, cracked a walnut between his eyelashes and glared around the shell fragments at his accusers.

"I never took no stereos," he said. "An album here, a single there, sure. But I was just a kid. Besides, I already had a stereo."

"Mr. Beefcake, we are not here to discuss your musical preferences. We would like you to explain how you grew from a 98-pound weakling to a 287-pound wrestler."

"Exercise! Sure, I remember those days when I weighed 98 pounds..."

"You should. It was three weeks ago."

"Well, I'm a quick study. Once I risked that stamp and Charlie Atlas sent me the course, I put on muscle so fast I changed jock size overnight."

"And what about the injections?"

"The what?"

"The needles, Mr. Beefcake. The injections given you by that South African witch doctor you saw once a week."

"Psoriasis, your honour. I was sufferin' from the heartbreak of psoriasis. The itchy, dry-scalp feeling, not to mention the embarrassment of all those flakes on your shoulder just as you're about to put a move on some chick. Well, I figure you never get a second chance to make a first impression, so..."

"You expect us to believe that, Mr. Beefcake?"

"Hey, you guys run pro rasslin' and you're hassling me about credibility? You wanna stomp on the steroid freaks, why don'tcha go after that Turtle mob?"

"Turtle mob?"

"Yeah, those turtle kids with all the muscles and the street-gang names: Lennie, Ralphie, Mikie and Nevertello."

"You mean the Teenage Mutant Ninja Turtles? You're saying the Turtles are on steroids?"

"Hey, they were two inches tall and just like that they're 5'10", wearing masks, carrying weapons and showing tendencies toward random violence. I rest my case."

"Mr. Beefcake, the Turtles are not on trial here, you are. And speaking of random violence only last night did you not pin your opponent, Corporal Punishment, to the canvas?"

"I'm a wrestler, for Pete's sake! That's what wrestlers do!"

"With industrial staples?"

"Okay, so I got a little excited. But what I want to say, your honour, is that I ain't takin' my psoriasis stuff any more and I've joined the fight against stereo abuse."

"In what way?"

"I'm workin' with the kids. My company, Bulk-Up Productions, is coming out with a whole new line of Bulk Beefcake action dolls. Only instead of selling add-on accessories, the kid starts with the complete doll with removable muscles.

"See, now that you guys are policing ... uh, now that I've seen the light and aren't taking my medicine no more, I'll start to get skinny. Every time a kid watches me on TV and sees where I've lost weight, he removes the corresponding muscle. The objective is to be the first kid on the block to get me down to human-being size."

"Commendable, Mr. Beefcake. And what happens then?"

"That's the whole point, your honour: I wrestle, and I lose."

"And then?"

"Well, the kid starts buying new replacement muscle parts. He can keep watching me fight to regain my title, and put them back one by one."

"And what will you accomplish by all this?"

"Well, for one thing, your honour, I'll sell a hell of a lot of dolls."

THE PRIDE OF BILLY GAULD

July 7, 1989

He first caught their eye on their early-morning jog, a boy in his late teens or early 20s delivering *The Province* at as fast a clip as his dragging left leg would allow. He never stopped, they said. He jogged in and out of the yards, he jogged down the street, always smiling, always upbeat. There was obvious physical impairment: the leg, a left arm that wasn't functioning quite right, a slur to the voice. But whenever they talked to him, they went away feeling good.

"His name is Billy — Gould, Guard, something like that," they said. "We think he's a great story, but we can't get anybody interested. They say it's no big deal. And we thought maybe you..."

I did, and I owe them. This, then, is the story of an athlete named Billy Gauld...

Billy Gauld is 24 years old. He has cerebral palsy, some mental retardation, and three jobs.

He delivers *The Province* in the morning, the *Sun* in the afternoon, near his home in the Kerrisdale area. In between he was working four days a week, 11 a.m. to three p.m., walking a sandwich board advertising a shaver shop. He's cut that back to two days a week now, because he's about to start job training as an assistant stock boy at a 7-Eleven store in Richmond. If that works out, he says he'll quit one paper route. One, not both.

But there'll be no work this weekend.

Today, Billy Gauld is in Campbell River, competing as a soccer player in the B.C. Special Olympics Summer Games 1989. He'll be one of 570 athletes and 150 coaches billetted in two schools, sleeping in the classrooms and the gym according to sport: soccer, power-lifting, track and field, bowling, rhythmic gymnastics and swimming. He could have entered the track and field or power-lifting events, but it's one competition per athlete, and he opted for soccer on the "B" team, where he plays forward.

It is a major event, and he went in confident that all that jogging would pay off. He'd be strong. He could run all day. He was ready — and if the team won, there'd be a spot in the national championships.

But before he left, he took care of business: He checked with both newspapers for permission to take the weekend off. When they asked who'd do the route, he broke into a big grin.

"M-O-M," he said.

Mom is Janet Gauld and yes, she admits, she does the route sometimes. But not often. John Ko of *The Province* circulation department gave Billy his route eight years ago. "When the weather was bad and we had kids phoning in sick, Billy would be out there doing his job," he says. "Billy didn't just have the route. Billy had pride."

He's kept that route without a break. Five years ago he decided he could handle an afternoon route, too. They, and the Special Olympics, have been a major force in his life.

"Special O brought him friends," Janet Gauld says. "They do things together. The paper routes — we go to the Arbutus Mall and people know him. We walk in Kerrisdale and they stop to talk to him. He's accepted."

Special O...

Janet Gauld is secretary for the Vancouver chapter now. They get a small government grant and some private donations, but mostly they hold car washes and garage sales, sell raffle tickets and work to carry their own weight. And they see the results every day in the eyes of athletes like Billy Gauld, who set Olympian goals and learn faster than any of us that the reward is in the pursuit as much as in the capture.

No, it's not a big story. There are hundreds out there like it. The sadness of Special O is that it never runs short of competitors. But when you're up to here with steroids and gambling and tales of sulky millionaire jocks, give yourselves a break. Close your eyes, and think of Billy Gauld.

Chapter Six

ANIMAL CRACKERS

For a guy who hates cats, fears snakes, loathes insects, doesn't go to horse races, distrusts any dog but his own and once sprained an ankle jumping off the bed because a sparrow flew in the window and landed on his pillow, I seem to write an awful lot of stuff about animals.

I'm not sure why. They just seem to show up, like the cows in the Far Side cartoons. Or maybe it's traumatic reaction to the Dude Ranch Episode.

The short version, minus the years of analysis, goes like this:

We took the kids to a dude ranch. On the first day, while sitting in quiet contemplation on the outdoor biffy, I was attacked from below by a mosquito. I must have scratched during the night, because by morning I had a lump on my butt the size of Don Cherry's ego and every bit as aggravating. Naturally, that was the day we went horseback bouncing. It did wonders for my festering mosquito bite.

They gave me a horse with stomach trouble. Every time I bounced, the horse would wheeze. Every second bounce he would fart, much to the distress of the people riding behind me. Before long I was bringing up the rear, numb with chagrin. Did Randolph Scott's horse fart? Did you ever once hear Champion or Trigger wheeze? Did Lash LaRue or Roy or Gene or Tex ever once get butt-bitten by a mosquito? Would this agony never end?

Yes, it would. It ended after about 45 minutes when my horse decided it was time to go back to the barn for lunch. Without warning, he did a 180 and galloped full-tilt back to the ranch with my arms around his neck and my groin pounding into the saddle horn, not stopping until he was in the barn, in his own personal stall, munching leftovers from the morning hay.

I fell off. The maid hadn't yet cleaned the stall. So there I was, on the second day of my vacation, my knees covered with horse poop, my butt festering, and my groin feeling like my next job would be harem guard.

"Don't worry," the foreman said kindly. "You'll get the hang of it."

The horse had one fart left.

ELLA-PHANTASTIC

April 6, 1988

So I'm sitting there on this elephant wondering how I'd look in a loincloth. The jungles of Thailand beckon. My nostrils flare as the beast within me stirs restlessly. Only the risk of injury keeps me from pounding my chest.

"*Ungowa,* Tantor!" I bellow. "*Ungowa!*"

"Jusaminute, sir," says Jeffrey, the faithful guide. "Seat belt not done up."

My elephant had a seat belt. I wanted to die.

"Did Tarzan have to wear a seat belt?" I whined. "Did you ever once in any of his movies see the Ape Man swing through the jungle, land on Tantor's back and yell 'Ungowa, Tantor — no, wait a minute! First I've got to buckle up for safety!'?"

"Tarzan wasn't a spastic who got motion sickness and threw up on the playground swings," my wife said sweetly. The next time I need a Jane, I shop Central Casting.

The driver — they wouldn't even let me steer the thing — jammed a nail into a link of the rusty chain that now kept us from sliding out of the box into which we'd just scrambled. We lurched off into the jungle, trackless if you ignored the highway 100 yards or so off to the left.

Going uphill was fine. Gravity forced you back into the box. Going downhill, the elephant picking its way daintily down a path about two squirrels wide, offered ample opportunity for profound thoughts like "What a truly wondrous creature, the elephant!" and "If this sucker slips, I'm jelly."

At the narrowest point on the trail, our elephant made a pit stop.
"Uh, it's pretty narrow here," I squeaked. The driver shrugged one of those "You-wanna-tell-the-elephant-he-can't-do-this?" kind of shrugs.

"Please, God," I begged silently, "don't let him lift one leg."

The elephant sighed contentedly and shifted into low. Gazing back at the wonder he hath wrought triggered one of those bursts of insight so blinding they must be shared. "You know, it's a good thing we had horses on the prairies and not elephants, or hockey would never have caught on. Pile that size, the kids would have had to take up soccer."

"Thank you for that," she said.

The elephant affair began early on the three-week holiday that was grudgingly allowed to include a little sports watching. I'd seen some Thai kick boxing, although perhaps not the best, since it was held on the second floor of the Marilyn-A-Go-Go (hard by the 24 Hour A Day VD Clinic) and featured women who looked as though they were still fresh after the mud wrestling. On TV I'd watched Elephant Soccer (neither striker had a left foot) and Elephant Sucker (Tony Tubbs, bigger than either of them, being accepted as a contender against Mike Tyson).

But to *ride an elephant,* that would be something. I could pretend the elephant was a horse and I was Lester Piggott after taxes. For only a second mortgage, Jeffrey fixed it. And as we stepped down off the beast, he filled us in on elephants.

"In Thailand," he confided, "all elephants are called Chang." At least, it sounded like Chang.

"What a coincidence," I marvelled. "In North America, all elephants are called Gerald."

"Ger-ald," he repeated. "How come?"

"In honour of world's greatest jazz singer, Elephants Gerald."

"Ah, I see!" he said doubtfully.

My wife was looking at me strangely.

"Another thing, Jeffrey," I said. "You ever wonder how Tarzan was able to grab those vines at just the right height to swing down and land perfectly? I mean, if he grabs too high he just hangs there; if he grabs too low, he could land in the elephant apples. But he always gets it just right! You ever wonder about that, Jeffrey?"

She took me by the arm. "It's time to go home, isn't it?" she said. And it was.

KITTY LITTER

July 23, 1987

This week I went to see *Cats*. Not Katz the bookie, *Cats*, the musical. The lighting was brilliant, the staging magnificent, the costumes out of this world. So why didn't I like it?

Possibly because I hate cats. In my humble opinion, God put cats on earth to make tennis racquets, and the decline of civilization began with the development of the nylon string.

Admittedly, the relationship between cats and sport is tenuous at best. There is no real justification for writing this on a sports page, except possibly that some species of cat are hunted (although not nearly enough) and hunting is considered a sport by those too young to have seen *Bambi*. That will have to do, because I'm going to write it anyway.

Cats the musical has the same problem as cats the animals. Once you get over the golly gee, isn't that (she, he) beautiful, nothing happens. On stage, a bunch of cats dance and sing or recite poems by T.S. Eliot. We are told that one cat has to die (I'd heard that — it was the only reason I went) and sure enough, about two hours later, one does.

"One down," I muttered. The cat person next to me sank an elbow into my rib cage. I love her, but she irks easily.

Even then, the cat comes back. That's another thing about cats: They always come back. Every day you read about some cat that was lost two years ago on a family vacation and found her way across three states and six provinces to get back home to little Marvin or Janie. Nobody ever interviews Marvin or Janie's father, who'd wasted a lot of time accidentally tying the cat to a tree.

Other than "Memory" — maybe the most beautiful piece of music written in a decade — that's about it, although I did note a couple of striking similarities between the stage cats and those that infest the human home. The stage cats had stupid names like Tum Tugger and Skimbleshanks (our two are named Nosey and Pookie — I rest my case) and according to the programme notes it costs the touring company $50,000 per year just to replace light bulbs, which is about average for any home with teenage kids.

I watched, and found myself thinking: Why did they choose *Cats*? Why not *Dogs*? Why not *Lassie: the Musical*?

Dogs are far more intelligent than cats who — when they're not sneaking into the bedroom at night to lie on your face and smother you, or going out to mug some bird — basically just lie around waiting to be fed.

146

Put Lassie up there. She could at least fetch, or roll over, or bury a bone. Or Rin-Tin-Tin. Now there was a dog! The kid would say "Okay, Rinty, go to the colonel and tell them the Indians are gonna hit the fort at dawn and this time they must be serious, 'cause they're bringin' the Braves with 'em. Oh, yeah, and they've got nuclear weapons. Got that, Rinty?" And the dog would arf once and run off to save the regiment. Or what about Sandy, Little Orphan Annie's dog? Guided Annie out of many a fix, he did, which was a hell of a trick for a dog whose eyes had no pupils.

Could a cat do that? Of course not. Worse yet, a cat wouldn't even try. So, kids, listen carefully:

If you don't want to wake up with a cat on your face or get lost in the woods with no one around to save you but some smarmy little Siamese with a rhinestone collar and a voice like Streisand on steroids, go stand in front of Mommy and Daddy and cry until they trade the cat in on a dog.

If they won't, just write to me. I'll send you instructions on how to make yourself a nice new tennis racquet.

LASSO 'ROUND A DREAM

May 10, 1978

Between little girls and large horses is a magical, invisible rope. It may stretch, but it never, ever breaks. If you are truly lucky, you may be there when the loop is thrown.

For me it started with a small girl bursting into a kitchen, puffing and dishevelled and dirty beyond belief, the eyes huge with wonder, the words a waterfall:

"Daddy-I-was-at-the-stables. *And-they-let-me-clean-the-stalls!*"

She probably cleaned about a thousand stalls — other people's at first, labour in exchange for time on someone's horse — dream time in a ring, magic at a trot. And then, one incredible day, the ecstasy of the first, soaring leap over a one-foot jump.

The work didn't matter. It never does. A little girl who'll have 50 reasons why she shouldn't take ten minutes to clean her room will spend two hours shovelling hay and manure for the right to climb into a saddle she needs a fence post to reach, and count herself among God's more fortunate creatures.

"Daddy, they let me clean the stalls..."

Kathy Wedge knows about the magic rope.

It caught her when she was a little girl in Saskatchewan. For the right to ride a farmer's horse she has swamped stables, unloaded manure, sold peanuts, begged rides on other horses, worked more hours than she can begin to count.

Now she rides for Canada's Olympic team, giving lessons and schooling other people's horses to earn her keep and the time to do it. Nothing changes. The objectives and costs soar together. When you ride, you scramble. But you don't mind. The rope tightened a long time ago...

"Daddy, could I take riding lessons? I know it costs money, but I'll use my allowance and baby-sit, and..."

There is a picture on the wall, but I don't need it. Every detail is etched in the mind. It was Horse Christmas, as it had been Horse Birthday six months earlier. Parents and relatives had been carefully primed. Each gift was horse-oriented: the jodhpurs, the jacket, the hard hat, the riding crop and ("Oooh! Grannie!") the saddle.

She posed in front of the fireplace, a princess set for the hunt. All she needed was the horse. The dream was already in her eyes...

At Southlands Riding and Pony Club it is a picturebook day. Starting Friday there'll be 400 riders performing here in the 20th annual spring show, but now there are only two horses going through the jumps as Kathy Wedge and Shirley Hills put them through the Gambler's Sweepstakes event for the edification of the mystified media.

The press conference is a try for a break-through. The good riders are athletes, they insist. The meet is an athletic event, not a social weekend for the idle rich. It's time, they feel, to get their competitions on the sports pages where they belong.

Their image is against them. It costs upward of $200 a month to stable a horse in the city. Sometimes you get lucky. The horse Kathy is riding she got for nothing. She found it on a farm, pulling a stone boat. But to get a good, sound horse with its training behind it can cost $3,000 or more. So they must be rich people out there fooling around. Swells, the lot of 'em...

"Daddy, do you suppose...is there any way...I mean, if I worked...could we please...?"

Her name was Ye Arba Samantha. Sam for short. She was not destined for greatness. Sam was five, the girl 11. They spent three years teaching each other.

It was 1972. Sam cost us $600, which we couldn't afford. Because we had friends with horses and an extra stall, the board was $75 per month. We could afford that, but barely.

The baby-sitting money went to the horse. Odd jobs were hunted down. She packaged the manure she swept from the stalls and peddled it to friends as fertilizer, 50 cents a bag. We'd tease her, sometimes, that it cost more to put it in the front end than she got for taking it out the back. But she worked — willingly, joyously.

She was not alone. We heard all the stories — the horses gone lame, the scramble for vet fees and show fees, the jumps refused, the tragedies large and small.

When Sam spooked at milk cartons — the targets in Pony Club races — the girl cried a little, thought a lot, and hung one from the centre of Sam's stall and left her cowering in a corner until she grew used to it. Education is not all found in schools.

We watched them grow, a tangle of kids and horses bound together by golden, invisible strands. Some of the girl's friends will be riding at Southlands on the weekend — older now, but with dreams and love intact. They are not spoiled, or no more than most. At the level attained by the Kathy Wedges and the Barbara Simpson Kerrs they *are* athletes, they *are* competing in a demanding sport.

But I'd have to disagree with those who say they're not rich. They're all rich. They just don't have any money.

THE BABY-KILLERS

March 3, 1985

I've discovered a wonderful place to watch whales. It's called the ocean. Maybe you've noticed it on your way to the aquarium. Big, roomy place. Old, sure, but the plumbing works and you don't have to scrub, drain or refill it. And as far as I know there hasn't been a single instance of a whale getting a bruise on its brain by bashing its head into the wall.

The whales seem to like it, too, probably because they were born in it. You know how it is when you grow up in a neighbourhood.

Funny thing about whales. They never run away from home. Oh, they wander around checking all the rooms and poking in the corners. But, barring the occasional crazy or careless type who gets washed up on the shore and can't get back, you don't hear much about the kids running away from home to have a look at the big city.

There are no street whales hanging around the corners offering to do it for a fin. Whales don't knife each other to raise money to suck strange chemicals up their blow holes.

But little whales do disappear. One day they're there, the next day they're not. The People get them. They throw nets around them and haul them off and stick them in jails called pools so more People can come and stare at them and make them parade themselves for pay, jumping in the air to earn the fish they eat while the Person at the wicket takes all the money.

I don't know what the whales call that, but I know the People term for it.

I wonder what the other whales think, back there in the ocean? I wonder if there are any who still remember Sanaq, the year-old baby who was kidnapped near her home off Churchill, Manitoba, in 1976 and carted off to Vancouver to do her tricks for money? I wonder if any of the old beluga group remember her or Kavna, the little boy beluga taken at the same time?

Is there a case file somewhere, listing the unsolved disappearances? I suppose not. Whales would have no way of knowing that five of their number have died here since the Vancouver Aquarium first got involved in kidnapping and confining whales in 1967.

They just disappeared. Swam off one day and were never seen again. And what the heck — they were only whales.

But still I wonder. Do whales cry? Do they mourn for the lost ones? Are their lives ripped apart, as human lives are torn by the disappearance or death of so many kids?

The scientists tell us no. They give the kidnap victims cute names, sometimes chosen in contests by newspapers or radio stations. They put them in tubs and tell us this one is frisky and this one is playful and this one really enjoys jumping up and grabbing that fish.

When one of the whales gets sick and dies, the scientists have all the answers. It was a parasite or a fever or some sort of pneumonia. They lay the whale out as they did Sanaq, and they slice it open and do a postmortem and come up with a good, scientific reason or guess as to cause of death. And then they get themselves another whale.

They have the pat answers, the People do. They have the numbers to show how many People came to see Sanaq and Kavna. They talk of the "impact" the close-up view of a live whale has, and how it's so much better than a picture in a book or on TV.

It's all very glib and professional — and a lot easier than discussing a nine-year-old female kidnapped at one and caged in a tub until she died.

REVENGE OF THE DEVIL

April 19, 1988

I've always believed that when it came time to design the thoroughbred race horse, God took the day off and gave the job to the Devil.

He probably said something like "Look, I know I've banished you to the depths of Hell and all that, but no hard feelings, right? So on your way down, how about stopping in on Earth and doing one last Good Thing? Who knows, (well, I do, naturally, but who *else*?) come Judgment Day it might do you some good. At worst, it shouldn't hurt."

"What in Hell have I got to lose?" the Devil snarled. "Whadya want?"

And the Lord sayeth unto the Devil: "Build a creature designed to race around in circles so that Man may have sport to behold at the day's end to his tilling of the fields, and perhaps even place a friendly wager on the outcome."

"You got it," the Devil promised. And for perhaps the first and certainly the last time in history, he kept his word. He did, indeed, design a creature that would race around in circles for the sport of Man. But he was, after all, the Devil. So, he built in a few flaws.

First, he took this barrel-sized body and rested it on four legs so slender and delicate they could have done ads for pantyhose. Briefly, he considered adding training wheels, then shrugged it off as too Christian.

He added flowing mane and tail accessories, all part of the package price. Then he built a gorgeous, big-eyed head with generous lips and sexy whicker — and placed in it a brain so tiny that small men had to climb aboard during races to show the silly thing which way to go. And even as the earth opened to swallow him forever he added the final touch: feet so devilishly fashioned that men had to pound nails into them to keep their shoes on.

151

The Lord put in the heart and the courage and the spirit, the Devil having none in stock. You can get arguments over which side brought in the tote board and the bookie, or, worst of all, implanted in the mind of man that watching the creatures race in circles didn't matter as much as having the money down on the right one. Maybe it was the Devil, planting the seed of temptation. Maybe it was the Lord, testing his flock as to righteousness and handicapping skills. It matters not.

From that moment, the creature called Horse had no say in its destiny. It was there to run for money, eat oats, provide fertilizer and keep its trap shut. It was proved again on the weekend when the jockeys at Ex. Park refused to ride because they considered the track conditions poor enough to be dangerous. Six races were called off on Friday, along with all of Saturday's card. Reporters, some of whom were counting on the weekend to get even, rushed around taking statements from all concerned.

The jockeys were quoted. So were the trainers and the track operators. We heard nothing from the horses. They probably weren't even asked.

The trainers don't have to tramp around in the mud ruining two pair of brand-new shoes. If they choose, they can watch from the clubhouse and get plastered while they're doing it. The jockeys get muddy and wet — but at least they're dressed for it. And when they don't feel like riding, they stage a walkout. The horse has to go out there stark naked except for a bitty little blanket, a saddle and a sweaty jockey who keeps saying things like "Whoa," and "Atta boy," and is heavily into whips and leather. Everybody talks about cushy stalls and stud fees and candle light and whinny, but nobody ever mentions *that*.

Just once — maybe this time when the jockeys are ready to go back — I'd like to see the horses go on strike. It would be worth it, if only to see, in this sport of kings, how many would pay to watch the jockeys race.

THINGS GO BETTER WITH...

February 16, 1989

The headline in the afternoon paper was a shocker:
Trainers face hearing into coke use by horses.

Well, I guess so! Since the "c" in coke isn't capitalized and hasn't got that teensy little TM near the bottom, we can safely assume we're not talking soft drinks here. We're talking cocaine, which is horse of a different colour.

And if it's true that several California horses have flunked urine tests and stand charged with running on cocaine booster shots, questions arise that must be dealt with immediately.

How do they pick up the razor blade with their hoofs?

Snorting would be no problem — not with nostrils that size — but how do they roll up the dollar bill to form the tube? And the urine tests. You ever take a close look at a horse in action? What did they use for sample bottles — wine barrels?

The story says the samples were frozen. Was that done while they were in the horse — in which case I suppose the sample could be squeezed out like a popsicle — or later, which would allow the horse to claim they got them mixed up and that wasn't his at all, it was that cheap little claimer's two stalls down?

More importantly, what made them do it? They had everything: fame, fortune, posh stalls, the best of hay and grain, grooms and trainers to wait on them hand and hoof. And, at the end of the rainbow, retirement at age three or four to a lifetime of the choicest fillies being led to the finest studs like an endless parade of Playboy bunnies to a four-legged Hugh Hoofner.

What drove them to dance with the White Lady? Boredom, perhaps. Or, the old story, the drive to compete. The neigh-sayers deny the stuff has ever touched their muzzles, but get them under oath before the California Horse Racing Board and it'll be the same tired excuse:

"Some of them eastern horses use the stuff alla time, so any western horse that wants to do better than show money has gotta use it or scratch.

"Me? Nossir, never touch it myself, but I know horses that do. It's the pressure. You either use it or finish up the track with nuthin' left but a moth-eaten blanket and a milk route. All that trainin', you think they wanna wind up carryin' some fat New York cop through Central Park, chasin' muggers with knives?

"So maybe they take a chance, y'know? Grab a garden hose and switch urine with some wimp track pony or somethin'. I mean, what are the odds? Everybody knows all those stories about side effects are garbage ... what's that?

"Well, yeah, those are teflon implants in my nostrils. Sinus condition, judge. I usta sniff somethin' terrible. Why am I shakin'? Well, I gotta see a groom about a curry job, and I'm late, so if you don't mind could I leave like, right away?

"My oath, judge, I never used the stuff. Not knowingly, anyway. The white stuff those other studs say they saw around my nostrils? My trainer did that, judge. Told me it was face powder, make me look good in the winner's circle. Me, I'm as pure as the driven snow..."

THE DUCK STOPS HERE

April 10, 1990

Mr. Tony Eberts
Outdoors Editor
The Province
Tony:

There are ducks in my swimming pool. Three, counting the decoy. We discovered them Monday morning. My wife looked through the sliding-glass doors and made a funny sound. "Ooh!" she cooed. I was immediately suspicious. The last time she cooed like that we wound up owning a cat.

"No more cats," I snarled.

"Not cats, ducks," she said.

"Don't call me ducks. Call me disturbingly handsome, call me sexy, call me..."

"Real ducks," she said. "Two of them. In the swimming pool."

I looked. She was right. There was the wooden one and two others that looked even stupider. One with a green head, the other looking fat, smug and know-it-all.

"That's the female, right?" I asked. "So how come she's so fat?"

"I think she's getting ready to..."

"She already has," I said, peering into the pool. "See, there's some over there, some by the drain, some by the skimmer ... Jeez! All the ducks in the world and we have to get two with the trots."

"Idiot! I mean, I think she's looking for a place to nest."

"You mean, like...?"

"That's right. Little ducklings."

"Ducklings, hell," I said. "I took Biology. Before you get ducks you get eggs, right? And then, you get ..."

"Cute little ducklings," she nodded.

"... breakfast," I concluded.

"*Breakfast*???"

"Yeah, breakfast: Fried duck-egg sandwiches. Duck omelet.

Scrambled, maybe, with a little salt. Or maybe over easy on toast. I know they aren't exactly Grade A large, but if we get lucky and she lays a lot of them..."

"But they're so *cute*! I bet if we gave them some bread and stayed very quiet, they'd come right up to the door. Wouldn't that be nice?"

"Go ahead, coddle them," I said.

"You mean, maybe cake instead of bread? I'm not sure ducks like..."

"Ducks, hell. I mean the eggs. We find 'em, we put them in the hot tub, and bingo: coddled eggs. I'd say poach 'em, but that would make the tub too hot for the rest of us."

"You have no soul," she complained. "Eggs become baby ducks. Baby ducks become adult ducks. Adult ducks..."

"Become dinner. You're right. Eating the eggs would be crazy. We let the eggs grow into big ducks, and then we eat *them*. It's just like hunting, only with home delivery. And you don't have to get up at obscene hours and freeze to death in a duck blind hoping some other hunter doesn't think you're a mallard."

We stopped talking about then, which is why I'm writing.

Is it unusual to have ducks land in your swimming pool?

Why can't I shoot them or eat them or boil their eggs? If I do, will Greenpeace picket my house?

Am I really expected to feel sorry for birds who fly south every winter — which, by the way, I can't afford to do myself?

Please hurry. My wife already wants to name them. I suggested Poopsie and Poopsie.

"Why the same name for both ducks?" she asked.

"Look in the pool," I said.

PSSST! BUDDY! WANNA BE A MOOSE?

March 1, 1990

Well, yes, there is a major baseball story that does not involve strikes, walkouts and big-league bitching.

On Sunday, the Seattle Mariners are auditioning moose.

Right there on stage at Seattle Centre House, 15 would-be moose (mooses? meese?) will dance, do backflips, walk funny and look as lovable as a moose can get — which I suppose is pretty lovable if you happen to be a moose of the opposite gender. Otherwise, they tend to smell bad, taste stringy and shy away from any attempts at housebreaking.

155

For the Mariners, not just any moose will do. They're looking for The Mariner Moose, the name chosen from about 2,500 submitted by school kids around the Pacific Northwest for a new Mariner mascot. In what Mariners' PR director Dave Aust assures me was "the closest ballot in the history of mascotdom," Mariner Moose beat out Seaward the Seamonster by *one vote*! When the going gets tough, the moose get going.

They were the top two in a field of five finalists that also included Bernie, the Mariners' Mongoose, Mightyball, the Mariners' Seal and Mr. Mariner, who would probably wander the field in a sincere suit handing out ticket brochures and suggesting we all do lunch.

Like the mascots, the 15 who'll attempt to fill the moose suit are finalists chosen after a write-in competition. How were they selected?

"On the strength of their *resumés*," Aust says solemnly.

"Dear Mariners: I would like to apply for the position of team mascot. I am small and agile and don't sweat hardly at all, which would save a lot of wear and tear on the moose suit. I have previous experience as a gorilla, a duck and the south end of a northbound horse. Am currently employed in Kentucky Fried ads, but will be free as soon as somebody tells me how I get out of this chicken outfit.

P.S.: If you would consider changing the mascot from a moose to a donkey, my wife says I make an ass of myself at least once every night and might as well be getting paid for it."

The Mariners, and the city of Seattle, are deadly serious about their mascot search, as well they should be. It's either that or think about the Mariners, assuming they ever get around to playing. Newspapers have written editorials about the talent hunt, and *The Sunday Times* wilderness writer has gone so far as to pooh-pooh suggestions that Seattle is not moose country, claiming evidence of at least 168 authenticated sightings.

The Mighty M's themselves have even half-promised that, all being well, The Mariner Moose could have a visitor at an early game. Yes, (*gasp!*) the sainted Bullwinkle himself could be at the Kingdome rutting for the home team.

Why a moose instead of a sea monster? Well, as Bullwinkle proved — and continues to prove in reruns with his friend Rocky Squirrel — moose are kind of neat and tidy and look like fun to be around. I'm not sure kids in the stands would warm up to something scaly and slimy looking. A mascot is more than someone in a funny animal suit or some pseudo-monster jumping around like a DNA experiment gone sour.

Mascots can flop. Fans can turn on them, boo them off the field, and the team with them. Who will ever forget the B.C. Lions' disastrous Jerome, the Gnome Who Lives Under the Dome. Or, God forbid, the Canuck Duck?

Besides, there's the moose track record. No matter how terrible things looked, Bullwinkle and Rocky Squirrel always beat Boris Badinoff and Natasha in the end. Given the Mariners' record, having a winner around shouldn't hoit.

STAY CALM AND PASS THE V-8

August 9, 1990

The Further Adventures of Macho Jim, Outdoorsy-Type Guy...

Okay, so I'm actually a City-Type Guy. So maybe macho is stretching it and I don't pound my whiskers in with the back of the axe and bite them off from the inside. But it is still possible to have outdoorsy-type adventures right here in the city. I myself have them all the time.

Did I not tell you of how the two ducks landed in my swimming pool and how we all sat enraptured for hours watching them use it as a poopeteria? Well, this one is even more exciting.

Yesterday, 2:30 a.m. We are awakened by the overpowering stench of burning rubber, or possibly smouldering wiring and insulation. It is so powerful we pull on dressing gowns, run out of the room, then out of the house. There is no escaping it.

"The house is on fire," my wife says.

"Omigod! My autographed picture of Cheryl Tiegs is in there! My complete set of Wayne Gretzky trading cards! My *Sports Illustrated* collection!"

"Your son," she reminds me, "and your 92-year-old mother."

"Them, too!"

She runs into the house and calls the fire department. (Well, somebody had to.)

Three minutes, several awaken-the-dead sirens and enough flashing lights for a movie premiere later, two fire trucks are parked outside the house and one of several firemen is asking my wife whether she'd like some oxygen. Nobody asks me anything.

I wait. They do not rush in to haul my mother and son from their beds. They do not pull down ladders, unroll hoses, chop a hole in my roof or do any of those other firemen things.

"Skunk," says one.

Hey, I know it's late, but there's no call to get insulting.

"Skunk," he repeats. "You can smell it clear over to the school yard."

Our dog wanders by, a purebred Highland collie who makes Lassie look like Roseanne Barr. She smells of burning rubber, or possibly smouldering wiring or insulation.

"Looks like your dog had a fight with a skunk," the fireman says.

The firemen look at one another, then at me. They pack up their oxygen tanks and leave. The dog runs into the house in case there are any rooms left that don't stink. There are. She remedies that.

"The dog," says my wife, "has to be cleaned. I read somewhere that tomato juice cuts skunk odour. Take her out back and bring me some tomato juice."

Crisis. We don't have any tomato juice. Fortunately, we Outdoorsy-Type Guys know how to improvise.

"Clamato or V-8?" I shout.

We settle on the V-8. I hold the dog. She empties this huge tin of V-8 all over it and begins to scrub. In seconds, the dog looks like a Rambo casualty.

"Her white ruff looks all bloody," I protest.

"It's three o'clock in the morning, my house smells of skunk and I'm pouring V-8 juice over a dog," my wife says sweetly. "Do you really want to continue this conversation?"

Not me. I'm camping out at the Pan Pacific until this thing blows over.

BILLIE JEAN, MEET VEAL CHOP

August 23, 1990

Two tales of blatant sexism hit the pages of the ever-vigilant *Province* Tuesday morning.

One of them was so heart-rending we ran it twice, once in the sports section, once in the People section. (Would that we could all be as tireless in matters sexual as this paper is in pursuit of them.) Billie Jean King needs to get from her highly-paid role of commentator for the U.S. Open tennis championship in Flushing Meadows,

N.Y., to Seneca Falls, N.Y., Sunday for her induction to the National Women's Hall of Fame, the timing was wrong for regular commercial flights, and — you're not going to believe this — *no one in corporate America will pay the $3,000 for a charter, or lend her a corporate jet!*

"It's partly a women's issue," sniffs Emilie Sisson, executive director of the Hall. "It's a failure of corporate America [that] shows how much more women across America must accomplish in order to prove themselves worthy of the honors and recognition they so richly deserve."

Right on, sister! One lousy corporate jet and those Fortune 500 companies won't pony up. Who the hell do they think they are? Sure, Ms. King will get to the ceremonies — but the Hall of Fame that nominated her and invited her is going to have to pay to get her there. How fair is that?

I was just reaching for my cheque book to send a donation when I saw the other story on Page 16, the one about Veal Chop, the newborn calf at the Pacific National Exhibition.

Veal Chop, we're told, probably will sell for around $80 — but "if the little critter had been a female it would have probably been worth $12,000."

Excuse me?

"Too bad it's a male," laments owner Fred Philps. "Females are worth a lot more. They can be used for milking or breeding. It takes a great male to service grand champion Holsteins. One bull can do a heckuva lot."

Oh, sure. A female swishes around the barn waving her tail and accessories and before you know it the farmer is bringing in some stud from the pasture to be used as a sex object. No cruising the discos for this baby. Oh, no. She's got home delivery.

More often, the poor male isn't even afforded the potential thrill of a blind date. Artificial insemination, that's the ticket. "See these tubes, Ferdinand? Fill 'em up." And nobody respects him in the morning. They just bring in another box of tubes.

We are talking major sexual exploitation here, not to mention the agony of watching those tubes being shipped out, never knowing who'll be the mother of your potential progeny, or whether they'll wind up as females in a barn or steaks in a freezer.

I say we rise up and save Veal Chop. Make him the symbol of a Cease Udder Discrimination movement (CUD). Ship him to fairs all over North America. Get a Canada Council grant. Put cows across railroad tracks until we're guaranteed equal pay for equal chops.

Who knows — maybe some Fortune 500 company will provide the corporate cattle car.

VICTOR HAD A LITTLE LAMB

June 16, 1991

KELOWNA — Out on the lush green turf of the Apple Bowl the would-be B.C. Lions cavort in the morning sunshine, perhaps relishing their final day of freedom before the veterans arrive to teach them the facts of pro football life.

On the sidelines, Vic Spencer is talking not of Lions but of lambs — one particular lamb, in fact: The one that became the Lions' first-ever mascot of their first-ever training camp right here, 27 years ago.

Mr. Spencer is an authority on the subject. If he hadn't had the DeSoto and hadn't been there to help sweet-talk the little girl into giving up her lamb...

But I digress.

Suffice it to say that Vic Spencer was a Lions' director before there were any Lions, back in the early 1950s when those s.o.b.'s from Winnipeg and Regina kept shooting down a Vancouver entry in the Canadian Football League, first because they didn't want to travel this far and later out of fear that with a stadium the size of Empire, the new team could generate enough money to buy the best players and (sob) win the Grey Cup every year.

But they got their franchise, and now here sat Spencer and a few of the other directors at that first training camp in 1954, eagerly awaiting the team's first intra-squad game the following day. It can safely be assumed that the odd glass was lifted in anticipation of the big event.

Somewhere in the course of the afternoon they had a great idea: What the team really needed was a mascot for the first intra-squad game. Lions being hard to come by on such short notice, they opted for a lamb.

"Well, we piled in my DeSoto and headed out into the country," Spencer recalls, "and eventually we came to this farmhouse where a little girl had a pet lamb, so young that they were nursing it with a bottle."

The little girl would not sell her lamb. After much negotiation, she did agree to rent it for the weekend, as long as they agreed to take the bottle, feed it regularly, and take really good care of her pet.

"Absolutely," they said. Then they drove back to the city and had it dyed orange and black.

"Vegetable dye," Spencer says virtuously. "Didn't hurt the lamb a bit and it made a lot better mascot wearing the team colours."

Now there was a problem. The game wasn't until the next afternoon. Where was the lamb going to spend the night?

"By this time she looked thirsty," Spencer says. "But that's all right, because so were we. So we took her back to the hotel with us and sneaked her into the bar while we talked it over."

They got a break. The bartender had his back turned, bending over digging out some ice. Spencer sat down on one stool and parked the lamb on the next one, front hooves on the bar.

"Scotch for me," he said, "and a double mint sauce for my friend!"

Strangely enough, they were asked to leave.

They retired to their rooms to mount the search for a proper place for the lamb to spend the night. Their choice was perfect: the hotel manager's bathroom.

"It got kind of messy, her doing what lambs will do," Spencer concedes. "But she stayed in there quiet as a lamb, you might say, and the next day we trotted her out for the game. She was a big hit, and we took her back to the little girl good as new once the coloured hair grew out."

We stood for a few minutes more watching the rookies — the talented, the tryers, the dreamers, the ones who'll make the first cuts and the ones who'll pack their hopes in athletic bags and look for another team or another line of work the way Lions' rookies have done now for better than a quarter-century.

"Vic," I asked, "why do you suppose they threw you out of that cocktail lounge?"

He gave it some thought.

"I guess," he concluded, "they only served lamb in the dining room."

Chapter Seven

LOVE AT FIRST DOWN

I became a sports writer for the best of all reasons: a journalism teacher named Stan Murphy threatened to kick my ass if I didn't.

I'd stumbled into journalism class in Grade 7 in Winnipeg, where I discovered that if you wrote a story you could work on the *Mulvey Mirror*, the school yearbook, which meant that you got to miss classes while you printed it on the old Gestetner machine in the hall outside the principal's office. (We also discovered that if you ran a sheet of paper through the machine backwards, it shredded and you could waste another half day cleaning it.) The *Mirror* or classes? No contest.

So I wrote stuff, and kept writing it. Now I was in Grade 11 at Victoria High, working on the school paper and vaguely wondering how I was going to worm my way onto a real one when I graduated.

"There's a part-time job at the Victoria *Colonist*," Murphy said. "Sports department."

"I hope whoever gets it enjoys it," I said, "because I don't want it." Sports writer? Not me. I was going to be Art Buchwald.

"Then you have a problem," he said, "because you've already taken it. I took it for you and you will accept it now or I will kick your ass until you do."

"But I don't want to be a sportswriter!"

"It will get you in the door!" he said in the tone reserved for village idiots. "Do well and maybe they'll take you on full time when you graduate. Once you're in you can always ask to transfer out of sports. Think of it as temporary. You'll be working for a newspaper!"

Hell, I already worked for the *Colonist*. I had a paper route — 105 customers. But I took the job. It was either that or face Mr. Murphy. I covered high school sports, lawn bowling, Little League, anything they wanted through school and summer holidays.

But I took no chances. I also kept the paper route. Up at 5:15, do the route, go to school, have dinner, cover a softball game, rush to the *Colonist*, struggle through the story, go home and grab some sleep, then rush for the paper the next morning to see what they'd done to it.

I don't think I ever turned in a homework assignment or served the detentions I got for ignoring them. To this day I don't know why they didn't throw me out of school. The teacher would say "Where's your assignment?" I'd say "I couldn't work it into my schedule," and around and around we'd go.

Heading into Grade 12 I faced facts: I couldn't write for it and deliver it. So: sports writer or paper boy? Reluctantly, I gave up the route.

Three days after graduation in 1955 I was a full-time reporter — in the sports department, but that was okay. I knew it would be only temporary. Twelve years later I'd had a paper (the Vancouver *Times*, 1965) fold under me after a year, almost died from the mumps (or maybe the pressure of the ice bag on my swollen nether regions during recovery), and had made an amazing discovery: I *liked* sports writing.

Mostly I liked football — football in general but Canadian football in particular, with its three downs, its 12 men, its Canadian-content rules and even that crazy part about giving a guy a single point for missing a field goal.

And here I was, the football-beat reporter for *The Vancouver Sun*. They were *paying* me to watch football. It couldn't get any better than that...

TIME OUT FOR ROMANCE

December 31, 1979

"You're going to do it again, aren't you?" snarled the former Deborah Easton. "You're going to watch football all day."

She was staring at me. Ice slowly formed on my considerable forehead. Instinctively, I knew her game plan: Hit him with the old You Never Talk to Me Anymore. But for every play there's a defence. George Allen says so. I opted for the full blitz.

"What's your beef?" I snarled right back. "I distinctly remember speaking to you Saturday afternoon between 4:15 and five. Vernon Perry had just intercepted his fourth pass for Houston and it wasn't time for *Hockey Night in Canada*. I even remember what I said: 'When's dinner?' "

"Do you remember what I said?" she asked sweetly.

"Of course, but that's stupid. You can't take a football and eat it."

"I didn't say eat it," she said.

There are wives who like football. *National Geographic* occasionally finds little pockets of them, usually in tiny villages so primitive the sets are black and white. Mostly, though, they hate it. Worse, they demand equal time, which can be rough. Take Sunday.

"When are you going to phone about the New Year's Eve reservations?" she asked.

"Look at that Steel Curtain!" I replied. "Three shots from the two-yard line and Miami can't get in."

"The furnace has stopped," she said. "The water in the aquarium is freezing the guppies."

"You ever see a guy as tough as that Franco Harris?" I asked. "Three guys just hit him — beat the crap out of him — and he gets up smiling. Super Bowl City! Nobody's gonna stop those guys. Nobody!"

"The neighbour's kids have just set fire to the cat."

That stopped me. "This could be serious," I said. "Cat fur smells when it burns. Tell them not to do it in the house. And when the cat's done, tell them not to forget we've got another one."

"What are you *saying*?"

"I dunno," I said wearily. "I've got a lot of things on my mind. Lynn Swan hasn't been in since the first half. The Steelers are starting to crack. They've already missed a convert and..."

I could see she was upset. So I made one of those considerate, tactful moves that help make a marriage work during playoffs.

"Let's forget football and talk," I suggested.

She looked at me, eyes shining. "Really?" she said.

"Sure. It's the two-minute warning. We've got 60 seconds."

She was silent. Obviously overcome.

"Let's use it constructively," I rushed on, one eye on the set. "Let's figure out when we're going to have some time to ourselves — you know, just the two of us. After all, it's almost a new decade."

The old soft soap. Gets 'em every time.

"Tomorrow, then," she relented. "I know you like watching the NFL, but it won't be on tomorrow and it's New Year's Eve. We can sit at home by the fire and..."

"Right," I said, flipping the remote to pick up the Rams and Cowboys while the Dolphins and Steelers were into commercial. "That's it, then. Home by the fire until 11:30. Then we'll eat lunch right there. Just you and me and the fire and the Peach Bowl."

"Peach Bowl? You know I don't make dessert."

"Uh, no," I explained. "The Peach Bowl *game*. Baylor vs Clemson."

Something told me she was disturbed. Nineteen years married, you learn to detect the signs. Maybe it was the way she picked up the poker.

"Not to worry," I added hastily. "It'll be over by 2:30. After that, no more football. Promise. I'll even skip the Blue Bonnet Bowl."

"No more football?" she asked doubtfully.

"Not a down," I said. "It's up against the hockey. Montreal vs Red Army. Oh, I could probably catch the fourth quarter when the hockey's over, but no way. This is your night."

"My night," she repeated. "We do what I want."

"Absolutely."

"Good," she gushed. "I've got it all planned. We go out for dinner at about eight. Then dancing. It's time you learned. The last time we went to a dance they stamped the back of our hands and made us take off our penny loafers. Then we come home and put another log on the fire. I'll have the champagne chilled. We'll drink in the 1980s. Maybe even have some friends in. We'll party through the night. We'll drink and laugh and talk until..."

"Twelve-oh-five," I interrupted. "Twelve-thirty tops."

She eyed the poker. "Why?" she said dangerously.

"Training," I explained. "The old eyeballs aren't what they used to be. Got to get my sleep. Sugar and Cotton Bowl games start at 11. I figure with the remote I can get the best of both. Then the Rose Bowl's from two to five and the Orange Bowl from five to eight..."

"Let me understand this," she said slowly. "You plan to usher in the 80s by lying flat on your butt on that couch watching football *from 11 a.m. to eight p.m.?*"

Her voice sounded funny.

"Well, sure," I said. "Oh, I was gonna watch the Rose Parade first, but that starts at 8:30 in the morning and I wasn't sure you'd want to be up that early."

"*Up?*" she screamed. "*Up?* Give me one good reason I should be up at 8:30 on New Year's Day when you're going to spend it all watching *football*!"

"To make my coffee," I said reasonably.

She's a nice girl, but kind of slow.

NEON LEON

November 3, 1977

Sometimes, when the letters on the page suddenly made no sense, when he knew the words were there but couldn't pick them out, Leon Bright would wonder if he'd ever make it.

He was 14 years old, trying to fight his way through junior high school against odds that made the game seem crooked. Five years later he would be Neon Leon, a legend in Florida high school football, a phenom wooed by every major college in the country. In eight he'd be a pro with the B.C. Lions, destined to be the Canadian Football League's rookie-of-the-year. But right then he had another nickname. In the two-bedroom house in Merritt Island, Florida, where he slept on the couch in the living room, seven younger brothers and sisters called him Pop.

His parents had separated a few years earlier, splitting a family of 15. His father took his five step-brothers and two step-sisters with him to Orlando. At 14, Leon was the man of the house. The younger kids looked up to him, depended upon him as they would a father.

And he had a bigger problem than any of them.

It is called dyslexia, a learning disability that has nothing to do with intelligence, a breakdown between eye contact and brain reaction. What it means is that you always have a reading problem. Sometimes you can't read at all. A page you read flawlessly on Friday will make no sense at all on Saturday. It can be a nightmare.

Life became a juggling act. Battling the dyslexia had left him painfully shy and unsure. The school was seven miles from home and football practice was every night, but Leon walked or ran home day after day because he was too shy to tell anyone he could use a ride. Books, football, home, books, football, home. Around and around, gaining on the field and falling behind in school, and wondering if it would ever end...

Leon Bright seemed faintly surprised that anyone knew about life in Merritt Island. He hadn't said anything. When the B.C. Lions brought him here last July, all anyone knew was that he'd quit Florida State as a junior and could run holes in the wind.

Attempts to interview him had failed miserably. He was too scared to be helpful, although he tried, and nobody asked the right questions. But get on the phone to Merritt Island. They'll talk for hours about Leon Bright, and the pride pours over the wires.

"Leon got through school because he worked like a dog and strove to overcome the dyslexia," says Harry Jennings, the high school English teacher Leon fondly calls "my key man".

"In college it was simply too big a handicap, but in junior high — where my wife was his counsellor — and high school he was one of the most respected and loved young men to go through the system."

If Bright was battered by the books, he found self-expression on the football field. In three years of high school ball he scored 75 touchdowns and had a career rushing record of just under 11 yards per carry. In his final two years he made All-American. Academically he had battled his grades up to a C average. When he graduated the college coaches were lined up and drooling.

"I could have gone most anywhere," Bright says. "There are still about 12 unused plane tickets in a drawer back home, for visits to schools. But I wanted to stay near home. Those visits — man, they scared me. So I went to Florida State."

It lasted three years, two playing football, one red-shirted while he fought the books again, this time losing out. He looked the situation over and decided to go home. Then assistant coach Jim Gladden, a buddy of Lions' coach Vic Rapp, suggested that if he was going to leave, he might as well leave and make money.

The prospect terrified him. "When we put him on the plane, I still hadn't told him how far he was going," Mrs. Jennings recalls. "We were afraid he'd panic and back off."

"Yeah, I might have, at that," Bright admits. "It's a long, long way from home."

Leon Bright is having a post-practice dinner. His friends in Florida have pieced his story together for the guy on the phone on one condition: If Leon is at all embarrassed at the mention of the dyslexia, the information will not be used. They are terribly protective when they mention Leon. Jennings is right: the kid is loved.

He's also grown.

"Go ahead and write it if you want," he says. "The dyslexia ... when I was young I felt bad. I wasn't one of the group. I felt *lost* — you understand? Then you kind of find out about yourself. The way I look at it, everybody had some kind of handicap. Now me, I'm pretty gifted athletically. With that, I figure I've overcome the other thing.

"I got a lot of help up here. When I came I was so scared, and when it got down to the last day and they told me they were going to start John Sciarra I was so sick and lonesome all I wanted to do was go home. But Larry Watkins and Jesse O'Neal, they said 'Hang in there. It's a long season.' So I stayed, and everything worked out great."

Next season is Bright's option year. When it ends he will be eligible for the National Football League draft. But he says he wants to stay here, get a job, and make a career. Then maybe in the off-season, dyslexia or no dyslexia, go home and work on the last two years of an industrial arts degree.

He is 22 now. He still gets homesick. But his mother is flying in today. Leon sent her the ticket to come see him play Saturday night against Winnipeg.

"She's kind of wondering how I'm doing," he explains.

Mrs. Bright, he's doing just fine.

500 AIR MILES FROM HOME

March 30, 1978

MONTREAL — Police say three-month investigation turns up no proof of plot to weaken key Edmonton Eskimo players with sex the night before 1977 Grey Cup game.

The next sound you hear will be the voices of 32 Eskimos trying to convince wives and girlfriends that they are not and have never been key players.

"Key player? Me? Hell, honey, I barely got out of training camp. I was a *rookie*. Rookies don't get to no parties, 'cept the rookie show, and even then all they let you do is drink and throw up. Aw, c'mon, honey! Open the door..."

Fortunately, winter is all but over in Edmonton. Had the Montreal story broken in February instead of yesterday, coach Hugh Campbell would have spent all summer chipping his starters out of the ice that had formed around them and their living-room chester-fields. As it is, the 1977 Eskimos — however innocent — will be subjected to a lot of winks and elbows in the ribs in the coming months. Nothing in sport titillates the imagination more than a suggestion that a man's playbook may be X-rated.

The story itself has just enough innuendo to conjure up scenes of lechery and debauchery, with booze flowing like water and hard-eyed girls plying football players with invitations to study their statistics.

Police in Montreal say their street contacts claim a group of girls had banded together on Grey Cup Eve to make sure the Eskimos left their game in the bedroom. Recalling that the score *had* been 41-6 for the Montreal Alouettes, and that the Eskimos did play like 32 guys who'd spent the night in a steam bath, they launched a three-month investigation which ended yesterday with assurances to CFL commissioner Jake Gaudaur that "nothing criminal had occurred".

In theory, that ends it. But of course it won't.

Disgruntled westerners who mortgaged the farm to bet on Alberta Crude will always wonder whether the dice were loaded, not to mention the players. They'll start asking questions — preceding them with "Of course, I don't believe it, but just suppose..."

There will be no shortage of questions.

Was it a plot by the bookies? Were the girls mob-hired or merely dedicated Alouette fans ready to give their all for the team, luring the innocent Eskimos with promises of a bi-cultural relationship that would melt the ice off their moustaches?

The suggestion is not without historical precedent — as commissioner Gaudaur is well aware. Legend has it that, in his days as general manager of the Hamilton Tiger-Cats, his team had a big game coming up in one of the other eastern cities against a club possessing an exceptional quarterback. And that several days before said game, a Hamilton miss with a leaning toward football players decided the team needed a little help.

She boarded a train, the story goes, rode to the rival city, struck up an acquaintance with the quarterback, stayed with him for several days, then sent Gaudaur a wire that said, approximately:

HAVE TAKEN CARE OF QB. REST UP TO YOU!

The Eskimos' problem is two-fold. No one is ever totally cleared of such a story, no matter how clean a bill of health the police and league officials issue. Besides, in matters pertaining to the pursuit and conquest of broad and/or booze the football player is the victim of his own image. Football players and girls *always* chase each other. Joe Namath said so.

Was it not Jim Young who said in his autobiography, *Dirty 30*, that the unwritten rule of all professional football teams is "Five hundred air miles from home, everybody's single"?

It's not true, of course. Some of them aren't married in the first place.

But the image is there, fleshed out yearly by curfew-breaking training camp escapades dutifully reported by the ever-vigilant media, who happen to be in the same hotel checking on the supply of Gideon Bibles.

I myself recall the memorable day a veteran player announced his retirement and, as a farewell gesture, listed on the dressing-room blackboard the names and numbers of girls he knew in every league city. The players, who'd seen the girls he dated, rose as one man, and rubbed them out.

Not that it's all the players' fault. Some of those girls just won't quit. They buy club press guides, which list the hotels of visiting teams, and lurk in the lobby ready to pounce. There was a girl in Winnipeg once they called the Avon Lady because she knocked on every player's door and offered samples. Then she...oh, never mind.

The point is, the poor Eskimos of '77 are left with Hobson's Choice. Do they plead innocent and blow the image just to keep peace in the family? Or do they snigger suggestively and blow their home life just to keep the respect of other teams in the league?

Will it be the ladies, or the Tiger-Cats?

If only the game had been closer. But 41-6... hell, they'd have been better off with a shutout. That way they could look their sweeties straight in the eye and swear they'd never scored at all.

DRAFT DODGER

June 14, 1981

Once upon a time there was a little boy who wanted to be a shoemaker.

All his life, while the other kids were out playing games or stealing hubcaps, he'd be at his little toy workbench making little toy shoes. Eventually, people were offering him scholarships to make shoes for them.

All the big schools — Vanderboot, Oxford, Arkanshoe, Mississlipper, LSshoe — had scouts on his doorstep promising him groupies, under-the-table leather and peach cobbler. But he was a California boy. For him there could be only one school: ShoeCLA.

Because he was on scholarship his course load wasn't heavy (Lacing 10, Leatherpunch 91) and the coach didn't seem to care whether or not he attended classes. "Just keep those cordovans coming, kid," he said. "You're our ticket to No. 1 in the polls — *Gentleman's Quarterly, Cobbler's All-America*, you're gonna make us the Really Big Shoe."

But college was not without pitfalls. He fell in with the wrong crowd at first. For a while it seemed that if the dean didn't get him the Dubbin would. But he persevered, because he had a dream: He was going to turn pro! He'd already picked the spot for his shop, close enough to Beverly Hills to lure the high-class trade but not too far from the haunts of the leather-and-spike-heel set.

He graduated *summa cum toecap*. He'd given it his awl and now it was going to pay off. He was packing his apron and last when the word came.

"Congratulations, kid," his coach said. "You've been drafted by the Boston Bootblacks."

"Uh, gee, that's nice, coach," he said. "But I don't want to work in Boston. I've got this shop picked out right here in LA. All my plans are made. The Bootblacks will have to get someone else. A lot of good shoemakers have graduated this year. They'll have..."

"They'll have *you*, kid," the coach interrupted. "All the shoe factories are in on the draft. They take turns picking and they've agreed that no one tries to hire the other guys' pick. Cuts down overhead and makes it a hell of a lot easier to keep good help."

"But...but...I don't know anyone in Boston! Nobody asked me if I wanted to go there or work there or even visit there. I've *seen* Boston! Who wants to go through life making sensible shoes? I want to be on the coast where I grew up. I want to benefit mankind. I could be the guy who makes the big breakthrough: the beach thong that doesn't split the skin between your toes. I'm not *meant* for spit-and-polish! I won't go!"

"Oh, you'll go, kid," the coach replied. "You'll make shoes for the Bootblacks or you'll make shoes for no one. Because the National

Footwear League won't let you work for any of its other teams. It's Boston or nothing and you might as well get used to it."

"But that's restraint of trade! That's slavery! That takes away a man's freedom of choice! There's got to be a way around it!"

"Well, you could jump to the Canadian League, if you wanna spend your career making second-rate mukluks. Up there you're on the negotiation list of the Hamilton Highbuttons."

He signed with the Bootblacks. At least there he could make shoes. Hamilton meant a career in workboots. And after all, it was a two-year contract. He'd do his time, then move to California. He could do two years standing on his head.

Two years later he tried to move to the LA Lacers. They wanted him. They'd pay him far more than he was getting in Boston. But they couldn't take him.

"Compensation," they said. "If we take you we'd have to give up our entire pump line to the Bootblacks."

"You mean," the kid said, "that I can never work where I want to work — that my career is always going to be in someone else's hands? That's ridiculous!"

"Sure it is, kid," they agreed. "But that's shoe biz!"

PLEASE PRAY QUIETLY

September 10, 1981

But thou, when thou prayest, enter into thy closet, and when thou hast shut thy door, pray to thy Father which is in secret; and thy Father which seeth in secret shall reward thee openly. — Matthew 6:66

It's time to get God out of football games.

Not that He won't be there anyway. It's His world, His universe, His cosmos, and we learn from childhood that He is everywhere. But I wish football players would stop talking about Him as though He's stickum on the hands or the extra deep back on second and long. It's, well...*arrogant*.

Case in point: Brian Kelly, wide receiver, Edmonton Eskimos. Monday in Hamilton he made a marvellous, one-handed catch for a touchdown. "Congratulations on that great catch, Brian," said the TV man on the sidelines.

"Well, thank you," said Brian Kelly. "I guess the Lord had a hand in there, too."

Now, I am not a particularly religious man. I profess no special understanding of His eternal plan. But I doubt it includes much about a professional football player running a down-and-in.

I also question both the logic and the sincerity of a boxer who spends 15 rounds obliterating another man's face, then falls on his knees to announce that "God was in my corner". What happens when two good men of equal religious fervour and depth of belief fight one another? Is it a draw? Does God take sides? Or does He look down and say:

"I've given you the skills. I've put the desire in your hearts and the strength in your bodies. Go to it. Now, if you'll excuse me, I've got a universe to run..."?

The Jocks for God groups are sweeping through the ranks of professional sport. Fellowship of Christian Athletes, Athletes in Action...whatever the name, the game's the same: Play your sport, do your thing, then tell everyone you couldn't have done it without the Lord.

Well, of course not.

The Lord put us here, set up the rules, laid out the Commandments. It's like saying "If it wasn't for the air, I couldn't breathe." There's no need; it's self-evident.

Individually, Jocks for God tend to be good, bad or indifferent in about the same proportion as newspapermen, milkmen, insurance salesmen or plumbers. Collectively, I don't trust them — maybe because I've been unlucky.

Most of the ones I've met fall into two categories: Ex-drinkers, chasers, carousers and curfew-breakers who now run around polishing their halos; or guys who were jerks, got the halo, and feel that the fact that they've got it entitles them to go right on being jerks. It's like an insurance policy, a Pearly Gate pass.

"I try to live a good life *inside*," a guy told me once. Inside he was Oral Roberts. Outside he was Harold Robbins. Just following him, you'd get old.

Certainly there are athletes in AIA and other groups whose sincerity you cannot doubt. But of the Christian athletes I've come to respect, most didn't go around preaching about it. They just lived it.

It's almost become a game in itself. Athlete makes big play, athlete comes to sidelines, athlete gets in front of camera, athlete says God was there with him. It's become an annoyance, an interruption, another commercial. Head for the fridge, boys, here comes the God bit.

In the end they defeat their own purpose.

In 1975, Long Beach State had a running back named Herb Lusk. Whenever he scored a touchdown he'd fall on his knees in the end zone and pray. "I just love to get into that end zone so I can thank the Lord," he said.

A year earlier, the B.C. Lions had a running back named Johnny Musso. He'd come out of Alabama and Bear Bryant said he was the greatest football player he'd ever coached. Now he was packing to go try it with the Chicago Bears, and the things he packed most carefully were the Bibles belonging to him and his wife.

Johnny knew about the end zone. He'd knock you flat to get into it. But that was for touchdowns and talk and games and TV. The Bibles were for living. He never forgot the difference.

MS. QB KNOWS HER RIGHTS

April 18, 1985

All her life she'd dreamed of playing quarterback for the B.C. Lions. What could be so tough? She could yell "Hut one! Hut two!" as well as any guy. What else was there?

On the morning of April 16, she read the words that would change her life:

15. (1) Every individual is equal before and under the law and has the right to the equal protection and equal benefit of the law without discrimination.

And, buried in the big story about something called the Charter of Rights and Freedoms:

Discrimination based on race, national or ethnic origin, colour, religion, sex, age or mental or physical disability will be outlawed...

She thought it over carefully, chose her lawyer, and demanded an appointment with Lions' coach Don Matthews. When he refused, the lawyer read him the Charter clause covering the rights of women to equal employment opportunities.

She got the appointment.

She announced that she wished to try out for quarterback. When Matthews said "But you're a girl!" she called him a sexist pig, turned to the lawyer and said "Shut down this pop stand."

She got her tryout.

She couldn't see over the tackling dummies, let alone a defensive lineman. She threw a football as though she was shot-putting a beanbag. Sometimes she threw it up to three or four feet. When they threw it back she caught it with her head. When Matthews laughed, she threatened him with a charge of mental cruelty and sexual harassment on the job site.

She got a contract for training camp.

On opening day in Kelowna her time for the 40 was an hour and 10 minutes including coffee break. When Matthews questioned her speed she pointed out that she'd broken a nail after five yards and the Charter clearly stated that there shall be no job discrimination based on physical disability, and if he expected a poor girl to be seen in public with a jagged edge on a fingernail and the polish chipped to boot, well...

He listed her time as 4.4.

The day of the first exhibition game against the Winnipeg Blue Bombers she noticed she was listed eighth on the depth chart at quarterback and demanded to know why she wasn't starting. When Matthews pointed out that Roy Dewalt and Tim Cowan were returning veterans and the other five were graduates of top-rated college teams she sniffed enough to get the mascara running, conferred with her lawyer on the sidelines, and returned to Matthews.

"Coach," she said sweetly, "I can't help but notice that Mr. Dewalt and Mr. Cowan and all those other young men are Americans. I am a Canadian citizen. In giving them preferential treatment you are clearly violating both the spirit and the letter of the Charter in that this is a Canadian league and I am a Canadian and therefore I should be given first opportunity at any jobs available. Now, you are perfectly free to take this matter before the courts, but you know how they're backed up and I assume you want to start tonight's game before Christmas. Therefore, on the advice of my solicitor, I suggest..."

She was moved to No. 1 on the depth chart and named the starting quarterback.

When they handed out the game uniforms she refused to put on shoulder pads because they made her head look small, rejected her jersey because orange wasn't her colour, and asked for something chic and summery. When Matthews threatened to bench her she reminded him that job discrimination based on clothing or hairstyle was clearly another violation of her human rights.

She was given a charge card for a local high-fashion boutique and started the game in a yellow pant suit, the Lion logo on the side of her helmet replaced by a mug shot of Cyndi Lauper. And her number read "Like, One".

On the Lions' first play from scrimmage she tapped centre Al Wilson on the shoulder, demanding that he hand her the ball like a gentleman because no lady ever reached between a man's legs on the first date. Wilson picked up the ball, turned, and handed it to her. Linebacker Ty Jones charged through the hole, tackled her and threw her to the turf. She awoke in a chic body cast.

"Baseball..." she whispered to the battery of lawyers, civil rights and women's action group reps leaning over her bed. "I've always wanted to pitch for the Blue Jays..."

Two were trampled in the rush to the phones. She lay back on the pillow, a faint smile touching her lips. Baseball would be fun. Oh, she hated spitting and cussing and chewing tobacco, but she'd soon make them stop doing that. After all, she knew her rights.

GENESIS

November 14, 1985

1. In the beginning, there were Teams.

2. And Teams begat Cheerleaders.

3. And General Managers said "Let them be built, that our male customers would salivate and dream great dreams and pay money to come back and watch them inhale and exhale every playing day."

4. And they were built.

5. And it was good.

6. And the Marketing Men said "Lo, for the fans who are not of the male persuasion and dream not dreams of Cheerleaders builteth fore and aft, let there be Cheerleaders of the male persuasion.

7. "And let them dress in cloaks of many colours, or torn jeans and numbered sweaters; and let them waddle like ducks or cluck like chickens; or beat upon a drum and make a great noise, so that the multitudes will know when to create bedlam and confound our enemies."

8. And the Earth was struck by a plague of ducks, chickens, lumberjacks, gophers, dogs, bears, armadillos and humans whose elevators reacheth not the top floor.

9. And they clothed themselves in strange raiments, and waddled like ducks, and clucked like chickens, and smote upon their drums to confound the enemy.

10. And it was God-awful.

11. And the Leaders were a Chicken who was funny, and a Schoolteacher named Krazy George, who was not.

12. And the Chicken and the Schoolteacher begat Ralph the Dog, who begat Gainer the Gopher, who begat the Ipsco Goose, who begat Jerome, the Gnome Who Lives Under the Dome.

13. And from their figurative loins sprang a host of humans who made waves and funny sounds and clothed themselves in gorilla suits and did other things that caused attendants from nearby Hospitals to yearn for their butterfly nets.

14. And the People, being foolish, forsook the ways of spontaneity and cheered only on cue.

15. And the Lord looked down and said "Enough is enough. Let the Angel who created this abomination come down with the shorts."

16. And it was so.

17. And Krazy George awoke from his bed five days before the Big Game and learned that he was out of work.

18. And he was sore anguished, and just plain sore.

19. And Krazy said unto the Lions, "Why hast thou forsaken me? Have I not served thee well for a decade? What is this contract I see before me? Wilst not thou honour it?"

20. And the Lions said unto Krazy, "There is no more bread to cast upon your waters. Our Angel has tapped out. Thou art history, babe."

21. And Krazy rent his garment, and was sore afraid.

22. And a Radio Station, seeking to ride upon the fame of the Cheerleader, offered to pay his salary to cheer at the Big Game. But the Lions said "Nay! We will play the game without thee."

23. And it was good.

24. In fact, it was great.

GOD, FLEET FEET — AND THE GIZ

November 27, 1987

Counting his parents, there were 11 people in the three-room house in the Memphis ghetto where Henry "Gizmo" Williams was born and spent the first 15 years of his life. All but four are now dead.

Multiple sclerosis took his mother first, but not without a fight. It dragged her down slowly and moved on to claim his brother

Milton and sister Barbara. Two years ago it took Edgar, the eldest, the one who'd become a father to the rest of the family when the parents divorced. In the years between, sister Charlene died of a drug overdose, brother Ross was shot and killed by a stray bullet from a robbery across the street, and his father died in a fire.

"I used to think about it," admits the Giz. "You know, wondering whether I had it [MS], whether it was going to get me, too. But I quit that. Now I just let the Lord guide me."

He says it matter-of-factly, minus the me-and-God overtones of post-game jockdom. "When I was 15 I moved from Memphis to live with Aunt Urshalean Dorsey in Tunica, Mississippi. She was a strong, church-going lady. When I didn't want to go, she made me. And every time I came out, I felt better. I don't know why, I just did."

The house was bigger than the one in Memphis. It had to be. Urshalean had her own kids and family. "About 21 of us in three or four bedrooms," he recalls. He spent four years there — happy years, because while there might not have been much, there always seemed to be enough.

But then, happiness always did come easily to the Gizmo.

"In Memphis it wasn't the best house, but I had a place, and food and clothes. If somebody else had something better, well, that was them. I remember I wanted Converse running shoes, but they cost $16. My friend had them and I was running around in three-dollar shoes. But I just told myself his were new and mine were, too."

He knew about money and the things it could buy. ("My brother Otis and me were the youngest, so we were really tight. We shared everything, and it had to be even. If he had 25¢ we'd split it, ten cents each, and throw the nickel away so nobody had more.") But only once was he tempted to take the easy way that was a way of life in the mean streets of the ghetto.

"About five of us decided we'd steal a bicycle. We did it, and we got caught, and they took us home in a police car. I was sitting there in the back seat like in a steel cage. I told myself 'I'll never do this again.' I wanted my freedom."

Drugs were also something for someone else if that was their choice.

"What I learned was, find out who you are. I know how to adjust to people. I started to learn in high school. If you're my best friend and do drugs, that's you. I'll still be your friend. I'll have a beer, but if my friends see me with one they might come and take it from me and say 'Man, that's not you!' "

Given the conditions, it was an attitude that had to be built on a rock of pure stubbornness. And that the Gizmo had in spades.

Football had grabbed him in elementary school, where he played only because the coach paid the $30 registration fee. It never let go. Coming out of high school as a track specialist with world-class speed, he was 5'4" tall, weighed 155 pounds, and resented anyone who suggested he was too small to play.

The football coach at the University of Mississippi tried it and Gizmo went home and tore up the four-year track scholarship the school had given him. His lady gym teacher did it, and when he turned pro with the Memphis Showboats after two years at Northwest Mississippi Junior College and two years at East Carolina University leading the nation in kickoff returns, he rushed back to the school to tell her.

He chose the Showboats for the same reason. "I always said if there was a pro team in Memphis that was where I'd be," he said. "Just to show them."

There were NFL clubs interested when the Showboats folded, but by that time he'd talked to the Edmonton Eskimos' personnel man, Frankie Morris. He didn't know where Edmonton was — "Take a map," Morris advised him, "and look on top of Montana" — but he agreed to come anyway and now he's in the Grey Cup game Sunday against the Toronto Argonauts.

He is a pleasant picture, sitting in an easy crouch against the wall at B.C. Place stadium. He smiles a lot, tells his story matter-of-factly, and talks of Otis and Larry, the brothers still alive, and of his five-year-old daughter from junior college days, Paris Nicole, who lives with her mother.

He says he will teach his children that life is a gamble, that things don't come easily, and that the best things won't be there because Daddy is a pro football player. Life, he says, is for living and trying and remembering all that is good.

The Gizmo: bigger now than in college days — two inches taller and 26 pounds heavier — muscular, but still without the look of a pro football player, a fireplug who's been clocked at 4.1 to 4.9 seconds over 40 yards and says he doesn't believe there's a man in football anywhere who's faster.

Some day, in a year, perhaps, when his contract is up, he may go to the NFL to find out. All it will take is someone to say he can't.

FIRST AND LIFE FOR THE FLEA

August 4, 1988

Terry Evanshen punched his wife last week. She was so happy, she cried. He wasn't supposed to be able to punch her, or hold her, or maybe even speak to her. In the minds of a lot of people, he was supposed to be dead.

One month ago tonight the paramedics hauled what was left of Terry Evanshen out of the wreckage of his car, did the best they could while rushing him to the intensive-care unit, and began thinking of him in the past tense.

He was in a coma. He had eight broken ribs, collapsed lungs, a spleen damaged beyond saving, a broken ankle and a right arm that had to be opened end-to-end because it had blown up like a balloon. Those were the injuries they knew about. The brain was jungle country, with unknown tigers crouched and waiting in the darkness. The only thing anyone knew for sure was that if he hadn't been an athlete he'd be dead.

Some day, Lorraine Evanshen will give her husband all the gruesome details of the accident his mind has blocked out, the July 4 nightmare outside Oshawa, Ontario, when a man drove his truck through a red light and smashed Evanshen's car on the driver's side.

But not now. Not when he is standing up in front of the TV set, dropping into a boxer's crouch and tossing mock jabs at any shoulder within range. Not when the doctors say he's got 65% of his mental faculties back, with a good chance of regaining most of the rest. Not when they say that far down the road after restructuring and therapy, the right arm could be almost good as new, that the vision in one eye is normal and that some of the blurring in the other could recede.

Now is for letting go, ever so slightly, of that breath she's been holding for a month. Now is for daring to allow the luxury of real hope. "That old bugger of mine," she says fondly, "I always said he had nine lives, and I guess he's used up half of them on this one."

There is a waver in her voice, a threadbare sound that tells of the daily 14-hour stretches at the hospital, so many of them beside a loved one in a coma from which he might never recover. But mostly there is amazement mixed with joy.

"He wants to jog," she says. "He's using those grips to exercise his hands. He wants to be out and doing things. We're not kidding ourselves. We know there's a long way to go, and no guarantees. But he's up, and he's *talking*."

For those who knew Evanshen in his 14 years in the Canadian Football League, that's the most encouraging sign of all. He always was a yapper, a needler, a flea of a flanker who'd never use one word when 30 would do. Tongue-tied, he'd never have played. "He's talking a mile a minute," Lorraine says. "Not all of it makes sense. There are periods where he'll just — go away — in mid-sentence. And he'll need speech therapy. But it's coming back. It's coming back!"

She can only shake her head at the response to word of her husband's injury. Prime Minister Brian Mulroney called. So did Harold Ballard. Bernie Faloney, who played his last season in Montreal, dropped in to talk to him. Bernie recalled a play they used to run, and gave the signals. "Sure," Terry said, "but how about this one?" — and made the calls for another route.

Wires and letters arrived by the hundreds, mostly from B.C. and Calgary, but some from all over Canada and one from Australia. "Tell them thank you for me," she says. "They'll never know how much it meant."

The miracle comeback is a daily, ongoing battle. And every day there are little signs of progress. The other day, Lorraine Evanshen took her husband to the washroom.

"They need a urine sample, honey," she said.

He thought it over for a minute. "The people around here are crazy," he complained. "There's nothing wrong with my urine. It's my goddamn head!"

Hang in there, you guys. Both of you.

"NOBODY ASKS ABOUT MY BRAIN..."

June 20, 1989

In mid-sentence, the fog rolls in to blanket one of the lights in Terry Evanshen's mind. He clenches his fists, shakes his head in frustration, and wills it away.

"The words," he says. "I reach for them sometimes and they're not there."

It is not an apology. His brain is damaged, parts of it pounded into the shadows by an accident the doctors can't believe he survived. Fourteen years of pro football taught him what you do to whip an opponent like that: You scout him, you face him, and you keep going at him until somebody blows the whistle and says it's over.

181

He is gaining, yard by yard. But Lord, it must be hard.

"The other night they showed a videotape of the highlights of my career," he said. " 'That's you,' they said. And all I could do was say 'All right, if you say so, it must be me.' And I *know* it's me, catching that pass or scoring that touchdown, but..."

He gropes for the words that will make his listener understand.

"I can't remember the excitement," he says wistfully. "The tingle of making the play. The *emotion* of that particular moment. It's gone. So much of it is gone..."

When they pulled Terry Evanshen from the wreckage of a car broadsided by a light-runner at 90 km/h a year ago outside Oshawa, the paramedics were speaking in the past tense. Eight broken ribs, collapsed lungs, ruptured spleen, undetermined head injuries, right arm so swollen by internal pressure that doctors opened it, wrist to elbow, lest it explode.

"The doctors said later that when they opened him up, some of his organs had literally been pushed high up into the chest cavity," says Fred Evanshen, gazing across the lunch table at his brother. "They moved them back down. They looked at the ribs, all broken. They looked at the arm and knew it had to come off. But through all that the body was twitching and moving like it was already fighting back, so they held off. Now the ribs are healed. They look like boomerangs and he's got scars you wouldn't believe — but look at him."

He's right. The exterior remains unchanged. A few days past his 45th birthday with the wife and three daughters back home on the farm in Ontario, he retains the boyish good looks of the kid whose numbers and tenacity carried him to the CFL Hall of Fame in 1984, the youngest player so honoured: Eighty touchdowns, 600 receptions, two Schenley Awards as the league's top Canadian player, all done with a self-confidence that sometimes passed cockiness on the curve.

But inside...

"People don't want to know about brain damage," he says. "They say 'You look great' and ask about the arm, and they're happy for me. But inside ... that's different.

"You want to be the same as you were. You try to camouflage the problem. But I'll be holding a conversation like this, and trying to remember something or get the right word, and it's *exhausting*. I'll be trying to fit the pieces together and I'll grab one and it just *goes away*. And I have to fight to get it back.

"It's like driving in a fog and you know if you veer left or right you'll wind up in the ditch, so you concentrate everything on just going straight ahead, and all the while you're praying there's nobody parked up ahead."

He is blessed, and knows it, by a wife and kids who hung in through the coma and the trauma and the pain of the past year. His athlete's body and will have brought him this far, but it's not a mountain you climb alone.

"Fourteen-, 16-hour days in that hospital," he said. "Lorraine would be there. And because I'm used to doing things myself I've become a nit-picker and a pain in the ass. The other day she was taking a break, visiting her folks in Montreal, and I was walking around the farm and all of a sudden it me, really hit me, how much she'd been through. And I was on the phone with her for half an hour, crying my eyes out and telling her how much I love her."

He cannot work. Not yet. The executive position he held before the accident may be out of reach. He sticks to the physiotherapy, listens to the doctors, and never asks when, or if.

"One year, four years, five ..." he says. "Maybe all the lights will come on, maybe they won't."

And maybe, some day, he can look at that highlight film again, and feel the sting of the pass on his hands and the jar of a tackle seconds later. It's there, in the shadows, and he'll never quit looking.

MY SISTER HAS 65 ROSES

August 29, 1989

In the dozen years since it first was told, the story has touched millions of hearts.

The little boy was trying to explain why his sister was coughing and had to take all those pills and undergo the daily therapy and medical treatments just to stay alive. He couldn't pronounce "cystic fibrosis," but he tried: "My sister has 65 roses," he said. And every birthday thereafter, the parents presented the girl with roses, as a gesture of love and remembrance.

"My sister has 65 roses..."

Five words from a little boy, but they became a battle cry.

In 1977 Don Baylor, then with the California Angels, gathered his teammates and fans and formed the first 65 Roses chapter to raise money for cystic fibrosis research. Today there are chapters in more than 60 North American cities, supported by major league baseball, NHL, NBA, NFL and CFL clubs.

The newest is here in Vancouver. Yesterday, the honorary chairman, Lui Passaglia, was asked to explain why he'd gotten involved, why he and Ottawa's Dean Dorsey are taking pledges and competing to see which scores the most points in the upcoming home-and-home series between the B.C. Lions and the Ottawa Rough Riders.

"I have four healthy children," he said.

That's what it's all about, really: the lucky reaching out to the unlucky. There is a chance now that cystic fibrosis will be cured in the next three or five or ten years. There's been a major breakthrough: the isolation of the gene that triggers the destroyer that takes the lives of more Canadian children than any other hereditary disease.

But it is a chance, nothing more. Doctors describe it as a base camp at the foot of Everest. They've identified the mountain that must still be conquered. In the meantime, children die, or live with the knowledge that few make it to 21.

"I have four healthy children..."

Dean Dorsey and Lui Passaglia are hamming it up a bit on the conference call set up in an effort to generate publicity for the 65 Roses challenge.

Dorsey, who is 32, calls Passaglia "Sir" in deference to his age. Passaglia, who is 35, says that B.C. fans are going to bury Ottawa fans. It is a soft-sell exercise, because the cause should need no selling.

Thursday night in Ottawa, fans will sign pledge forms promising so much for every point Dorsey kicks against the Lions in the two games. Next Tuesday, B.C. fans will do the same for Lui here. Pledge forms will be circulated through the city and handed to fans as they enter.

Neither man gives a hoot who "wins" as long as the dollars (tax deductible) are there in large amounts and the right (i.e., his) team takes the points. In the struggle for the donation dollar it is a method of grabbing public attention, of laying before the public the case of children whose lives centre around daily rehabilitation and treatment and trying to shut out the ticking of that invisible clock that is stealing their future.

You see, they know the story of the little boy who said his sister had 65 roses. They know all of it.

They know that the little boy, so protective of his sister, had cystic fibrosis himself. He was 12 years old when he died. His sister reached 21. She was, they know, one of the lucky ones.

BIG DAY IN TURKEY NECK BEND

October 18, 1990

"Oh, they'll be a-whoopin' and a-hollerin' in Turkey Neck Bend come Saturday," I assured everybody. "Mind you, a few noses might be out of joint down the road a piece in Bug Tussle and Black Gnat, but what do they know?"

"The net," somebody whispered. "Get the net!"

"Eagle Keys is going into the Canadian Football League Hall of Fame," I explained. "You know Eagle — coached the Edmonton Eskimos and the Saskatchewan Roughriders and the B.C. Lions? Once said he loved his wife Joyce so much he'd keep her even if she was an import? Well, he was raised in Turkey Neck Bend, Kentucky, and when they get the word down there..."

Right then came The Great Idea: I would phone Turkey Neck Bend and tell somebody the big news. It would rage like wildfire down the entire street and maybe all 27 people (unless there's been a population explosion) could sign a card or something.

I called Kentucky information.

She'd never heard of Turkey Neck Bend. "The closest I have," she said, "is Turkey Foot."

"Try Bug Tussle," I said. "Or Black Gnat. They're just down the road."

No Bug Tussle. No Black Gnat. Something was rotten in Kentucky.

I phoned Eagle. Over 25 years he's fibbed to me sometimes, like when he said he got his name because his father liked birds. ("And I got me three sisters: Robin, Sparrow and Crow. Crow, she's the ugly one.") But I knew he wouldn't lie about his roots.

"Can't find it!" he said. "Well, shoot, it's right there just across the Cumberland River outside Tomkinsville. You got to drive through Fawbush Hollow. You'll come to other places like Mud Lick and Possum Trot, but keep goin' and you run right into the Cumberland, and right across it there she is, Turkey Neck Bend."

It is, he conceded, kind of off the beaten track. "One time we went back and I wanted to show Joyce where it was and I got on the wrong road. We pulled up to this little gas station that looked familiar, but it wasn't Turkey Neck Bend at all. Danged if it wasn't Bug Tussle!"

I told him about my plan to let Turkey Neck Bend know that one of theirs was in the Hall of Fame. Eagle kind of figured it might be a waste of phone money, him not being back for a lot of years, not even the time they threatened to secede.

Secede?

"Yeah. They wanted a ferry across that river that ran all the time, because if it was shut down you had to drive 50 miles around to get there. And when people said no, Turkey Neck Bend was all set to secede and join up with Tennessee."

It was, he conceded, a near thing.

So I scrapped the search for Turkey Neck Bend and remembered how much fun it was talking to Eagle when he was coaching, and how he'd talk football forever if he thought you really wanted to know. Newspaper guys in Saskatchewan say he'd sit all night swapping stories, then drag them off to his place with the dawn, open the door and say "Joyce! Company! How 'bout some bacon and eggs?"

I remembered the rare times when, under duress, he'd rummage in the kitchen drawer for a couple of big spoons and start slapping them over his knee. Lord, he could make those suckers fly.

And I remember the time in his talent-poor days with the Lions when he explained the whole coaching profession in one sentence.

"It's amazin' how bad a coach I became," he said, "when I didn't have a quarterback."

QUINTUPLE THREAT MAN

January 21, 1990

As a 1983 B.C. Lion, Sammy Greene was a quintuple threat — kick returner, pass receiver, boozer, pill-popper and cocaine snorter. "If it would make me feel good, I'd try it," he says.

Feeding his abuses cost him about $2,000 a week — probably a lot more than the other users on that 1983 team that went to the Grey Cup game without him. "Yeah, I wouldn't say I was the only one," he admits. "We kept it in the closet pretty good. I'd do something [get drugs] for them; they'd get something for me. We were a close-knit family."

He is speaking quietly. We are, after all, in church...

"Sammy Greene's turned preacher," the caller said. "He was at the Lux Theatre over on East Hastings, on the stage with the microphone talking to the street people. They say he's found God."

Sammy Greene? The B.C. Lions' Sammy, who tried out with about 14 teams in three leagues and was chopped by all of them? Sammy Greene, who tore up the CFL for 14 games in 1983, then got cut, and Don Matthews would never say why? Sammy Greene, who tried a comeback in 1988 and was doing pretty well at training camp until he told coach Larry Donovan that he couldn't play with Matt Dunigan?

You're kidding.

"Another one," I thought. "Another jock in big trouble who probably found God 20 seconds after the cops found him. A scam. It's got to be a scam…"

"I have trouble watching football games on TV," Sammy Greene says. "It hurts too much. I look at Merv [Fernandez] playing for the Raiders, and I know he wasn't that much better than I was. Ronnie Lott [49ers safety], he'll be in the Super Bowl. I played against him in college. And I know I could have been there, and I threw it away."

The face above the shirt and tie with the blue blazer looks less lived in than abandoned. In 48 hours he'd be hitting the streets of Skid Road again — talking to the hookers, the homeless, the winos, the drug pushers with whom he used to deal. After that, he'd be on the stage at the neighbourhood Salvation Army branch, trying to pass along the message he says has worked for him.

But now, sitting on one of the fold-away metal chairs that stretch row upon row at the Vancouver Christian Centre that has become a home and refuge, Sammy Greene is laying out the other story, the one about the football career he couldn't handle.

"The day coach Matthews cut me, I'd come to practice under the influence. I said I didn't see why I should have to go play the next game in Regina when we already had a playoff spot clinched. Heck, all I wanted to do was get back to my room and finish what I had. We argued, and I said some rude things, and he cut me."

Matthews took a lot of flak for refusing to say why. "He was protecting me," Sammy says. "The coaches always protected me. I was spending more than I was making, so every time I reached an incentive point in my contract, for passes caught or something, I'd go in and ask for it then. And they'd give it to me. They were protecting me. I just wish that once somebody would have quit protecting me. Because then maybe I'd have gotten some help and …"

187

"Sammy's crazy," one of the '83 Lions told me back then. "You know, one time he left his helmet in front of his locker and somebody peed in it. He put it on, got all that stuff all over him and yelled. But then he just went on out to practice."

"Every team I went to it was the same," says Sammy Greene. "Every team! I'd start off good, but I'd always feel like there was something missing. And I'd go to the booze and drugs trying to find it, and my confidence would go, and I'd be gone."

But no one ever blew the whistle. Not on him, not on the teammates he says were using the same stuff, although perhaps to a lesser degree. Even in college, they were "helping" him. Because Sammy Greene could play football, and if you could perform between the white lines on the field, the white lines you were snorting didn't matter.

As a high school hotshot in Santa Barbara, he went on a recruiting visit to the University of Las Vegas-Nevada in 1978, and came home with five bottles of Jack Daniels. When the college coach questioned him, he said they were for his mother. "Okay," said the coach, and he got his scholarship.

Stardom in college was a two-edged sword, because now it wasn't just booze, it was drugs. "People gave me things," he says. "Money, everything. And my dosage increased with my popularity."

The Miami Dolphins drafted him third in 1981. ("There I was," he says, "a guy with a cocaine habit, in the drug capital of the world.") He played the pre-season, then bounced from team to team, league to league. In Regina, on one of his last kicks at the cat, he met a girl named Carol who became his wife, hung in there through the troubles and a move to Vancouver, and eventually led him to the church.

"If you ever play again," she said, "it's going to take an act of God."

By this time he was trying to quit, and even telling himself he was making progress. He'd go to prisons to speak out on the dangers of substance abuse. On the way home in the car, he'd have a drink.

Crunch time came at the church.

"At first I sat in the very back row," he says. "Then, gradually, I started moving up. And then I back-slid."

That was when Pastor Henry Hinn took him aside.

"You need a change of environment," he said, and hauled him off to Florida for a church convention. There he heard Jimmy

Swaggert, Oral Roberts and other evangelists, and came home determined to carry the word to Skid Row. "That is Hell down there," he says. "I know it. I've been there."

Sammy Greene removes the TV mike from his lapel. "Thank you," he says, and shakes hands. His life, he says, is just beginning. In two weeks, he'll be 30 years old.

Chapter Eight

TAKE ME OUT OF THE BALL GAME

Someone (I suspect Bob Krieger, our resident cartoonist and baseball nut) has painstakingly compiled a list of 35 of Tom Boswell's *99 Reasons Why Baseball is Better Than Football* and left it in my mailbox.

There are approximately 12 billion major league games on satellite TV, all of them involving people named Manny, Jose and Reggie. If they held a massive uniform swap, hardly anyone would notice.

And Jeani Read, one of our Womenpersons of the Opposite Sex columnists, has published an ode to Opening Day. Now, I like Jeani. She looks good and smells better and it isn't her fault that God put her on earth to show other women how to wear blue jeans. We get along fine because both of us know that I am old and married and harmless.

We have our differences. Jeani thinks people who watch football or hockey can't put on their CAT tractor cap without turning the brim sideways to set it on Lock so it shouldn't fall off. No one will ever convince me that Ms. isn't short for mistake. She thinks football is a game played by savages. I think baseball is a game designed to give millionaire jocks a time slot on TV to complain in public when they get a bwister on their wittle fingie.

And once a year, she writes about the joys of Opening Day.

Normally, I say nothing. I forgive Krieger his passion because he is on the way to being the best cartoonist in the land and some day I may want to buy an original, cheap. I even forgive him for his brother, one of those guys who, if you ask him how many redheaded shortstops are currently hitting over .225, looks at you and says "Hitting right- or left-handed?" And then he tells you.

But this time JR has gone too far. I quote:

"I opened my favourite baseball book, a book of poetry and prose and random pieces, exceedingly romantic ..."

Right there, you have what's wrong with baseball: Not the game, the people who watch it. They're not satisfied to accept it as a game like any other game, sometimes good, sometimes bad, sometimes mediocre. They don't dare, because if they did that they'd have to admit that on a lot of nights the game packs all the excitement of marathon clam-shucking.

So they justify a sport in which each team plays 162 games before the important stuff starts by crediting it with some sort of ethereal quality, some aura only the true fans can perceive.

Baseball writers reel off things like "There is no clock except the events of the game. Baseball's time is seamless and invisible. Since baseball is measured only in outs, all you have to do is succeed utterly... and you have defeated time." And "The business of baseball is dreams."

Translation: This game is so slow that you have to line the players up against a stationary object to make sure they're moving.

Baseball fans sneer at football, which requires a huddle to call the next play. This from a sport in which a guy who has only three pitches shakes off four signs.

Football is so slow, they say, then cheer when a guy who's just hit a baseball out of the park trots around the bases tipping his cap. In a perfect football game there are great catches, great passes, great hitting. In baseball's perfect game, two guys play catch.

I do not hate baseball. Alexander Cartwright or Abner Doubleday or whoever invented the game made a major contribution to North American society: a nice, quiet way to fill in time between hockey and football while catching up on your poetry. And remember, you pitchers, watch out for those fingie bwisters.

WAY TO GO, WINFIELD

August 7, 1983

Never mind the pennant race. Did or did not New York Yankees' outfielder Dave Winfield deliberately aim the baseball he hurled at the skull of that seagull, thereby rendering it dead?

Lord, I hope so.

I hope he sighted in, reared back and let fly with malice aforethought. I hope he screamed "This is for the statues! And the bald guys! And my car! See how good it feels when something lands on *your* head, you bleeping feathered flush toilet!"

And if he'd missed, I'd hope the ball boy would have the common decency to throw the ball back and let him keep shooting till he got it done.

There's been a lot of sanctimonious claptrap since Winfield put the hit on the seagull during the Blue Jays-Yankees game Thursday night in Toronto. "Omigoodness! He killed a helpless little bird! You'll burn in Hell for this, Winfield! You'll get traded to the Mets! God sees the little sparrow fall, you creep!"

What he should have received, of course, was a standing ovation. Officials estimate that there are 88,000 mating pairs of seagulls within one mile of Exhibition Stadium, most of whom use it as a missile range when crowds gather. So one less is a big deal?

Two nights earlier, one of them spent an entire game in centre field. I assume it fell asleep about the third inning. If Winfield had tripped over the bird and broken his skull, would the cops have come out to grab the bird, drag it to the police station and make it hang around for three hours while the paper work was done so it could swear to come back to Canada on a specified date to face charges under the Criminal Code of "causing unnecessary suffering to a human"?

Substitute "bird" for "human" and that's exactly what happened to Winfield. He threw a practice ball in the general direction of a seagull sitting on the grass some 75 to 80 feet away. More than likely he was trying to make the damned bird get lost. But he hit it, it died, and some yo-yo laid charges. Until they were dropped yesterday, Winfield faced a possible $500 fine and/or six-month jail sentence for doing by accident what we've all yearned to do a hundred times.

Monday night the Blue Jays are in Yankee Stadium. Toronto city manager Paul Godfrey plans to walk to centre field and apologize to Winfield personally. And well he should. The issue is not whether God sees the little sparrow fall. It's whether He sees what the little seagull drops. If He does, Winfield can quit worrying.

NO PLAY, HONEY, NO PLAY!

August 8, 1985

The major league baseball strike was settled in a bedroom, not a board room. It was settled at approximately 11:55 p.m. Tuesday by Mrs. Claudel Jefferson, wife of the well-known outfielder, in a ploy as old as the labour movement: threatened withdrawal of services.

History will not likely record her contribution. The Peter Ueberroths, the Don Fehrs and the Lee McPhails will be taking the credit today, the commissioner blushing becomingly and saying "Aw shucks" a lot at suggestions his intervention was the key, Fehr and McPhail each insisting his side won. But this is the way it really happened:

The Jeffersons were just settling into the king-sized waterbed in their $500,000 town house. Tammy Jefferson, already warmed by the marvellous Bordeaux she'd discovered in the specialty shop to serve with the steaks at dinner, swirled her brandy snifter and reflected on the wonderful way things had worked out.

"Just think, Claudel," she sighed. "Three years ago you didn't know whether you'd get out of high school, the hubcap market was down, your dad had cancelled your allowance and we barely had enough money to keep the ghetto blaster in batteries. Now here you are making $360,000 per year for seven months work, we've got this lovely home — and, you marvellous man, you told me to order the mink for my birthday."

"JEEZ!" he groaned. "The mink! I forgot about the mink!"

"What's the matter, darling?" she cooed. "You don't have to do anything about the mink. I've already ordered it. Did I tell you I got the white one? Costs more, but like the lady at the store says, tray cheek."

"Uh, honey," he stumbled, "I bin meanin' to talk to you 'bout them minks. I think we gotta put the little suckers on hold."

"On *hold*? Claudel Jefferson, what do you mean, on hold? You said..."

"I *know* what I said, woman. But that was before. That was when I was workin'. Right now I ain't workin', I'm walkin'. We're on strike. No pay, no play."

"No *pay*? You're making $360,000 a year! If you weren't just an average player, if you could hit or at least talk like that Reggie Jackson, you could be making two million dollars and I could have mink underwear if I felt like it. Who *says* you're on strike?"

193

"Donald Fehr. Like, he's our lawyer. He says we ain't gettin' our fair share and we gots to make some sacrifices now in the interests of long-term gain and to put an end to major league slavery."

"And Mr. Fehr," she said sweetly. "Does *his* salary stop while you're on strike?"

" 'Course not, woman! He's a lawyer! Now, while you're can-celling them minks, you better maybe stall them off for a month or two on payments for the Rolls. We ain't gettin' no strike pay, so..."

"Claudel," she snapped, "you listen to me and listen good. You ain't in this world on no scholarship, honey. You don't play baseball, you got a great future pumpin' gas. Guy hadn't noticed you playin' stickball on the street and hittin' the damned thing over the apartment block you might still be gettin' our DE-ssert by boostin' a pushcart.

"You wanna talk negotiations? Okay, here's my final offer. You go tell that smartass Mr. Fehr and your smartass teammates that I am gonna be on the phone talkin' to the other wives all day tomorrow. You walk, we walk. We walk with half of everythin' you got, forever.

"And one more thing," she snarled as she slammed the bedroom door behind him. "When you're workin' in that filling station and we walk by, you ain't gonna have no trouble recognizin' me. I'll be the one wearin' the *mink!*"

Fourteen hours later the strike was over. Mr. Ueberroth praised both sides. He did not mention Mrs. Claudel Jefferson. When it comes to playing hardball, the commissioner knows diddly squat.

THE OLD BALL GAME

October 12, 1989

American League umpiring supervisor Marty Springstead has fired back at the Toronto Blue Jays and their post-playoff whining that Oakland relief pitcher Dennis Eckersley was doctoring baseballs with an emery board.

"What did they want us to do, strip-search the guy?" he fumed. "Did they really want us to dig down in his pants and check the guy's crotch in front of 50,000 people?"

Well, yes.

Not that I see anything wrong with Eckersley using an emery board. In the macho, full-contact world of professional baseball, where brave men grit their teeth and laugh at the risk of pimple or wart, the ever-pre-sent danger of improper cuticle care cannot be over-emphasized.

But strip-searches would bring a new dimension to a game sadly in need of one. In the case of a matinee-idol type like Eckersley, the mere thought that he might be stripped down in a search for performance-enhancing equipment might increase the Oakland gate by 10,000 per game. And that's just counting the girls.

The marketing possibilities are endless. Morgana the Kissing Bandit could expand her field of operations and hire out as the Designated Searcher — although, given her build, she could be in grave difficulty if she had to straighten up.

Or, in the case of the Blue Jays, they could let Fergie Olver do the play-by-play:

"Eckersley checks the runner... now he checks his nails... Wait a minute! Eckersley's got something in his hand! What is that thing, Buck?"

"Uh, it's a baseball, Fergie."

"So *that's* what one of those things looks like! Gee, no wonder we can't hit it. It's so round and everything. And — it's *used*! It's got stitches all over it! Boy, you'd think for an important series like this the umpires would make sure our guys had new balls to hit...

"HOLD IT! We've called time! Obviously we've seen something we don't like about Eckersley's delivery. Cito Gaston is talking to umpire Marty Springstead... now he's waving to the bullpen...

"Let's see, we've got a lefty and a righty warming up. Probably anticipating another one-two-three inning for our guys... No! Cito must be calling in Morgana. He's holding both hands in front of his chest!

"Yes! Here she comes! The Jays will send the Bandit against Eckersley!

"It's a dangerous move, Buck. I don't think she's had time for a warm-up, although even from here, Tom Henke does look a bit flustered. Now she's approaching Eckersley on the mound...oh, migawd, Buck, she's inhaling and holding her breath! Does she let it all hang out or doesn't she?

"She's checking his shirt for vaseline. Now she's got his mouth open, looking for slippery elm or tobacco. A lot of your pitchers will do that, Buck: Pretend to chew because they like it, then spit the stuff all over the ball when the umpire isn't looking. A little inside baseball stuff for you Blue Jay fans out there... Certainly *our* guys would never try anything like that, but these Athletics, well, I dunno...

"She's got him stripped to the waist now... The organist is playing bump-and-grind music and I think... yes, Eckersley does seem to be twitching along. Probably trying to distract Morgana, Buck, but an old pro like her won't fall for it. See, she's pulling the pants down and...

"Now she's reaching for the jockstrap. She's peering under it... Wait a minute! They're leaving! They can't do that! There's a *game* on! Buck — where are they going?"

"I dunno, Fergie. But wherever it is, they're going hand in hand."

BLIND JUSTICE

July 20, 1990

"The children with whom Mr. Rose will be working need a role model with whom they can identify in order to make the most of their chances in life."
— U.S. District Judge Arthur Spiegel, on making 1,000 hours of community service with inner-city youth part of Pete Rose's sentence for federal income-tax evasion.

Pete Rose, role model, cheated on his income tax, gambled on sports events in direct violation of baseball's rules of conduct, lied about it, then copped a plea when the feds had him cornered. Part of the income he didn't declare came from selling memorabilia of his great baseball career. He did that with such fervour that there's a joke among collectors that goes:

"You want the uniform Pete was wearing when he got the hit that broke Ty Cobb's record? Sure. What size, and do you want the road unie or the home?"

Nothing personal, Pete — but pick somebody else's inner city, okay? I'm just a tad tired of athletes who find remorse and/or God shortly after the authorities find them.

Ben Johnson cheated. He knew he was cheating when he was doing it. He says he's sorry and no doubt he is — but I haven't noticed him giving back any of the two million dollars or so he made at least partially as a result of that cheating.

Pete Rose cheated, and he is going to pay. The sentence — five months in jail, three months in a half-way house and a $50,000 fine — is compassionate. I've known compulsive gamblers, and it is a disease every bit as destructive as alcoholism for the gambler and the people he loves. The law has knocked him down, but not out. Fair enough.

But let's leave the kids out of it.

You want to send role models into the inner city, judge, send heroes, not instantly-reformed jerks. Send men and women who *came* from the environment, who hauled themselves out of it without bending the rules or betraying a trust. Send people who look upon autographs as a thank you, not an income supplement. Send winners, on and off the field.

Pete Rose could walk into an inner-city school and say "Hey, I did all those things, and I was wrong, and I'm sorry." The answer, spoken or not, would be the one I got last year from a bunch of 12-year-olds who asked me about anabolic steroids.

"They're harmful and they're illegal, and if you use them you're a cheat," I said. "Look at Ben Johnson. He cheated, and he got caught, and he's paying for it."

"Yeah," a boy answered, "and he's got about two million bucks and a Ferrari."

What's Old Pete going to tell them — that he was doing fine until he got caught, and that when the feds closed in he agreed to plead guilty to two years' worth of tax-evasion charges if they'd drop charges on two other years' returns? You listening, kids? When they've got you cold, plea bargain.

How about the values learned through competitive sport? Hey, kids, when you're a baseball star you can flog everything: your hat, your bat, your baseball — and let's face it, who really knows one baseball from another? Sell one, sell 20. Who gets hurt?

No, thank you. Let Pete Rose serve his sentence and yes, put him in the Hall of Fame because there's no way he could have cheated on even one of those 4,256 career hits. But don't set him up as Role Model (Reformed). The kids deserve the real thing.

THE GOSPEL ACCORDING TO CHARLIE
November 29, 1990

The Cincinnati school-board official in charge of finding a teaching job for Pete Rose at five inner-city schools says there'll be no special treatment for Charlie Hustle even if he was a world-class baseball superstar.

Rose's venture into the halls of lower learning for 1,000 hours of community service comes at the insistence of a federal court judge. Apparently he figured Rose could serve as a shining example for kids on the way up, having done five months in the slammer for evading taxes on money earned gambling and selling old uniforms, bats and his autograph.

He's to work a regular teaching shift, under the supervision of a certified teacher, running physical education classes and doing whatever other tasks he's assigned. All serious, teaching stuff.

Uh-huh.

We take you now to Watson Elementary, where Pete Rose is about to begin his first day as teaching assistant.

"Hi, Teach. I'm Pete Rose. You want my autograph? Five bucks. Eight-to-five you can get $20 for it without even leaving the teacher's room. Twenty bucks for five... let's see, that's double your money, right?..."

"Mr. Rose, I have been a teacher for 35 years and frankly the idea of your teaching the children here has me..."

"Thrilled to death. Yeah, I know. But listen, Teach, I'm kinda busy. That five months in the pen really shot my timing. Can't hardly sign more than 20 balls an hour anymore. You know what that'll do to my take on my next gig on the Home Shopping Network? First the wrist goes, then the spelling..."

"Mr. Rose, I fail to see what this has to do with..."

"Yeah, that teaching thing, right? Well, the way I figured, you could maybe get all the kids together right off while they've still got their lunch money. I tell 'em a couple of baseball stories, maybe do some health stuff about the dangers of jock itch and picking the right hair colouring, give 'em a discount on the autograph, and split."

"Split?"

"Yeah — like, go home. I got things to do, balls to sign. Listen, you do this for me and I'll give you something really special: the uniform I was wearing the day I broke Ty Cobb's base-hit record. You just tell me what size you are and whether you want road or away colours, and it's yours."

"Mr. Rose, I am not interested in your uniform, your hat, your bats, and most definitely not in your balls. You are here by court order to teach the children, to give them the benefit of your recent experience, and by heaven..."

"Geez, lady, what are they putting in that chalk dust? Okay, you want the kids to learn from what happened to me, trot 'em on over. Yo — you kids! Get your butts over here!"

"Thank you, Mr. Rose."

"No problem! Okay, kids, as you all know I was the greatest baseball player who ever lived. But this judge got upset because I got caught making bets and then lied about it. So I had to do time in this awful joint where the team was lousy and we weren't allowed to do road trips.

"But I overcame! And you know why? Because I knew that when I got out it would make a hell of a book and even a movie and I'd get rich all over again! So, the moral is, if you're gonna get caught doing stuff that's against the law, remember to be a superstar first. Okay, Teach?"

"Go home, Mr. Rose."

"You mean I'm excused?"

"Never, Mr. Rose. Just go home."

IT AIN'T IN THE CARDS

March 27, 1991

I do not often ask favours of you.

Mostly, I'm delighted to hear from you, even those among you who write or phone to call me a sexist pig, a know-nothing, big-mouthed jerk, a no-good, Gretzky-loving bleep-bleeper or all of the above. All it means is that you're reading what I'm writing. That being the case — hey, I've *got* you.

But this one time I beseech you on bended knee:

Please, no more calls about baseball cards. Or hockey cards. Or autographs of famous ex-jocks which might now be worth enough to put your kid through college so where do you write to find out how much you can get and how do you know the person you ask isn't lying through his or her teeth?

Thank you for sharing your heart-warming memories of the drawer full of Bee Hive corn syrup cards or Ace Percival Wheaties cards or old major league cards that your mother threw in the garbage while you were overseas defending our shores or working in the oil patch or doing time in the slammer.

I ask this for one important reason: I don't care.

If your mother threw away the cards that might have made you rich, take it up with your mother.

If you dimly recall having a Honus Wagner card that looked just like the one Bruce McNall and Wayne Gretzky bought for $451,000 only some big kid conned it from you for a Roger Maris and the gum that came with it, go steal it back.

If you once trashed a mint-condition Mickey Mantle rookie card by clothes-pinning it to your bicycle spokes as a pretend motor, go look in the bathroom mirror then beat your head against it while screaming "Stupid! Stupid! Stupid!"

Tell Dear Abby. Hit the confessional booth. Go to a shrink. But save the phone call or the 39¢, because I don't want to hear about it.

In the first place I am not a collector.

No, that's a lie. I do have an autograph from Ella Fitzgerald, a great and classy lady from the pre-lip-synch days when the instruments didn't have to be plugged in. Come May 7 I probably will try to get Mel Torme's when he plays the Orpheum.

But not to sell. Not to slip into a see-through plastic shell to cart off to the next card show to flog it if the price is right. I heard Ella sing when she had a range bigger than the Rockies. Torme is still the best around. They're not for selling, they're for remembering.

What bothers me about the sports-card craze is that it is no longer a hobby. It's become a stock with enormous growth potential.

Kids shouldn't be thinking that way. They should be trading and dealing their doubles in bedrooms full of footballs and baseballs and all the neat junk whose value is measured in use and memories, not flogging commodity futures at a trade show with adult sharpies looking for a steal.

If it's your hobby and you enjoy it, good for you. If you're the kind of person who delights in slapping your forehead and screaming "Omigod, Ma! That shoebox I had when I was a kid — *what did you do with it?*", have a ball.

But it ain't my department. It has nothing to do with sport. It did once, but not anymore.

Chapter Nine

FACES IN THE CROWD

It was spring. There was a Man at the Door.

"Man at the door says he's a football scout," the switchboard person reported. "Wants to see you."

It was a code we'd developed to screen out the wing-nuts. If the switchboard person thought the visitor was legit she'd say "Someone here to see you." If she thought we were dealing with a potential bowl of Froot-Loops, she would say "Man at the Door".

"Tell him he's 20 years too late. I'm donating my body to Goodwill. Science didn't want it."

Not all Men at the Door are bananas, although the percentage is high. They tend to wave their arms and shout a lot when you refuse to publicize their scheme to destroy the Russian hockey team by parachuting in a crack team of Commando groupies.

But I'd never had a Man at the Door football scout, and the hockey Men at the Door had grown tiresome. The last one had shown up in a Skid Row tux, waving a hockey stick. His plan was to curve the blue lines in at each end so the wingers could be ahead of the centre and not be offside. I sent him away with the phone number of a guy who wanted to end arguments over whether a puck actually crossed the goal line by running a laser beam from goalpost to goalpost. When in doubt, cross-pollinate.

A football scout Man at the Door could be different. "Okay," I relented. "Send him in."

He came in, a nondescript little guy in wrinkled clothes, about 36 hours behind in shaving. The first thing he said was that he wasn't really a football scout.

I fingered a copy spike.

"I'm a player agent," he said. "I got this kid, he's another Tony Dorsett. But he's a junior, see, and he wants to go for the money right now. I need to know the best team to take him to. The one with the most money."

Well, you never know.

"What's his name?" I asked.

He shook his head. "No way," he said.

I pointed out that before any pro team would negotiate to sign a kid they'd probably want to know who he was.

"But if I tell them who he is," he protested, "they won't need me! They can just go straight to the kid!"

He was, he admitted, new to the agent game.

You meet a lot of them in this business. That's the fascination of it: toilers, schemers, con men, dreamers, stars, unknowns, and innocents who lost when Fate played with loaded dice. They come from all walks of life. Some of them, like Nick the Matchmaker, are right out of Runyon.

Some of them make you laugh until you cry. Sometimes, you just cry.

Oh, yes — about the Man at the Door. Later, I found out he was a night janitor at a Seattle bank who'd written to a bunch of football players offering to be their agent. Fraud? No, just a little guy with big dreams. Everybody has to have dreams...

THE COMMISSIONER CRACKS DOWN

February 15, 1975

"Yes," the Commissioner admitted regretfully, "we had to disqualify the Chinese. They were using the old toothpaste-on-the-balls trick."

Windsor Olson was phoning from Seattle, agreeably fielding questions about a tiny item all but lost on Friday's sports pages:

PORTLAND, Ore. — The National Table Tennis League has ruled that the Republic of China men's team placed toothpaste on ping pong balls during the recent world championship matches. The decision stripped the Chinese team of its world title and awarded the championship to the Seattle Sockeyes.

The man who made the decision was Windsor Olson. Now he sounded a little tired — optimistic, but a little tired. It hasn't been the best year for burgeoning professional sports leagues and Windsor Olson, Commissioner of the NTTL, has had his problems.

"We've had a few disasters," he admitted. "There's been more teams dropping out than dropping in. But we've got nine now — Cedar Rapids, Spokane, Portland, Seattle, one in the midwest someplace... it's growing."

But what about the world championships?

"Well, what happened was, the NTTL brought the Chinese team over for a tour. When it came time for the world championships, we held them in a school gymnasium in a town called Hubbard, Oregon.

"What we didn't know was, the school needed a new lighting system. First the PA went out. Then the lights went out in the middle of the matches. Matter of fact, they went out eight times. We had 1,300 paid, but just before the last match the kids came racing out of the stands and stole all of our flags and some of my records.

"Now, after the first match, the Sockeyes' captain, Tom Ruttinger, started complaining that there was a foreign substance on the balls. He was still complaining when the whole thing was over and the Chinese had won. Then, when we started taking the tables down, we found toothpaste on the under-surface."

Toothpaste?

"Old Chinese ping pong trick," he explained. "Just like a spitter in baseball. The ball is so light that with a foreign substance on it, it will do almost anything. So I had to take the title away and give it to the Sockeyes."

Windsor Olson runs an armoured car service in Seattle, and is not a rich man. In 1972 he and a couple of buddies launched the NTTL, which he runs with a fanatic's zeal and a candour that is refreshing.

During the current hassle over Seattle's domed stadium, with baseball and football interests battling to keep the issue alive, Olson told a Seattle reporter that "The NTTL isn't too concerned with the stadium issue."

"We're not looking for 100,000 spectators," he explains, which is probably a good thing since his record crowd to date is 1,800. "Our game is probably best at 900 to 1,100. Everybody can see, we've got lights dropping down to the stage like a fight ring, the table's wired for sound, there's a lot of leaping around..."

Like the World Football League, the NTTL may have started too big. When you have franchises in Florida and Oregon and you do all your travelling by car, it can present problems. Like the Florida trip last year.

"Because of the energy crisis I hauled a big trailer full of gasoline drums behind the car," Olson recalled. "But in Blythe, Utah, a trailer bearing gave way and we had to leave it, gas and all, and push on. Wound up in an orange grove in Florida, out of gas, sitting there eating oranges and wondering how in hell we'd get home."

This year, Florida was out. But Anchorage was in, and the Chinese and Sockeyes drew an $8,000 gate, which isn't bad at $3.50 to five dollars. "We are on a five-year plan now in which we figure to outdraw minor baseball in the U.S.A.," Olson says modestly.

And there has been progress. The world championships, for instance, were worth $6,000 per man, which explains why things got pretty tense in Hubbard, Oregon.

Oh, by the way, Olson, how did the Chinese take the disqualification?

"Tell the truth, I'm a little embarrassed about that," admitted the man they call the King Kong of Ping Pong. "See, I'm not sure they understood. I kept explaining to their captain, but there was a language problem and he just nodded and smiled. Now they've gone home, and I won't be in contact with their people for a week or so.

"I think," he added, "they might still think they won."

Then he brightened.

"One thing, though. They haven't got the money yet."

And $6,000 per man will buy a lot of ping pong balls. Not to mention toothpaste.

GREENHORN AT WEMBLEY

March 23, 1978

He was a little man in a blue trenchcoat who looked like he might pick your pocket or cop your watch. He spoke like a man wearing novocaine lipstick.

"Yrlookinfrtickets?"

"I beg your pardon?"

"Tickets," he muttered, peering fearfully around the mob. "Yrlookinfrticketsornot?"

Well, you know how I feel about ticket scalpers. Bloodsuckers, they are. Jockstrap vampires. Should be folded, stapled, spindled and mutilated. Two little holes punched in their lower orchestra.

You know that business about the guy who paid $50 for two tickets to the Canucks-Canadiens game, then got escorted out of the Pacific Coliseum by the police because the tickets were stolen? I read that and laughed. Serves him right, boy. Anybody who'd deal with a scalper...

But this was different.

I was standing on the concourse outside Wembley Stadium — *Wembley!* — an hour before the Liverpool-Notts Forest League Cup game. We'd flown over specially, just to see it. *And I didn't have a ticket!*

That's how I met my first tout.

We were standing among a couple of thousand semi-sober, late-teens, early-20s soccer fans, many of whom were looking for tickets themselves. I don't know how he picked us out. Maybe it was because none of us was carrying anything red and white. Then again, maybe it was because none of us was carrying a beer bottle.

But there he was, materializing as though just beamed down from the *Enterprise*.

"Yrlookinfrtickets?"

Well, I was pretty excited.

"Hey," I yelled to my friends, "there's a guy here with..."

"Shuddup!" he hissed. "You tryin' to get me killed?"

He pivoted away from us and stared fixedly at the twin towers of Wembley. With his back turned, he gave me the facts of life.

"Don't show nuthin'," he whispered. "No money — nuthin'! These people sees me with tickets or takin' money, they'll beat me up and take it all — the tickets and the money."

"How come?" I whispered back.

"They don't like the way I makes me livin'."

We got down to the negotiations — five tourists trying desperately to look casual and one little man in a trenchcoat who'd fade into the crowd at every passing bobby.

"Y'want five seats, right? No standin'. Y'don't wanna stand, y'know. Cheaper, but uncomfortable in there with all them drunks wavin' flags and singin'. Tell ya what — I got five good ones you can have for £25."

Well, that seemed fair.

"Each," he added.

"*Fifty bucks a ticket?*"

Instantly he was ten feet away, staring in another direction.

"Talk it over wiv yr friends," the word floated back. "If you want 'em, gimme a nod. But don't flash no money, and *don't say tickets!*"

We talked it over. All but my wife, who didn't want to see the game and thought ten cents would be exorbitant. She just stood there, her mouth working but no sound coming out.

For five of us, we needed £125. We didn't have it.

I myself was ten pounds short due to an earlier sage investment — the purchase of 15 Liverpool hats for a kids' soccer team at home. (I wanted the winners' hats, but they had to be bought before the game because the trailers with the souvenirs were always taken away before it ended, lest they be turned over by the more fun-loving members of the departing mob. But I wasn't worried. Everybody knew Liverpool would win.)

"No way I can work it," I said sadly. "Not unless he'd take a traveller's cheque."

Like that, there he was.

"Sure, I takes 'em," he said.

We made the deal and reached for the tickets. He didn't have them.

"Can't carry 'em on me," he explained, pointing over his shoulder at the mob. "They'd take 'em and break me legs. You come with me. I'll take you down where you can get a cuppa while I go get the tickets. You don't want the ladies stayin' up here. These people turn ugly."

"You want tea?" I asked my wife.

"Fift...fift...fift..."

"Speech impediment," I explained.

He nodded sympathetically and escorted us to the Wembley Squash Club coffee bar, ignoring a sign that said Members Only. "Wait here," he said. It took him 30 minutes. When he came back he was clutching five tickets.

"Best in the 'ouse," he assured us. "They oughta be. They go for five pounds each."

"Five pounds," my wife said faintly. "And for two we're paying fift...fift..."

He looked at me questioningly.

"She's overcome," I said.

So, for only five times face value, we sat in historic Wembley and watched a two-hour scoreless draw.

But at least I had the hats. Liverpool would certainly win the replay. The kids would love me. Imagine — hats of the League Cup champions.

Wednesday afternoon the score came over the wire: Notts Forest 1, Liverpool nil.

I phoned my wife.

"The hats are no good," I said.

"Fift...fift...fift..."

THE CHICKEN PECKS HIS SPOTS
August 7, 1979

The giant orange chicken with the purple, yellow and orange head and the spindly yellow legs and griddle-sized yellow flat feet flopped seductively back on the hotel room bed. "Where do you want the girl?" the manager asked.

The chicken opened one wing. The delectable little honey recruited from the willing dozens in the hall crawled obligingly into his embrace. Flashbulbs popped as they cuddled beak to cheek. For Ted Giannoulas, it was the end of another hard day at the office.

Friday night he was at a baseball game in Tacoma. This was Saturday afternoon, spent poolside entertaining the mob at Superflop V, the bellyflop diving salute to cholesterol. In three hours he would catch a plane to Chicago to open a supermarket. He didn't have a day off in July, won't likely have one in August. It's why he makes $100,000 a year jumping around in a chicken suit.

"Five or six more years like this," he says, "then I see The Chicken picking his spots. Like Sinatra, y'know? He doesn't play Caesars Palace every night, right?"

For those who've dropped in from another planet, The Chicken — *née* The KGB Chicken — is the mascot-for-hire who plays pro football, baseball and basketball games, turns up on national TV a lot, and has turned cheerleading into an art form.

He is the feathered fowl who runs the bases backwards and ends with a Pete Rose bellyflop slide; the barnyard badgerer who follows umpires around with a noose and puts the whammy on opposing pitchers; the Pulitzer pullet who sticks his beak into basketball huddles when there are seconds left in the game and somehow emerges unfried.

He was born in March of 1974 when San Diego radio station KGB hired a journalism and communications major named Ted Giannoulas for two dollars an hour to climb into a chicken suit as a promotion and hand out Easter eggs to kids.

It was supposed to last two weeks. Four and one-half years later he was still laying 'em in the aisles and turning down a $100,000-a-year offer from Ted Turner to bring his act to Atlanta. Eight months after that he was being sued for $200,000 by KGB and within a month — in a brand-new suit — "I became a born-again chicken." Not bad for a kid from London, Ontario...

Ted Giannoulas pulls off the chicken head and wearily tosses it on the bed. The publicity photos are finished. The suit feels like a furnace. But he is still hyped by his performance — or rather, The Chicken's.

"I don't see The Chicken as a mascot hanging around banging a drum and going 'Hi, kids!'," he says. "The Chicken is a comedian in the Harpo Marx sense. He gets away with things others might not because everybody knows The Chicken is his friend. He doesn't intrude. They can see he means no harm. His biggest fans are the referees and coaches — his biggest fans!"

When Giannoulas speaks of The Chicken it is in the third person. You can hear the capital letters. "How long can The Chicken go on? Well, Mickey Mouse just turned 50." It is Dr. Jekyll and Mr. Chicken. "I view The Chicken," he says, "as my son."

In many ways he is correct. There is Chaplin timing in some of his routines that makes him far more than a man in a chicken suit. When KGB and The Chicken parted company in May after a lawsuit over who owned the rights to the suit (the station won the decision but not the money), it put another guy in the suit and sent him out at a baseball game. He lasted 15 seconds. The crowd booed him off the field.

Giannoulas has his own explanation of the differences.

"The Chicken has an inbred sense of comedy, a high energy level and a thorough knowledge of sport. I know the games. I know when to get in, when to get out, when to improvise. I'm not a Chaplin freak, although I love some of his stuff. I appreciate the Three Stooges more now than I did as a kid. And Popeye, and vintage Bugs Bunny cartoons. See, nobody ever beat old Bugs. And nobody beats The Chicken."

Nobody beats him, nobody hates him, and nobody sees him. Like Batman, Spiderman and the four guys in the Kiss rock group, he changes to Ted Giannoulas, 5'4", 24-year-old from San Diego by way of Windsor, in the privacy of his room. The Chicken had to battle his way down the hall, averaging about two bikinied popsies per door. Ted Giannoulas can make the walk back unscathed and unnoticed.

"Movie stars would give millions for what I've got," he says. "Stardom and privacy at one time."

The act brought him recognition. The split with KGB and the resulting lawsuit gave him national impact.

"It was a philosophical difference," he shrugs. "The station saw The Chicken as a commercial tool, I saw him as a career. They'd taken the suit off a shelf in a costume shop. After The Chicken caught on they had a guy in Salt Lake City design the real Chicken suit, but they didn't copyright it. So in 1978 I flew up there and got the rights."

When KGB wouldn't let him freelance, he took the station call letters off the suit and worked anyway. The station sued and won. The Chicken went underground for a month, only to emerge in an outfit virtually identical except for the colour — orange instead of red.

He stayed in San Diego, where he was given the keys to the city, where the mayor phoned and asked him to come out in support of his campaign, and where his autobiography, *From Scratch*, has sold 15,000 copies in the city alone.

"The Chicken was born out of their laughter and support," he says. "He couldn't leave them."

He is a phenomenon of his time. Women want to hold him, to cart him off to their rooms and take him to bed like a Teddy bear. "I'm like the guy at the party who puts on a lampshade and makes people laugh," he says. "There's nothing like the feeling. It's the greatest thing in the world."

And when the party is over he can take off his Chicken suit and walk away. Just like Batman.

ONE STEP ALONG THE ROAD

August 17, 1980

JOHNSON — Peacefully at rest on July 3, 1980. Nathanial Aaron Lloyd of Port Moody, aged five years, joyfully remembered by his loving parents, Glen and Gaye Johnson...

Nathan Johnson had leukemia. It was discovered at 17 months and from that moment Glen and Gaye Johnson lived a death watch laced with dwindling hope. They saw other kids die and still others live, and they clung to the statistics that gave their son a 50-50 chance.

It ended in Edmonton, in a hospital where they specialize in that last, desperate chance. Nathan Johnson died — not of leukemia, but of spinal meningitis. It is the final, knifing cruelty of leukemia: that so many who die do so from something else caused as a side-effect.

He was five years old. In a year or so he'd have been learning to kick a soccer ball, perhaps working his way through the juvenile ranks as his father did before becoming, in 1974, one of the first players signed to a professional contract by the Vancouver Whitecaps. Or maybe he'd have gone in a different direction entirely. He wasn't granted time to face the choice.

Glen Johnson thought about that a lot, and about the kids who'll be coming into the cancer wards as Nathan did. Because they never stop coming. Progress is being made. In 1970 a child with leukemia had a five per cent chance of beating it; now it's 50% and as high as 60% for other types of cancer in the young. But every day, somewhere, there are other Nathans, and will be until it's whipped.

So, when Nathan Johnson died, his parents went to the J.R. Nicholson Cancer Research Foundation for Children with a big plan and a small hope: if they could do something to help the Nathans to come, then maybe, somehow, their own Nathan wouldn't have died for nothing. They would raise $20,000 and buy a cell separator for the new Children's Hospital.

They didn't have the money — their own medical bills over the past three and one-half years had been prohibitive — and they didn't know how they were going to get it. But if the foundation would look after it and set it aside until there was enough, they'd get it somewhere. Because they knew what it could mean.

"On Easter weekend Nathan was really in bad shape," Glen Johnson recalls. "He needed white blood cells. But there are only two cell separators in B.C. They're both in the adult section at Vancouver General. You have to book time on them. You can sit there and watch your child dying and know there's something that can be done that might help, and you know where the machine is, and you have to book time, like you book a dinner reservation or a soccer ticket."

He got his time on the machine — Glen Johnson's time, not Nathan's. That's what a cell separator is all about. They stick a needle in the arm of a donor, pump the blood through a machine that separates and removes white cells, then pump the depleted blood back into the other arm.

Glen Johnson was on the separator five hours a day for four days.

"I wandered around like a zombie," he says. "But they got the cells for Nathan, and for a while he went into a state of remission. It *helped*."

They were only buying time, and they knew it. But for the hopeless, time is all there is. Time, and all the known treatments and finally the ones that aren't known — the experimental drugs tried because they're all the hope that's left. At the end, Nathan was on the newest one, Interferon.

For Nathan, it wasn't enough. It may not be the answer. But Glen Johnson speaks of looking down the road, then looking back to see how far you've come.

"We saw a dozen kids — three years old, four, ten, 12 — being admitted. We saw some die. The night Nathan died he'd been in the same room with a boy 12, just admitted. Then Nathan had to be isolated. Fifteen minutes later the father of the new boy came in to see how we were doing, and Nathan was dead. The man was almost in shock. Up 'til then, he hadn't looked down the road.

"But they gave Nathan two years. He lived four. He made some progress on the new drugs. We went a step further than anyone else. That's something, I guess..."

A week later at a Whitecaps game, kids in soccer uniforms collected money to help buy the cell separator. Had the dice rolled another way, Nathan might have been one of them.

Some reached for money. Others passed them by, forgetting that there will be too many other Nathan Johnsons, and there are still too many steps along the road.

STILL WORKIN' HIS SIDE OF THE ROAD

April 28, 1981

At nine he was a ridge-runner, roaming the Appalachian Mountains of Virginia trapping fox, coon, possum, mountain hawk and, on a good day, skunk.

Skunks were best, says Sam Snead, " 'cause you trap one of them, you weren't goin' to school that day. No way!"

There wasn't much money — but then, there didn't have to be. The table in the house in Hot Springs, Virginia, was covered with wild game, "turkey, chickens, two or three kinds of preserves," and the five Snead boys and the sister would sit on the long bench next to it and there was always plenty for everybody, even if you were mostly barefoot.

"On skunk days," says Snead, sitting in his hotel suite sipping on a brandy, "my momma would meet me at the door and yell 'Don't you go bringin' them clothes in here! Take 'em outside and bury 'em.' That was how they'd get clean, you see. In the dirt.

"My mother," he said. "Lord, but she was strong. She could lift a barrel of flour up onto the wagon. You know what a barrel of flour weighed? 192 pounds.

"Happy days, y'know?" he sighed. "Really happy days."

Samuel Jackson Snead has come down the road a fair piece from Hot Springs, but he's carried the soul of it with him. He will be 69 come May 27, a living, breathing legend who plays the seniors golf tour and could still shoot the lights out if the putter would hold still. But he's at his best when he speaks of the tour that was, as opposed to the tour that is. Speak of Jack Nicklaus and there will be respect and admiration. Speak of Ky Laffoon or Lefty Stackhouse and the lights go on in his eyes.

"Laffoon was a tobacco chewer," he said. "He was always spittin'. Hit a gnat at 20 paces. Play behind him and you had the stuff all over you and your ball. Stackhouse, he'd get so mad he'd bite his own hand. One time I saw him throw his clubs in the lake. 'For five cents I'd jump in with 'em,' he says. And some guy says 'I'll give you five bucks.' 'Put it up,' says Lefty, and jumps in. He came out wetter'n a duck, took the money and said 'At least I beat this sumbich game for five dollars!' "

Those were different days, of course. The pro tour was just getting started when Sam Snead joined in 1937. In the early years you put up your own prize money — $50 a head — and played 36 holes in three days. You stayed alive as best you could, hustling when you had to, and California and Florida stops were best because you could pick oranges from the groves and hide them in the rough to save on meal money later. The professional golfer had not yet become America's guest when the kid from Hot Springs ambled onto the scene.

He was to win 135 tournaments and earn $620,000 in a career that's been reborn with the seniors tour and the Legends of Golf tournaments like the one he'll play June 8-14 at Capilano. But back then he was just Sam Snead, who'd swung his first sticks at rattlers and copperheads at home, then graduated to rocks and finally to golf balls, by accident.

He was a good high school halfback, a baseball pitcher and basketball player. He could run a ten-second 100, and got his start at play-for-pay in tennis earning 50¢ each time he whipped a spoiled brat, paid by the kid's father.

When he broke his hand playing football he began swinging a golf club because he thought it would knit better that way. Fuel for the legend was there almost from the start.

His first job was at the Homestead course in Hot Springs, as a club-maker. It lasted, he says, two weeks and four days, until he was offered a job as pro at the nearby Cascades course. "No salary, just what you could hustle plus a sandwich and a glass of milk at lunch. I didn't make enough to pay for my laundry that first year, but boy, did I beat on them golf balls!"

He almost shot the job out from under himself. One day Alva Bradley, owner of the Cleveland Indians, was bending over on the fifth green when a ball delivered by Snead bounced once and hit him on the rear. He was going to have the kid fired for hitting his second shot while the foursome ahead was still on the green. "It wasn't his second shot," Snead's partner explained. "It was his drive." The hole was 335 yards long. "I really caught that one," he says with relish.

He has caught a few with that honeyed, rippling swing. He has over-driven a green 360 yards away. In 1959, at the Sam Snead Festival, he shot an outrageous 59. "For pure animal grace," wrote the late Grantland Rice, "the sight of Sam Snead murdering a tee shot is the acme of tigerish reflex in human form."

In 1945, on a bet, he shot successive rounds of 83, 82 and 81 — playing with one hand. His left. Nine years later, recalling his boyhood days, he trimmed a piece of swamp maple with a bulge on one end, had the head balanced, and used it and a wedge to shoot a 76.

He is a horn player (1960 scouting report: "Can't improvise much, but he'll be in there blowing his brains out on the melody"), a man who made the coconut straw hat famous, a man whose earnings in today's dollars would be $8,500,000. But mostly, he is a legend with memories.

Dutch Harrison, whose biggest purses came from the wallets of club members who thought they could play, recalls the day he met the pre-legend Snead. He talked the kid into playing for money, shot his usual solid round — and got taken to the cleaners.

"Say, sure do thank you folks," the kid twanged to Harrison and his partner as he collected his money. "What time tomorrow you folks gonna be out here?"

"Son," Harrison said, "you work your side of the road and we'll work ours."

He's been working it most half a century now. He fishes a little and golfs a lot and spends his home time on a farm tucked against the forest in Virginia. And when he closes his eyes and inhales, he can smell his momma's preserves.

ONE LAST ROUND FOR BYRON

September 16, 1981

We said good-bye to Byron Scott Tuesday morning at the church, the cemetery and the Piccadilly Hotel pub.

He'd have liked the funeral. Mind you, the morning air at the cemetery might have gotten to him because, as Pam Glass said in opening the eulogy, "It's a little early for Byron to be up." But he would have loved the wake.

When Byron Scott died last week his body was 70, his heart was 21, and his liver was 306. He was a drinker, was Byron — not a mean drinker or a slobbery drinker or a trouble-making drinker, just a drinker — a guy who'd done it for a long time and always enjoyed the laughter and the stories as much as if not more than the booze. And they were telling Byron stories at The Pic.

No one knew him, really — not his drinking buddies or the newspaper and radio and race track and street people who gathered to see him off. He was just a stocky, brash little guy who materialized one day in the 1950s and stayed forever. He claimed a newspaper and radio background and straddled the poverty line by cadging free-lance assignments. He had an ex-wife somewhere and a son some-where else. Until he died, that's about all anyone knew.

Byron didn't help. When he spoke of himself it was usually a put-down. He brushed off his army career by reporting that when he came home "that's when we started to win the war." Until yesterday, we didn't know about the Distinguished Service Medal he had won in 1943.

He lived in the cheapest quarters he could find. For years that meant the Kingston Hotel — "Where the celebs meet the debs," he'd explain. When he moved into the Sunset Towers, a subsidized senior citizens' complex, Byron called it "going uptown."

He'd keep track of the sports press conferences and crash as many as he could because the sandwiches and companionship were free. But he'd also keep track of the birthdays and the expectant mothers, and there was money for flowers or candies when there was barely money for food.

He was just...Byron. The phone would ring and a voice would say "Byron Patrick Scott!" and you knew he was there with curling results or basketball results or word that he was going on the wagon for two weeks because he'd be covering the horse show. He was always on the wagon for that one. When he fell off, the crash was awe-inspiring.

He claimed he got his clothes from the coroner. "Great coat, eh?" he'd say. "Just this one little spot of blood on the sleeve."

One day after a press conference, none of the guys he usually rode with was going his way. "No problem," he said, "I'll call an ambulance." He made the call, told a reporter to clear a spot on the floor, and lay down to wait. "He'll be here soon," he said. "The service is really quick."

He could drive you crazy.

A few years ago we were sitting at the press table in the Pacific Coliseum for an exhibition basketball game. The legendary Bill Russell was coaching the Seattle Supersonics. Suddenly, during the warm-up, Byron leaned over and waved frantically. "Bill! Bill!" he yelled.

Russell thought we were part of the scorer's table. He unfolded and ambled over.

"Yes?" he asked.

"If you need any help," Byron said, "just call."

215

He used to phone Bud Poile, the Canucks' then-general manager, getting past his private secretary by announcing himself as "Byron Patrick Scott, representing the provincial government." When Poile rapped him for it he was indignant.

"I am with the provincial government," he said. "I'm on welfare."

He drifted in and out of our lives, and the harsh fact is we didn't care as much as we should have. If we had, we'd have kept better track. It shouldn't have taken four days to confirm rumours that his heart had given out and he was in the morgue. His drinking buddies knew right away.

They flocked to The Pic yesterday, maybe 100 of them, scoffing sandwiches and booze and remembering Byron in the way he'd have liked best. They figured there'd be more at 4:30, when the second shift came in. He couldn't have asked for a better good-bye.

CHRISTMAS STORY
December 11, 1981

The kids in the journalism classes always ask: "What's the hardest column you ever wrote?" It is this one.

This is a Christmas column, sort of. I play the Grinch.

No doubt you've noticed that this newspaper has a Christmas Fund drive. Most newspapers have, and a lot of radio stations. Maybe that's part of the problem: Because there are so many there's a tendency to glance at the picture, skim the story, cluck the tongue — and turn the page.

Oh, you'd give at the office or send a cheque, but most times it never really got to you. Sometimes you didn't read it at all. Because there were so *many*.

When I started out in this business I drew the assignment of writing those stories. It did not make me happy. Heart stories, we called them. Sob stuff.

They were approached with a certain cynicism. We'd sit around, some of us, and sneer at the commercialism. "You're ever gonna lose your wallet, lose it at Christmas," we'd say. "With donations, you'll get back double." I was 20 years old, and knew everything.

That particular fund was to raise money for the 500 most needy families in Victoria. When it closed, the total raised would be divided by 500 and distributed. I got the assignment because I was new.

"Fresh approach," they told me, which meant low man on the totem pole.

So I wrote stories. Every day, another story about someone in trouble or a family that couldn't afford presents for the kids. Day after day.

They got to me, but not the way they were supposed to. Oh, they were sad cases, all right, and it was too bad, and hopefully there'd be enough money so the kids could have presents. And sure, somebody had to write it. But why me?

After two weeks, I tried to beg off.

No way.

So I decided to bring it to a head. I'd show them how cynical I was. They'd *have* to take me off. I wrote a fake story and turned it in as I'd turned in all the others. It started out like this:

"Your name is Mary, and the only thing coming down your chimney this Christmas is soot."

It didn't work. The city editor scrunched it up and told me to quit fooling around. But we all had a good laugh. I remember that.

I especially remember it each Christmas, when I look at my daughter in a wheelchair.

She was 14 when the skiing accident occurred. There have been five Christmases since. She cannot walk. She has some use of her arms. Her mind is locked away, hopefully in a better world than we can give her. It opens your eyes.

You see, Christmas funds are not just desirable or marginally necessary; they are vital. Whether they help provide care or treatment or presents or food or that tiny extra that can give a family without one a touch of Christmas and a tinge of hope, they *must* be filled. To say no is to turn your back on kids who, but for a turn of the wheel, might have been yours.

They lend themselves to cynicism. It is easy to say, and there is some truth in it, that they shouldn't be necessary, that people have problems 12 months of the year, not just in December, and where are all the charitable people in the other 11? The problem in totally accepting them is that you have to be there.

When you're lucky, accidents and need are things that hit someone else. Other people's kids suffer, never yours. All the newspaper stories, all the TV and radio pleas, are about other people in another world.

Then one day something happens, and it's not their world, it's yours. Until you've been there, you can't possibly know.

This is not a sports page column. It doesn't belong here, really. Maybe it's just a try at erasing the other story about the girl, the chimney and the soot. Oh, it never got published — but I wrote it.

The lesson, I suppose, is that happiness is fragile, and it's not always the other guy's that breaks. Hug your kids and fill their stockings. But remember the ones that are empty.

THE FUN LEAGUE

July 30, 1982

A chap in our office has a twisted knee. "Stretching a single into a double," he says, leaning proudly on his crutches.

Down at the radio station a sports reporter is learning to type one-handed until the sling comes off his separated shoulder. "I was dribbling through the box just ready to shoot," he says, "and POW! Two guys sandwiched me." His boss is sympathetic, and should be. He did the same thing diving for a line drive.

I tell you, it's a disease. Participaction Backlash, the new madness of the masses.

In offices and supermarkets and factories all over the country, eager-beaver ex-jocks or wannabe jocks run around with clipboards, or hang signs on the wall:

FUN! FUN! FUN! SUPERMARKET SOFTBALL LEAGUE! NO SKILL NEDESSARY! SEE GLADYS IN FROZEN FOODS!

Pretty soon Gladys is hanging over the checkout counter checking out the muscles on the bag boy.

"Hey, kid, you comin' out for the Canadian Kippers practice tonight? We got a big game Sunday against those Prime Cutters turkeys from Meats."

"Uh, sorry, but I've already signed up with the Green Bayleaf Packers over in Condiments. They outbid the Tony Tigers from Cereals. Offered me parsley, sage and thyme, but I held out for Rosemary. You know, the one with the..."

"The Packers! Listen, kid, you wanna go through life sniffing cinnamon that's your business, but at least hear our offer. And don't you believe that stuff they say about Frozen Foods. We're not all frigid. Let's drive over to my place and discuss it, okay? Your cart or mine?"

There are two great flaws in the Participaction Theory. The first is that the average person is physically equipped to handle it. The second is the idea that pick-up team sport is based on fun. It's not. It just starts out that way.

Someone decides to form, say, an inter-departmental softball league. They scrounge around for a few bats, a couple of balls, throw some jackets around the field for bases, and start. The wives or husbands join in, and the kids, and it doesn't matter if the score is 146-2, because who's counting?

Then the rot sets in. You can almost graph it.

Someone calls a practice — and shows up with a team list and league standings. The kids don't play anymore because the other team will come loaded, right, and they're not gonna pull that crap on us. The wife with the good swing can play but the one who can't see her shoes, let alone first base — "Uh, honey? Why don't you be in charge of watching the cooler?"

Then someone gets an idea:

"Hey, why don't we get *hats*? You know, so we'd all look like the same team!" After the hats come the T-shirts with the name on the front. But these things cost money, so why don't we get a sponsor? Maybe the supermarket would do it — employee relations and all that.

One day the wife in charge of the cooler notices a stranger. The pitcher, maybe, or a guy who stands 6'5" and holds a bat like he's done it before.

"Who's that?" she asks. "He doesn't work at the store."

"SSHHHH! Fred from Canned Goods brought him in. It's his cousin. Used to play senior "A". Hit .500 and has a sinker they'll never see. This is the big one, honey. We're playing the Stock Room Reds for all the marbles. This is no time to take chances!"

They trot out on to the field and Fred's cousin hits three home runs. The only batter to touch his sinker is a guy nobody knows who hits four homers and says his job in the stock room is to feed the cattle.

Meanwhile, the ones still playing for fun are throwing their out-of-shape bodies in front of line drives they can't catch, swinging at pitches they can't see, and wearing their bandages like medals of honour.

"Okay, so we lost this time," says the guy with the clipboard. "But next year, boy, I'm bringing in five guys from the House of David. Next year, we're gonna have *fun*..."

IRONPERSON

August 16, 1983

The Canadian International Ironman Triathlon is now the Canadian International Ironperson Triathlon, and I trust you're as excited about that as I.

The entry of two ladies from Banff in Saturday's event in Penticton, the press release tells us, "brought to the surface an obvious issue that had been lurking in the background for some time. With both men and women competing, was it proper to call the event an IronMAN? After considerable, and at times heated, debate, the Canadian Ironman Race Committee reached a consensus that the name should be changed to IronPERSON."

Well, I should think so. I myself have long been a supporter of an Ironperson whose record in the triathlon stands as a challenge to those who pursue excellence in this most gruelling of all events.

As Ironperson her work on collars and cuffs is exemplary. As Dishperson she leaves behind a trail of cutlery bright as a diamond tiara. And in the final event, well, visitors have been badly cut walking through glass doors, so brilliant is her performance as Windowperson.

The fabulous Mrs. D. (to reveal her full name would be to risk her kidnapping by jealous neighbours) is in heavy training this week and may also enter the triathlon, providing that some confusion as to events can be cleared up in time.

The press release says competitors "will swim 2.4 miles, bicycle 112 miles and run 26.2 miles consecutively." Surely they jest. If my Ironperson did that, she might not have enough strength left to sprinkle my shirts. That way lies chaos.

Swimming, cycling and running a total of 140.6 miles also raises the issue of technology. It took Aussie yachtsmen five years to develop the keel for *Australia II*. Where am I going to find a 140.6-mile cord for an iron in less than a week? Besides, can an Ironperson reasonably be expected to do all that and still deal with the dreaded Wall of Pain — that agonizing moment when she discovers ring around the collar?

I'm not certain I want to put Mrs. D. through all that. As the press release itself says: "The magnitude of such an undertaking begs the question: 'Why? Why would anyone do it?' Each triathlete has his or her own answer. But phrases such as 'ultimate challenge', 'unforgettable accomplishment' and 'spiritual victory' invariably creep into the responses."

I wouldn't want my Ironperson to get too close to people who think like that.

ONE PUSH AT A TIME

March 22, 1985

Hunched down in the wheelchair, the useless legs tucked almost to his chin, he suddenly looked so frail.

The muscles on the arms were still clearly defined under the striped T-shirt. The bulk of shoulder still showed promise of the strength he would need so desperately in the 18 months to come. But he was down there at waist level to the hundreds pressing around him to say good-bye, and as he ran his grease-encrusted racing gloves over the tires and blinked the moisture from his eyes, Rick Hansen didn't look like a hero at all. He looked like a small boy screwing up his courage to ride a pony or take a dare.

All at once, people in the parking lot at the Oakridge shopping mall were whispering the numbers:

"Twenty-five thousand miles!..."

"In 18 months! Seventy miles a day, three days a week. For 25,000 miles!..."

"Around the world! Hell, I couldn't wheel that thing around the block..."

If the figures had come to overwhelm Rick Hansen on this overcast Thursday morning it would be a temporary thing. Fourteen hours earlier, wheeling into the chaos of his West End apartment to find five people waiting to interview him or give him something or bring up another last-minute hitch in plans, he'd retreated briefly to the apartment block lounge, where there was a chance of some privacy.

"Tomorrow," he confided to a friend. "Tomorrow the easy part starts. Tomorrow, all I have to do is wheel..."

But yesterday, just for a second, he looked as though every one of those miles to come was a stone around his neck. It was an understandable reaction. The path that's brought him this far has been laced with minor miracles and major disappointments, each in its own way adding to his self-imposed obligation to succeed. They offer interesting contrasts.

A motor home was needed and there was no money. Suddenly, it was there, provided by Vanguard Trailers Ltd., and specially modified, right down to a hole in a panel so Hansen can slide off the end of his bunk and be in the bathroom. Expo 86, under whose banner Hansen will wheel as he tours the world, has provided some 200 Expo pins.

School kids sold oranges and washed cars to raise a few bucks for the fund. Prime Minister Brian Mulroney sent a congratulatory telegram — thus far in lieu of cheque.

But the people were there. Hundreds of them, picking up the fund-raising appeal carried yesterday morning on virtually every radio station, and re-routing to Oakridge to be briefly a part of something they sensed could be great.

Some came in wheelchairs they could move themselves, some in motorized models steered by joysticks designed to accommodate limited hand movement. Some — the silent ones trapped by fate or circumstance inside their minds — came with parents or friends, seeking a glimpse of the young man who wants to raise ten million dollars for spinal-cord research that may some day set others free.

For Rick Hansen it all added up to an emotional overload. He was excited, inspired, overwhelmed — and, I think, a little bit scared.

By now, as he pumps down the road toward San Francisco, that will have worn off. He's free now — free to focus muscle and mind and heart on a single goal, knowing that every turn of the wheels brings him that much closer to achieving it. But there was a moment there yesterday I will never forget.

The reception was held indoors. As he headed for the open doorway of the reception hall, the wheels of his chair hit the aluminum strip across the floor that stops the door as it shuts. The chair stopped dead.

Without a pause, Rick Hansen reversed the chair half a roll, threw it forward again, and rolled out to challenge the world.

BELLY TO BELLY

August 7, 1985

No, admits Tom Butler, there has never been a major league bellyfloppers' strike, nor does he anticipate one. "I hold all the cards," he said. "I've got all the tickets to the beer tent."

Speculation has been semi-rife that the bellyfloppers might follow the lead of major league players and force high-level contract negotiations as zero hour approaches for Superflop XI, the World Bellyflop and Cannonball Diving Championships on August 31 at the campground in Otter Springs, Florida. (For those requiring more detailed directions, Otter Springs is to Gainesville what Green Bay is to Milwaukee.)

Commissioner Butler merely smiles. He knows that for true floppers, the risks are far too great: potential loss of the magnificent 3 1/2-foot World Championship Trophy (simulated gold plate, $49.95 Canadian plus tax and engraving), the $1,000 first prize and, worst of all, the missed opportunity to don the Coveted Green Bathrobe, the Masters blazer of the wet set.

"There will be no strike," he says. "In fact, I have cabled my counterpart, Mr. Ueberroth, offering our assistance in filling the gap left by the absence of baseball during their strike. We stand ready to place one world-calibre flopper in each of the major league cities, each man ready to perform the full Superflop program for each of the remaining home dates. One show only, doubleheaders extra."

Does he feel Mr. Ueberroth will accept?

"It's debatable," he concedes. "After all, if we once get established he may never get his crowds back. Once they've seen a Butch Hilterson, a Rickey Henderson ain't all that much."

To aficionados of the flop, Butch Hilterson is legend. In 1980, the 325-pound plumber from Denver, Colorado, competed in the championships wearing a snowy-white tutu in tulle with chic scalloped bodice. Although he didn't win, he was named Ms. Congeniality and got to help take down the decorations.

Hilterson thus earned his place in flopdom's Hall of Fame next to the immortal Butts Giraud, the three-time champion who knew it was time to retire the day he went into his bathroom and blew himself up.

Strong men weep at the memory.

Giraud was getting ready for his final dive of the 1978 championships, riding a string of two perfect sixes. He knew he could collect enough points to win just by concentrating on height-of-splash and water displacement, two of the three elements of the flop. But inside that bulbous body lurked the heart of a Barnum. He would risk everything and pin his all on the third element: showmanship.

He had imported a Hollywood stunt man to design a body pack that would fit under his shirt, with a detonator wire running down the sleeve to his hand. At the peak of his dive he'd push the button and burst into flames as the shirt burned off his back, but hit the water and extinguish before he got hurt.

He was standing in the bathroom when he decided on an instrument check.

"I just push this button like this, right?" he asked — and exploded.

He was too big to stuff in the john, so they rolled him in a blanket until he went out, then reloaded him. Giraud strode to the board, ignited on schedule, and scored another six. Big deal, Reggie Jackson.

Butler, who owns the franchise rights to floppery, feels this month's show will prove that flopping is a sport whose time has come — the only sport where a guy goes into the tank and it doesn't matter. "If baseball strikes for three weeks," he warns, "it's history."

Giraud, now a mere shadow of his former selves, will not make it to Otter Springs, but old-timers are hoping for a guest appearance by Christie Wilson, the 450-pound former Miss WBFCDC. "She wasn't just our queen," Butler remembers fondly. "She was also first and second runner-up."

GOOD-BYE, JOE

June 3, 1988

The soccer boots are around somewhere, the keepsake-sized pair on a chain that Joe Johnson gave my son 16 summers ago. "For working hardest, Dad," he said. "I wasn't the best, but Joe says I worked the hardest." You could have read by the glow in his eyes.

He was eight years old, a quiet, introverted little cuss trying to come to terms with the fact that he was small enough to pass for six. Enrolling him in soccer school had been our idea, not his. He was well co-ordinated, bubbling with an energy that had to be channelled before it exploded. Soccer, we thought, was worth a shot.

It was more than that. We dropped him into a sea of boys at the UBC campus and he bobbed up a different kid. He'd found a game where size didn't matter, a team game requiring individual skills based not on strength but on co-ordination and agility, and it was love at first sight.

The love never died. It took us through house league — two years with shirts that hung skirt-length, playing for Nightingale Pharmacy, 11 kids converging on the ball as though the earth had tilted in its direction, and seven more years working up through the juvenile ranks.

I say "we" because I was fortunate enough to be there, leaning against the fence with the other parents at first, bringing the half-time oranges when my turn arrived, later as manager — a term meaning you fill out the forms, clean the noses, take the injured to the emergency ward and drive the forgotten kids home. And later, as the boy turned 17, a chance to start over with another group of ten-year-olds, him coaching, me still playing manager. Golden times...

We talked about them yesterday, when word came that Joe Johnson had died Tuesday night.

We remembered the little soccer boots, and the sea of kids out on the UBC fields, and how, no matter how many age groups were involved, Joe always managed to wind up the sessions playing with the littlest kids, running along barefoot and laughing, cheering them on, dropping deft little passes or doodling through them in outrageous games of keepaway. He'd had a great professional career with the Glasgow Rangers, but he never had more fun than in the summer romps with the kids.

There's no way of counting the number of kids who bubbled through the UBC camps in the Joe Johnson years, but it has to be thousands. Check any recreational league today, look at the 86ers or the coast league teams. They're loaded with players who were once Joe's kids. In its heyday, it was the only such camp around — classes in which Joe was the overseer and teacher and kids who'd come through the system themselves spent the summer passing along what they'd learned to the new crop.

When the camp wasn't in operation, Joe coached juvenile teams — sticking again to the little guys he loved most of all. He held strong opinions about how kids should be coached, how parents should be involved if they can enjoy and encourage without pressuring, and how, if they can't "they should bloody stay at home!" He knew his kids, knew their problems and their needs. "Sometimes they need more than coaching," he told me once. "Sometimes they just need a hug, and someone telling them they're doing fine."

Sitting here writing this, I found myself wondering if there'd ever be a statue of Joe out at the UBC soccer pitch. Then, as my son packed the car full of soccer balls and plastic triangles and headed off for another practice with another group of 11-year-olds, I realized how foolish that was. Joe doesn't need a monument. He's got thousands of them.

FOLLOW THE BOUNCING BALL

August 23, 1989

Naturally, somebody mentioned The Song. And, naturally, Alan Hinton had a story about it.

"The bloody song," he said fondly. "Did I ever tell you how we made that record? Well, they wanted the players to do it, and I knew they never could unless they were in the proper mood, which was not quite sober. So..."

> "White is the colour,
> Soccer is the game..."

For a moment, a guy could almost hear the voices — the triumphant, raucous voices of the best sports story this town has ever had.

Mind you, it was easy, because Hinton was there, and Bob Lenarduzzi and Derek Possee and Bob Bolitho, some of the Vancouver Whitecaps who stayed, the vanguard of the 1979 Soccer Bowl champions who'll gather here for a reunion match on September 8.

The Whitecaps. The team that grabbed a city by the heart with a grip we thought would never be relaxed...

> "We're all together,
> "And winning is our aim..."

"...so I hauled them all down to the No. 5 Orange Club and we got into the beer for the best part of the afternoon. And then we went off to the recording studio..."

Alan Hinton. The Old Fox. Has any other one-season athlete had the impact he had on this town in 1978? Trevor Linden last year, perhaps, but he joined the Canucks as a budding superstar. Hinton arrived as an assistant coach for Tony Waiters and, at 35 and in a shape most charitably described as "chunky", suddenly found himself a player again.

If there'd ever been any speed it had long since sped away. "He doesn't waddle, exactly," *Province* columnist Clancy Loranger said around his cigar. "But from the rear he does look like two pigs in a sack." But off a set piece he could put the ball on your head and name the eyebrow. He scored one goal — and drew assists on 30 more for a league record.

The next year, the championship year, he was coaching in Tulsa. I always felt that was a shame. He should have been there in New York, waving the Soccer Bowl...

"So cheer us on
Through the sun and rain..."
"...by the time we got to the recording part we were all ready. As the afternoon wore on they threw in a few professional voices to sort of help us along, and I remember the record people telling me later that they had a hell of a time — what do they call it? — editing the thing, because at the end of every line Bobby Campbell would yell out 'You (BLEEP)-er!' Nice bit of work, that, making it come out all right."

It came out fine. Every station in town — country, middle-of-the-road, rock, all of them — played this crazy record that was actually a steal from an Old Country team with the team name changed. And like everything else that year, it was magic.

"... the man at the studio said we'd sold about 7,000 and were making money on it, so naturally I went to [general manager] John Best and asked for some of it for the players. And, naturally, he said no..."

They're coming back. Almost all of them. Lofty Parkes, John Craven, Roger Kenyon, Trevor Whymark, Willie Johnston, Kevin Hector. They'll look at the Vancouver 86ers, who are building a similar story on a smaller, saner scale and, as The Old Fox said, there'll probably be some tears.

"They were glorious times," he said. "Glorious."
"For Whitecaps,
Whitecaps is our name..."

THE CRAZY CANUCK'S LAST RUN

October 25, 1990

The videotape was made in 1987 when only his closest friends knew how severely Dave Murray was already gripped by the cancer that claimed him yesterday at 37.

It begins with various clips of Murray in flight — yellow suit and red helmet, body tucked into that projectile package, the elder statesman of the Crazy Canucks playing bullet down the ski hills of the world.

Then comes the parade to the microphone: former national team coach John Ritchie and the other three Crazy Canuck originals, Ken Read, Dave Irwin and Steve Podborski, poking fun at their old teammate, telling stories of the days when no course was too steep, no party too long, and life was going to go on forever.

Periodically, the camera switches to Murray, longish hair neatly trimmed, slimmer by far than the slab-shouldered old man of the mountain who led them in the 1970s, but looking good in his tux with the red tie. And laughing. Laughing a lot.

Officially, it was a dinner to launch the Dave Murray Ski Foundation. As such it was an overwhelming success, raising $80,000. If the central figures knew it was also a bit of a good-bye they hid it well under the laughter and the obvious love.

Read claims Murray "set a new standard for longest hair and straggliest beard in the World Cup '74." Ritchie discusses a world class hemorrhoid and the novelty of giving coaching instructions that included "cheeks well spread." Irwin recalls the first time they looked down the hill at Kitzbuhl, convinced that no one in their right mind would ever design a course like that, and how much time Murray spent after they first tried it, going from bed to bathroom at each remembered fright.

Podborski praises Murray's ability to read while lying stark naked with the book flopped down on his chest, and the day he found the maids taking turns vacuuming in front of their room "because the door was open and Dave was in there, chest-reading."

The version of the tape photographer Pat Bell gave me ends with more scenes of Murray flashing down the mountain, sometimes falling, sometimes finishing, but always going full bore. The music is upbeat, the snow is flying, and every line of his body shows a man having the time of his life.

That's how we should remember him. I met him only once or twice in passing, but from what his friends have told me I suspect he'd want it that way. The battle with cancer was a private fight by a private man who didn't want it getting in other people's way or changing their approach to him.

"He didn't want people seeing him sick," Bell says. "The last time I saw him he was pretty bad, but he kept asking me how I felt and how things were going with me. 'Don't slow down,' he said. 'Keep your speed'."

There is another, longer version of the banquet tape. Bell put it together on his own hook as a gift. Murray didn't want it shown around because it might look as though he was blowing his own horn. Instead, he put it away so that, someday, it could be shown to his then-unborn daughter, to give her a memory of her father who might not be there.

It will be a beautiful memory. And when she sees him flashing down the mountain, she'll know her father was a good man who led a good life, and lived it every inch of the way.